RADIO

HAPPY ISLES

Radio

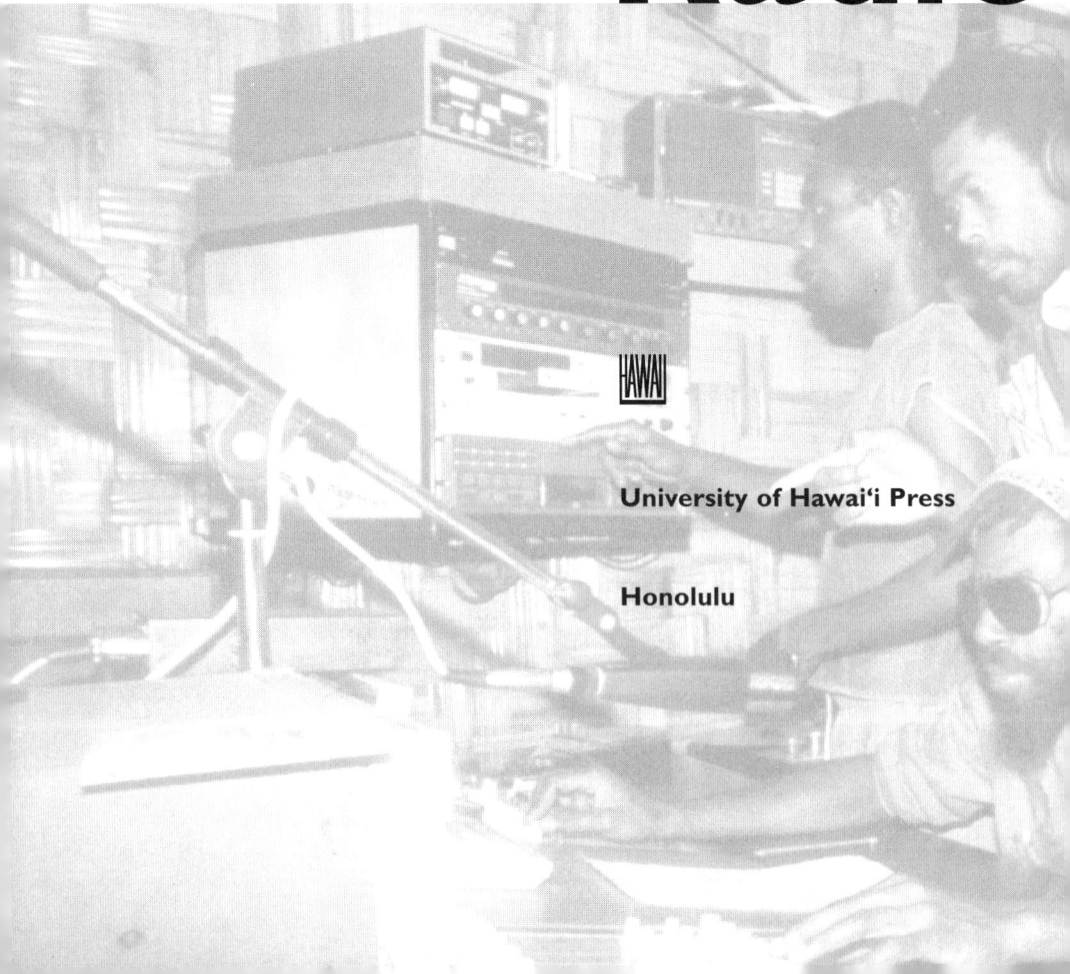

University of Hawai‘i Press

Honolulu

ROBERT SEWARD

Happy Isles

MEDIA AND POLITICS AT PLAY

IN THE PACIFIC

Printed in the United States of America
03 02 01 00 99 98 5 4 3 2 1

Permission to reprint passages from the following sources is gratefully acknowledged.

"KHBC," lyrics by Vicki I'i Rodrigues, © 1936 by the Estate of Vickie I'i Rodrigues. Reprinted by permission.

"Radio," from *Three Last Poems* by James Merrill, © 1995 by The New York Times Company. Reprinted by permission.

"Radio, Radio," by Elvis Costello, © 1978 Sideways Songs, administered by Plangent Visions Music Limited. Reprinted by permission.

"Oceania" map, by the CIA.

Photographs, courtesy of the Pacific Islands Broadcasting Association.

Library of Congress Cataloging-in-Publication Data

Seward, Robert, 1942–
Radio happy isles : media and politics at play in the Pacific / Robert Seward.
p. cm.
Includes bibliographical references and index.
ISBN 0-8248-2014-2 (alk. paper). —
ISBN 0-8248-2106-8 (pbk. : alk. paper)
1. Radio broadcasting—Islands of the Pacific.
I. Title.
PN1991.3.I75S49 1999
384.54'099—dc21 98-8624
CIP

University of Hawai'i Press books are printed on acid-free paper and meet the guidelines for permanence and durability of the Council on Library Resources.

Printed by Data Reproductions Corporation

CONTENTS

ACKNOWLEDGMENTS

In the course of listening across the Pacific, I have incurred a good many debts. My gratitude to Pacific broadcast professionals is great indeed. As I want to be careful not to embarrass anyone in what is really quite a small community of specialists—or worse, to put them at risk—I will say, simply, thank you to all. The reasons for this caution will become more apparent as the book unfolds.

In addition to this general note of thanks, there are a few people that I would like to acknowledge openly. Shiu Singh is one. Singh is the former senior editor of PACNEWS, the news exchange of the Pacific Islands Broadcasting Association, known as PIBA. He served in that capacity from the first days of PACNEWS until his replacement, Jonas Cullwick, took over in 1995. Editor Singh has been extraordinarily persevering and unstinting in the time he gave to me. This book would be impoverished without his newsman's eye and his radio ear. He generously permitted me to rummage through the PACNEWS archives dating back to the earliest stirrings of the news exchange, and Jonas Cullwick was equally helpful. I profited from numerous conversations and from sitting for hours on end in the PACNEWS editorial offices, both in Honiara, Solomon Islands, and in Port Vila, Vanuatu. I admire Singh's dedication to radio, his courage and integrity as a newsman.

Tavake Fusimalohi, general manager of Tonga Broadcasting Commission and the first chair of PIBA, granted me access not only to PIBA documents but to his own station and staff in Nuku'alofa. He patiently answered questions in Tonga, Vanuatu, and at a number of PIBA assemblies, providing essential background to the public documents about PIBA's founding. Fusimalohi is a legend in Pacific radio, and rightly so. His controller of news, Laumano Petelo, was no less generous. She allowed me to sit at the work table, which is the center of activities in her newsroom, and she also presented me with stacks of precious reel-to-reel tape, affording me a fuller appreciation of the singular nature of broadcasting in the Pacific. Our conversations began in Honiara and continued in Nuku'alofa.

PIBA officials and staff were helpful in any number of ways. They invited me to the annual meetings, where issues confronting broadcasting and the media are discussed with care and conviction. These assemblies are attended primarily by general managers from across the region and provide a setting for formal statements as well as informal conversations where more can be said than safely declared publicly. Hendrik Kettner, PIBA's technical coordinator, helped me comprehend the technical problems facing broadcasters in the salty heat and storm-driven Pacific. He caused me to listen to Pacific radio with new attentiveness, and I began to hear subtle differences as I traveled from island to island. Now I know to listen for the sound of downtown Apia and to distinguish that of downtown Suva, and I can pretty well guess if it's Port Vila or Honiara.

Bob Makin, former director of media services at Vanuatu Broadcasting TV Corporation (VBTC), before that a senior broadcasting officer in the colonial service and now PIBA coordinator, provided considerable detail as well as background on some of the darker side to Pacific broadcasting, much of which has not been profiled here. Makin was generous with access to PIBA archives and resources. I profited from his patient answers to myriad questions and requests.

Wolfgang Holler provided useful material on broadcasting in the Pacific, on PIBA efforts, and on critical financial support from the nongovernmental organization, Friedrich-Ebert-Stiftung (FES). When I first met Holler, he was the PIBA coordinator. He has since returned to Berlin, where he is currently head of a 24-hour radio station with multicultural programs.

Hendrik Bussiek gave detailed comments on the early history and formation of PIBA and PACNEWS. His correction of my text—in particular, the "Fax in Exile" chapter—and clarification of the record have been invaluable. Considering his careful reading, I think he was gallant to write that the chapter is "a fair account of the events and the PACNEWS story." I thank him for his courtesy and his help. Relocated to Zimbabwe, Bussiek attempted similar legerdemain with the Southern African Media Project, which was also supported by FES. He has now returned to journalism.

Reinhard Keune, of Friedrich-Ebert-Stiftung, ever a diplomat, provided background on his foundation's support of PIBA and relations with UNESCO.

Al Hulsen, former general manager of Hawaii Public Radio, deserves special mention. It was Hulsen's twice-daily reports of "Pacific Island News," before he became GM, that first got me on this Pacific quest. I had never heard the likes of such reportage over the air. Indeed, according to media theorists, I wasn't supposed to be hearing it. But five days a week, there were his five-minute spots about news developments in the widest variety of Pacific states—not just the larger islands like Fiji or Papua New Guinea or islands with political association to the United States like American Samoa. It was remarkable, enough so for me to go down to the station to find where that news was coming from.

Hulsen was more than forthcoming. He showed me the PACNEWS bulletins and began to fill me in on PIBA. Over time, he supplied tapes of programs, some containing his own breaking stories on nerve gas disposal at Johnston Atoll, and access to his own stash of PIBA documents. Hulsen has been unstinting with contacts and information, which have helped to clarify my own thinking about Pacific journalism and public service radio.

At the Solomon Islands Broadcasting Corporation, James Kilua, the general manager, kindly allowed me to visit his station on more than a few occasions and to hang out in the newsroom. He was generous with tapes of local music produced by SIBC, tapes of the program "Radio Happy Isles," and a review of the regulatory environment of his station. Dykes Angiki, news director at SIBC, met with me over the course of several years in Honiara, Suva, Port Vila, and New York, sharing his insights on the specific challenges journalism faces in the Pacific. Sam Seke was helpful both when he was editor at PACNEWS, later news editor at SIBC and now as a freelance journalist. Indeed, all the editors and reporters in the SIBC newsroom patiently answered questions and left me to read over their stories and shoulders—George Tausiria, Walter Nalangu, Alfren Inomae, George Atkin, Charles Stennett Kereau.

At Radio New Zealand International, Adrian Sainsbury and Rudi Hill furnished valuable background, Hill forwarding tapes of early efforts to provide interisland communication.

Russ Willey, of BBC Tropical Tapes, provided information, as did Don

Budd, Voice of America, Worldwide English Division, who supplied tapes of "VOA Pacific," some of which I coincidentally had heard on travels around the area.

The Honorable David Tupou, attorney general and minister of justice of the Kingdom of Tonga, provided detailed and nuanced information on the Kingdom's Defamation Act and its amendment, useful because it was somewhat at odds with outside media reports concerning rights of free speech and press.

Others who were generous with their time include Prue Moodie, Australian Financial Review; Antari Elbon, V7AB, Radio Marshalls ("The Heartbeat of the Marshall Islands"); Bill Reihr, manager of the Broadcasting and Publications Authority, Republic of Kiribati; Ephraim Tammy, National Broadcasting Corporation, Papua New Guinea; Larry Malinowski, Central Pacific Network; Martin Miriori, Bougainville Interim Government; Bishop John Zale, Gizo, Western Province, Solomon Islands; Dusty Frederick, Pohnpei Public Broadcasting Corporation; Nina Ratulele, Pacific Islands News Association; Warwick Boyd, Albuquerque, New Mexico; Joe Boyd, Rykodisk London; the late Robert Ohman, AP journalist; and Briar-Rose Nagaya, director of Nauru Media Bureau.

Meiji Gakuin University, Tokyo and Yokohama, granted sabbatical-year support, and the Institute for International Studies, Meigaku, afforded further research assistance. Kaneko Yoriko was unfailing in response to data searches, and pleasant about it too. And colleagues in the Faculty of International Studies were most encouraging during this process of research and writing.

Finally I acknowledge Elmer Luke, who was almost always patient throughout this process, ceaselessly steady in support, dedicated to clarity and a pellucid account, and an editor with a firm and tireless hand.

My appreciation to Pamela Kelley, University of Hawai'i Press.

There are many others whom I have not named here, for reasons stated earlier. But to them, again, much gratitude.

Portions of "Radio Happy Isles" appeared as an occasional paper of the Institute for International Studies, Meigaku, and sections of "Fax in Exile" appeared in *International and Regional Studies*.

Tokyo
1998

INTRODUCTION

When I first visited Vailima, the home of Robert Louis Stevenson in Samoa, I was a bit disappointed. It wasn't anything like what Graham Balfour, in his *Life of Robert Louis Stevenson,* had written:

> At this height the beat of the surf was plainly to be heard, but soothing to the ear and far away; other noises there were none but the occasional note of a bird, a cry from the boys at work, or the crash of a falling tree. The sound of wheels or the din of machinery was hardly known in the island: about the house all went barefoot, and scarcely in the world could there be found among the dwellings of men a deeper silence than in Stevenson's house in the forest.[1]

It seemed to me a marvel that the waves breaking on the reef could have been heard so clearly, for Stevenson's house is six hundred feet above sea level and about three miles inland. I couldn't hear a thing.

Balfour had gone to Vailima during Stevenson's lifetime and observed the writer's quotidian routine; surely he had not gotten the description wrong. Had the "din of machinery" long since obscured all sound of the ocean? The next day, I walked my way up a hill adjacent to Vailima with Al Hulsen, then president and general manager of Hawaii Public Radio. We rounded a bend in the road and paused to rest and get our breath. Suddenly, as if out of nowhere, we were met by the unmistakable measure and cadence of the

Pacific Ocean. Focused like a beam of light from a lens, the sea was now there to be heard. A little lower and the sound could not be discerned. A little higher and it faded out again.

Hulsen and I had set off that Sunday in 1994 after the conclusion of the Pacific Islands Broadcasting Association Assembly in Apia, Samoa, to hike to the top of a hill and from there approach another hill, where Stevenson is buried. Our imagined itinerary from the top, where the Apia Telephone Exchange and the Postal Radio Facility are situated, was to walk across a saddleback, ascend the summit of Mount Vaea—the site of Stevenson's tomb—and from there head on back to town. We made it around the chain-link fence of the Postal Radio Facility, but the overgrowth was more than planned for. The only way across to Mount Vaea seemed to be bushwhacking down the saddleback. On a warm day the summit seemed a fair struggle away, so we retreated back up the hill. After climbing the fence, we sat for a long time under a tree on a high spot, looking out over the mountains of Upolu in one direction and the breaking surf in another. Mulinu'u Peninsula and the radio transmission tower of the Samoa Broadcasting Department were clear in the distance.

As we rested, gazing out and talking, the sounds from Apia drifted up to us. Certain sounds seemed to rise above others—the barking of a dog, singing, cars seeming to hit the same bump in the road, a solitary voice, someone chopping wood, children laughing and playing. At that location we could hear nothing of the sea.

This book is a little like that trip up the mountain, where sound seems to focus at this place or that, depending on where one happens to sit. That is, in part, the book is about sounds, sounds heard over a period of time, a stretch of five or six years during which I listened to the radio wherever I went, and listened to the people who work for and run the radio stations. The narrative isn't limited to the aural realm, but it is strongly influenced by it.

I observed, and I listened . . . in a taxi in that unlovely part of Fiji where every traveler waits to go someplace else. I was on my way to buy tape cassettes in a dark retail store in Lautoka, listening to the radio, Fiji Gold, over the sound of fallen sugarcane being crushed under tires. It's Ricky Lee Jones—

CHUCK E.'S IN LOVE . . . AND IT'S TRUE! IT'S TRUE!

The taxi slows for speed bumps; a woman chases a chicken across a swept yard. Mangroves punctuate seaside sand, and a mirage of silver storage tanks reflect midday glare. Segue to "Banana Boat" with Harry Belafonte, switch to another frequency and "Siga Ni Sogo 'Fiji Day,'" by the group Kabani with George Tuinasaqalau on his steel guitar. "How Bizzare?" Yes, next up is OMC's Pauly Fuemana.

PELE YELLS WE'RE OUTTA HERE.

The ear is given a revelatory experience.

In these pages I use the term "local." I intend it in much the way someone in Hawaii might to identify a person who has ties to the community, to a common place and custom. In Hawaii you will often hear the question, is he local? And more often than not, you will hear a ready answer. The distinction is between our here and your there, sorting us from other. While nearly impossible in charged discourse, I mean the term without nuance and in no other fashion, only to fix the point of view. To be sure, the paradigm allows no room for a binary identity, and in the end, the distinction between mine and yours may hardly be emancipatory. However, in examining the ever-shifting boundaries in which we are all locals to someone else's other, perhaps the distinction helps approach an understanding of the system and complexity of differentiation that Pacific peoples themselves make. In most cases, "local" is used here to describe a Pacific, place-to-place, regional voice, as distinct from the "other" of metropolitan powers, perceived to be outside. It is also the distinction around which this book is organized.

I think the distinction, as I have tried to explain it, is a little akin to what happens to sunlight as it passes through water when you get to a depth of about ten meters: a cut finger bleeds green. With increasing depth, the component colors of sunlight are absorbed. And although the brain makes certain compensation, we become red-blind—which is why many nocturnal reef fishes are shades of red. For those of us who are immersed in the media world of North developed nations—plopping CD-ROMs into our PCs, downloading software, and e-mailing around the world—it is difficult to imagine the circumstances of a South less-developed world. We become a little media-blind. Media habits have to be relearned, particularly in this case of listening.

The opening chapter, "Radio Happy Isles," attempts to set the local tone. For those of us used to reading, however, the idea that radio could carry, beyond neutral facts, something of a tribal memory and exist as the telephone party line into which communication is passed seems more than a bit fanciful. But hearing is believing, and music is a prime example. To paraphrase, local is what local does, and from comparisons of radio music within the Pacific and without—on a Brooklyn station, say, or in France or New Zealand—one may begin to develop a sense of the uniqueness of Pacific radio. Music may be a cultural expression, but it is also a peculiar demonstration of what can constitute local programming. What a station programs reflects local taste and choice within the constraints of funding.

Pacific island nations display great contrast one from the other. But there are some broad similarities in the area of broadcasting. For example, many radio stations have evolved out of a public service model established by colonial authorities. Many countries, but not all, are small in terms of population and must provide service over a wide geographic area. Equally wide is the age and socioeconomic range of the audience that must be served, which is quite different from programming in Europe and the United States, where audiences are targeted and narrowly defined. Where private stations are now permitted in the Pacific, public service media have had to adopt new strategies for survival as governments corporatize and privatize these formally government-backed broadcasters. The chapter "Distantly from the BBC" details some of these trends, providing comparisons outside the region as well. It ends with an examination of the Solomon Islands nationwide station, SIBC, and suggests that categories assigned to the licensing and supervision of broadcasting can be other than hard and fast.

When I began research on this book, Professor Yoichi Ito of Keio University gave me this advice: Don't do another media study on international information flow. What he had in mind specifically was another quantitative study about the issue of imbalances and inequalities in news flow between North and South—only one of the many issues that erupted on the international scene under the UNESCO umbrella around 1976 when the term "New World Information Order" (NWICO) entered the political vocabulary. By 1987, when the director general of UNESCO was replaced, the debate had cooled. NWICO is today a "fading controversy," but access to information that affects a country's security and well-being remains a heated subject.[2] The issue of international information and communication is still seen as a prerequisite for the "economic and political independence of the developing countries."[3] Not so many years ago, Pacific broadcasters who had to provide news to their audiences had dead air when it came to timely information about neighbor island states. Thus the chapter "Fax in Exile" takes a look at how a group of Pacific radio broadcasters combined efforts to establish the

Pacific Islands Broadcasting Association (PIBA) to address this particular need. The result was a watershed: the capability to share timely intraregional news on a daily basis—a fact of media life taken for granted in North countries. "Fax in Exile" details the origins of the resulting Pacific News Service, PACNEWS, the inauguration of which coincided almost exactly with a coup d'état in Fiji. This chapter, a longer version of which was published elsewhere, relies primarily on access to private files, archives, and confidences provided by regional broadcasters and governmental and nongovernmental officials.

It is one thing to set up an organization but another to gather and disseminate the news, especially in a Third World setting. The chapter "News Sources—Mostly Radio" takes a newsroom-eye view of how the thrice-daily PACNEWS bulletins covering issues and events in more than fifteen Pacific island countries are solicited, assembled, and put on the wire and on the air. Most of the material is provided by correspondent PIBA member radio stations, with innovations to round out coverage.

PACNEWS, as one might imagine, faces certain constraints in the active reporting of controversial events in the region. The insurgency in Papua New Guinea is one such example, where any news on the Bougainville struggle presents unique challenges in terms of sources and contacts. "News Sources—Mostly Radio" contains a studied look at procedures and problems in treading the fine line between governmental "official news" and alternative reportage on the conflict in the political climate of the contemporary Pacific. Bougainville provides, as well, a case study of difficulties faced in any Third World newsroom. Actual source documents for some news bulletins are included here to give a behind-the-scenes view of the issues at stake.

Moreover, because PACNEWS, a news exchange, must contend with unusual journalistic circumstances, I have introduced the concept of the "news net" here. The news that may be the "catch of the day" is in fact determined before PACNEWS editors get their hands on it. For this reason, it is necessary to consider the original source of the news stories that are submitted.

We listened to music in the first chapter, and here, in the chapter "In the Newsroom," we listen to the news. This is appropriate because the majority of PACNEWS stories originate in radio newsrooms. The research for this chapter arises from the novel perspective of days actually spent sitting in local stations. Background issues of news reporting in developing countries are discussed: government pressure on journalists, equipment constraints, the cost of news, news values, who gets into the news, and so on. In some sense, then, we return to local programming. Tune in, and you might be surprised to hear a nonlocal voice. It would be understandable, I suppose, to conclude the voice to be evidence of North dominance. But before you turn the dial, listen again. You may hear a surprising echo that is quite local after all.

"The Storm," the final chapter, concerns what most of us *read* about the Pacific region, from the perspective of the outsider. The storm occurs as a metaphor here, but it is often literally the case in what we encounter when reading about the Pacific. Sometimes, in contrast to what one *hears,* this out-of-region perspective can be jarring. If you have been even slightly persuaded by what you've *heard* in the previous chapters, reading may no longer be believing. Headlines on the order of "Pacific Nation of Tokelau Gets Telephones at Last" will seem far less quaint and exotic than before. These three atolls, some 480 kilometers north of Samoa, will have become the authentic "voice" you know.

A few words about method. I have attempted to keep media theory from clouding these pages, leaving it as an underlying skeletal form on which to hang the narrative. Where specific theoretical questions arise, owing to Pacific circumstances, I have sought to address the issues at hand, pointing out where form holds and where it does not. Rather than assault the reader with a barrage of facts and figures about the Pacific, I have layered information throughout the narrative. For those unfamiliar with the region, background facts will crop up in context. This mode was adopted as a reflection of the storytelling tradition in the Pacific, which seems to exhibit a circularity. Most of the chapters, however, can be read as free-standing observations on aspects of media and, in particular, news and radio broadcasting. For a quick summary, basic demographics have been provided in appendix B.

One of the points of this exercise is to understand how broadcast media in the Pacific necessarily differ from those in metropolitan, North countries—meaning Northern Europe, the United States, and Japan. But similarities, like differences, go far beneath the surface. If, for example, you were inclined to see the action film *Speed* the summer it was first run, you could as easily have seen it in Suva, Fiji, as in Sacramento or Atlanta. At that time, the Royal was a real theater, not a dozen-plex the size of a shoe box where you hear the film next door. Seats were reserved, FJ$2.50, a little over US$1.75. Ushers in uniform escorted you to your aisle and pointed a flashlight to your seat. No tipping. The Royal's curtain opened, the film began, and in the ample space, the sound was great. Screeches and the sound of car crashes careened off the theater walls to the tilt of the speeding bus.

While you could buy popcorn, Coke in a bottle with a straw, candy, and ice cream, dal and peas were also sold. The audience ate with abandon and laughed in all the right places. Given that the film was foreign and its star was of part Pacific ancestry, I wondered if the audience might share some delight in Keanu Reeves' heroics. There was, of course, no reason they should. This was a Fijian crowd, not Hawaiian. And alas, my favorite line—*Don't attempt to grow a brain*—didn't elicit much of a response.

Obviously, the same film seen in two different places does not a common media experience make. And to be sure, the Royal was something of an exception even in the Pacific, where video parlors stand in for theaters. Today the Royal too has been transformed into a video arcade, and the Village Six by the creek in Suva provides the latest fare. As with radio, the rules are rapidly changing.

Whereas a prevalent metaphor about the Pacific notes the vastness of the sea, with tiny island countries isolated one from the other, the map I have come away with is not a big blue sea with specks of brown, but a full space of overlapping voices heard on the radio. Before this gives rise to "snickers of static," as in the words of James Merrill, let me hasten to add that radio is the vital medium in a region where television is only beginning to make an appearance—in but a few capital cities—and the majority of newspapers are weeklies.

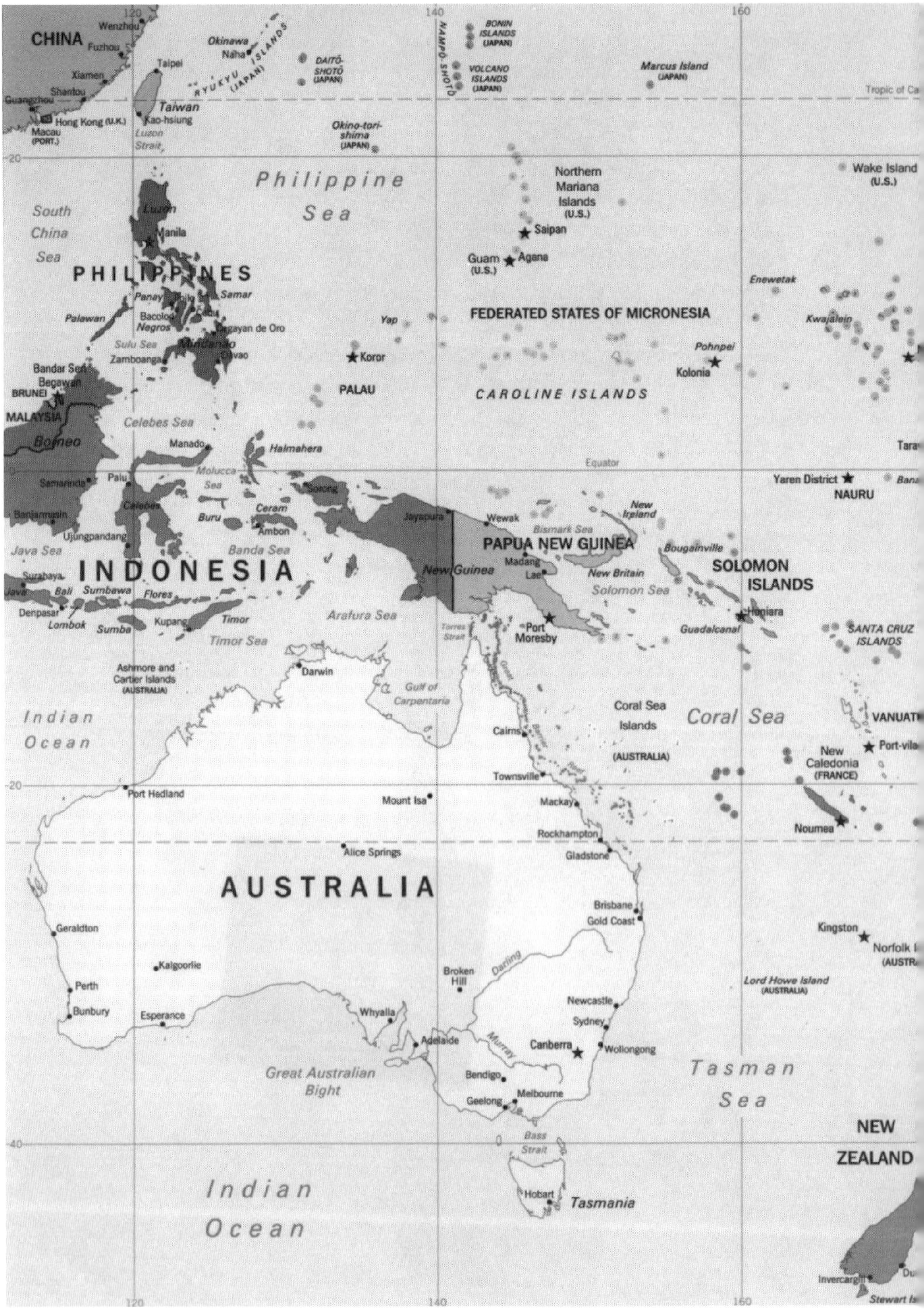
CHINA
Wenzhou
Fuzhou
Xiamen
Shantou
Guangzhou
Hong Kong (U.K.)
Macau (PORT.)
Taipei
Taiwan
Kao-hsiung
Luzon Strait
Okinawa
Naha
RYUKYU ISLANDS (JAPAN)
DAITŌ-SHOTŌ (JAPAN)
NAMPŌ-SHOTŌ
BONIN ISLANDS (JAPAN)
VOLCANO ISLANDS (JAPAN)
Okino-tori-shima (JAPAN)
Marcus Island (JAPAN)
Tropic of Ca
Philippine Sea
South China Sea
Luzon
Manila
PHILIPPINES
Panay
Samar
Palawan
Bacolod
Negros
Cagayan de Oro
Sulu Sea
Mindanao
Zamboanga
Davao
Northern Mariana Islands (U.S.)
Saipan
Guam (U.S.)
Agana
Wake Island (U.S.)
Enewetak
Kwajalein
FEDERATED STATES OF MICRONESIA
Yap
Koror
PALAU
Pohnpei
Kolonia
CAROLINE ISLANDS
Bandar Seri Begawan
BRUNEI
MALAYSIA
Borneo
Celebes Sea
Manado
Halmahera
Equator
Tara
Samarinda
Palu
Molucca Sea
Sorong
Yaren District
NAURU
Bana
Banjarmasin
Celebes
Buru
Ceram
Ambon
Jayapura
Wewak
Bismark Sea
New Ireland
Ujungpandang
Java Sea
Banda Sea
PAPUA NEW GUINEA
Bougainville
Madang
SOLOMON ISLANDS
INDONESIA
Surabaya
Java
Bali
Sumbawa
Flores
New Guinea
Lae
New Britain
Solomon Sea
Denpasar
Lombok
Sumba
Kupang
Timor
Arafura Sea
Torres Strait
Port Moresby
Honiara
Guadalcanal
SANTA CRUZ ISLANDS
Timor Sea
Darwin
Ashmore and Cartier Islands (AUSTRALIA)
Gulf of Carpentaria
Great Barrier Reef
Indian Ocean
Cairns
Coral Sea Islands (AUSTRALIA)
Coral Sea
VANUATU
Port-vila
New Caledonia (FRANCE)
Townsville
Port Hedland
Mount Isa
Mackay
Noumea
Rockhampton
Gladstone
Alice Springs
AUSTRALIA
Brisbane
Gold Coast
Geraldton
Kingston
Norfolk I (AUSTR
Kalgoorlie
Broken Hill
Darling
Lord Howe Island (AUSTRALIA)
Perth
Bunbury
Esperance
Whyalla
Newcastle
Sydney
Adelaide
Murray
Canberra
Wollongong
Great Australian Bight
Tasman Sea
Bendigo
Geelong
Melbourne
Bass Strait
NEW ZEALAND
Indian Ocean
Hobart
Tasmania
Invercargill
Stewart Is
120
140
160
20
0
20
40

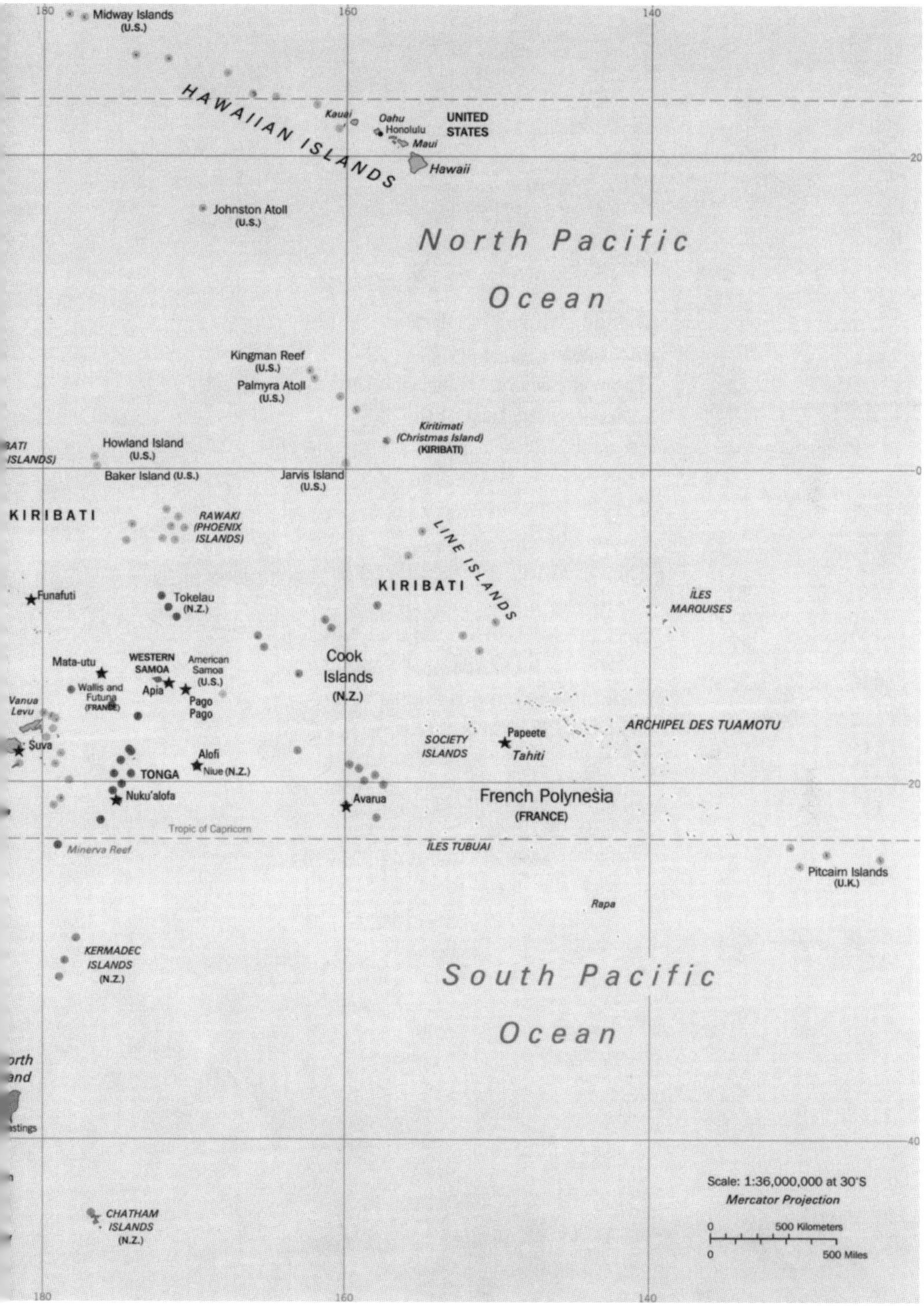
Midway Islands
(U.S.)
HAWAIIAN ISLANDS
Kauai
Oahu
Honolulu
Maui
Hawaii
UNITED STATES
Johnston Atoll
(U.S.)
North Pacific Ocean
Kingman Reef
(U.S.)
Palmyra Atoll
(U.S.)
Kiritimati
(Christmas Island)
(KIRIBATI)
Howland Island
(U.S.)
Baker Island (U.S.)
Jarvis Island
(U.S.)
KIRIBATI
RAWAKI
(PHOENIX ISLANDS)
LINE ISLANDS
KIRIBATI
Funafuti
Tokelau
(N.Z.)
ÎLES MARQUISES
Mata-utu
WESTERN SAMOA
Apia
American Samoa
(U.S.)
Pago Pago
Wallis and Futuna
(FRANCE)
Vanua Levu
Cook Islands
(N.Z.)
Suva
Alofi
Niue (N.Z.)
TONGA
Nuku'alofa
SOCIETY ISLANDS
Papeete
Tahiti
ARCHIPEL DES TUAMOTU
Avarua
French Polynesia
(FRANCE)
Tropic of Capricorn
Minerva Reef
ÎLES TUBUAI
Pitcairn Islands
(U.K.)
Rapa
KERMADEC ISLANDS
(N.Z.)
South Pacific Ocean
CHATHAM ISLANDS
(N.Z.)
Scale: 1:36,000,000 at 30°S
Mercator Projection
0 500 Kilometers
0 500 Miles
180
160
140
20
0
20
40

Radio

Behind grillwork (buff plastic
In would-be deco style)
The war goes on. With each further
Hair's-breadth turn of the dial:
"Kids love it—" "Sex probe in Congress
Triggers rage and denial,"
The weatherman predicting
Continued cold and rain,
Then high-frequency wails of
All too human pain.
Announcer: "That was a test. Now
'Nights in the Gardens of Spain.'"
A black man's mild, exhausted
"Honey, I could be wrong . . . "
Gives rise to snickers of static
—But wait. Listen. This long
Ghastly morning, one station
Has never stopped playing our song.

James Merrill

LOCAL

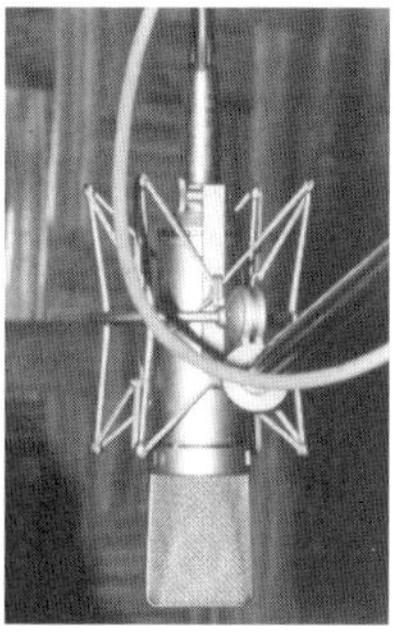

Out here they turn radios on when they buy them and never turn them off: they're like fishnets, set to catch whatever music is swimming around in the dark.

—P. F. Kluge, *The Edge of Paradise*

1

Radio Happy Isles

Programming Local Radio

THIS IS SIBC, RADIO HAPPY ISLES.

From Honiara, on the island of Guadalcanal, comes this announcement from the Solomon Islands Broadcasting Corporation radio station. Several time zones away, but just the same side of the international dateline, Radio Tonga on Tongatapu echoes with

KO E UI ʻE NI ʻA E ʻOTU FELENITE, MEI HE A3Z NUKUʻALOFA ʻA E KOMISIONI FAKAMAFOLALEA TONGA.

(THIS IS THE CALL OF THE FRIENDLY ISLANDS, A3Z NUKUʻALOFA OF THE TONGA BROADCASTING COMMISSION.)

And from Alofi on the island of Niue, the other side of the dateline, comes

THIS IS RADIO SUNSHINE.

On Saturday mornings the program from Honiara is a music request show. At first you might not understand the Pidgin the deejay is speaking. But if you persisted, you would hear familiar English words interspersed in the monologue—*hit record, top of the charts, Janet Jackson, Roxette,* and *U-2*. You would recognize the format as well. Even so, it's not quite the kind of format you hear on many music stations around the world these days. It's not the kind set by program directors or radio consultants who serve up a sort of convenience-store, fast-food music with complex formulas based on station demographics. There are no tight playlists, no frequent rotations. Still, this SIBC Saturday morning broadcast format resembles, vaguely, something you might hear on FM in Los Angeles or on a commercial station like J-Wave in Tokyo.

A radio listener from outside the Solomon Islands would recognize what has become a global approach to music radio: outcues, spot breaks for commercials, back-announcing of records or sets of songs—thematic sets, public announcements, topical comments appropriate to the music, and no time-and-temp. The sound is fairly sophisticated. Songs sometimes begin with the deejay's voice-over. Two or more songs are run together. There is easy banter. The feeling is more street-hype polish, more personalized, than flash.

Junior Adifaka is a handsome Melanesian deejay in his twenties with a sexy on-air personality. He looks his part too, knows his music, and manages a free-form format. Despite the program's name, "International Top 40," it's not Top 40 radio of the kind one hears in the United States. It's not underground radio either, and there is little in common with "urban contemporary," 98.7 KISS-FM in New York. Global charts are but a distant echo. This SIBC playlist would, in any case, be closer to Reach'n Records from Australia than to Record Shops (UK) or Dataflow (worldwide).

There is but one radio station in most Pacific island countries, often under some form of direct state management or control—even in a period of corporatization or privatization. So a listener does not expect a format reminiscent of the early days of KMPX-FM in San Francisco under Tom "Big Daddy" Donahue. But even so, although SIBC is a public service radio, the deejay is more or less free to choose what songs to play. His weekly mix is based on personal taste and what listeners ask for. Arbitron (a service that tracks radio stations) and similar sophisticated audience surveys are many miles away, across the Pacific. The pulse of the audience is in the streets and in the local clubs and, as with any station around the world, in the program manager's and general manager's offices.

The light in the control booth is dim. It enters through two layers of glass and looks onto the station's grassy courtyard, reflecting nothing off wooden bats and sisal-covered walls. This filtered light from the tropical sun sets a mood in the studio, where the deejay is alone. Adifaka creates the space for the music to fill in a seemingly effortless mix.

That is to say, there is a studio air booth, but the Saturday morning show, like most of the programs on SIBC, is broadcast from the control booth without a separate engineer—there simply are not sufficient personnel even if one chose to divide the responsibility. The deejay is surrounded by turntables, tape decks, control board. The rack contains a clutter of things to play.

He cues songs, does his own segue between songs, sees that one cut flows into another, manages the microphone, hits buttons that regulate turntables and tape decks—all on the fly. Junior Adifaka's noticeable confidence is an adrenaline-energy, induced by live-air play—an impressive choreography as electronics, voice, and music pour out in sound and tempo, everything held together by the embrace of a voice like cream. This part of the Pacific is locked in. The distance is spanned.

SIBC on AM and shortwave commands the demographics of the entire country. No one knows for sure what the "cume" is, the cumulative audience, nor even the ratings. We know that every second household in the Solomon Islands has a radio and that there is some spillover of the broadcasts into Vanuatu and Papua New Guinea. But if you walked out of the station, you'd find out what your ratings were, because, on the way to town, down Mendana Avenue, people would tell you.

A notable exception to the Pacific pattern of mostly public radio is Fiji, where FM 96 in Suva, run by William Parkinson's Communications Fiji, provides format radio in English and Fijian twenty-four hours a day. There is nothing eclectic, just lots of local emphasis, and the station is widely popular. Communications Fiji also runs the Hindi station, Navtarang, which serves the sizable Indian Fijian population.[1]

As a private station, FM 96 does not have to provide the "public service broadcasting" for which the public Fiji Broadcasting Commission, an independent statutory body, is responsible. (In 1997, FBC was in the process of being privatized. Government subvention will be a significant lever over what gets broadcast.) In the Solomons, SIBC is also charged with public service broadcasting, but public service broadcasting varies widely from country to country in the region. In New Zealand, for example, the Broadcasting Act mandates that minority interests be provided for. This includes the interests of women, ethnic minorities, the disabled, and the Maori community. A ministerial directive requires that at least 6 percent of the money administered by the public funding agency NZ On Air goes to Maori broadcasting; NZ On Air provides an even greater percentage. For most of the small Pacific island nations (small in terms of population but not in geographic area), the interests of an entire and sometimes widely divergent population have to be served by one station, from one studio.

Listen to Suva's private FM 96, however, and the sound is automated, like the formats provided by consultants. But then diversity is not expected in a successful commercial station, and Communications Fiji is prominent in its markets. Public service radio, on the other hand, has a wider spectrum of audience to serve, including economically unproductive markets in highland areas or outlying islands. Parkinson's private stations are typical, successful local radio: rip-and-read spot news, lots of regionally popular music, hometown sports, and advertisements for local merchants. FM 96 produces the advertisements in its own studios, and it wins regional awards for its efforts.

Not all radio programming in the Pacific is like Radio Happy Isles on Saturday mornings, nor, certainly, like Suva's FM 96. There is plenty of dead air space, old-fashioned programming—a pale and uninteresting allusion to a BBC-style—and little that hints at political controversy or debate. Safe, you would say: nothing to rile the prime minister or get the general manager (GM) fired. You hear a voice on the air and you can assume that the deejay is the general manager's cousin or the broadcasting commissioner's daughter. Still it's refreshing, because it is not the standard formats and syndicated programs that most of us in the developed world now hear.

In places such as the United States, Japan, and Australia, commercial stations make frequent use of syndicated programs for all sorts of formats—music, sports, news, even talk shows. Once mostly confined to late nights and weekends, this sort of programming now creeps into daytime and evening hours. Turn on a commercial station in Yokohama: you could be in Los Angeles for all the program differences—or New York for that matter. No wonder. Westinghouse alone controls something like 175 of the 10,000 stations in the United States.

In part, stations have moved to such syndication because of cost. For example, in Australia a night shift for a live deejay, which usually runs around four hours of air time, might cost something on the order of AU$25,000 a year.[2] If the program manager buys a syndicated program, which comes by satellite service to his regional station, the same program slot can be covered for about AU$5,000. These costs for commercial stations dictate a shift away from live-air play and regional programming and local content. The result is sometimes a sort of homogenized radio and bubblegum rock format. And sometimes programming that is far more interesting and sophisticated than could be produced locally. This is, however, a matter of taste, of choice.

Tight budgets for communications are a phenomenon not only of low-income countries. Radio New Zealand is being squeezed for funds through the allocation decisions of NZ On Air, which was established by the Broadcasting Act of 1989.[3] The public funding agency distributes the broadcasting fees it collects (NZ$89.8 million in gross income in 1993) to radio and television, specifically to individual producers of television programs. This funding on a program-by-program basis beyond simply bulk funding stations was taken in part to encourage more local programming. Radio suffered a loss in funding from NZ On Air but continues to receive its bulk funding. In 1993, NZ National Radio broadcast 28.6 percent New Zealand music.

A decade earlier, however, UNESCO studies showed that, as regards TV programming, local content accounted for only 25 percent of New Zealand's broadcasts. In contrast, for the United States the figure was 98 percent; for the United Kingdom, 85 percent; and for Australia, 50 percent. As former public service stations around the Pacific become corporatized—and are expected to return a profit—it is not unexpected that such foreign content slips into the program schedule. NZ On Air funds programs directly to work against this trend. Nevertheless, syndicated programming is a fixed feature of modern mass communications even where attempts are made to include wide ranges of groups and to maintain local programming. Radio is no different, either public service radio or commercial radio.

There are those who bemoan the trend and see danger in foreign over local content. The French, for one, have demanded a "cultural exception" under the General Agreement on Tariffs and Trade on imports of film and television programs. France seeks, in part, to protect its movie industry against imports from Hollywood. The French wish to retain the right to subsidize films and television in much the same manner that they subsidize ballet, theater, museums, and orchestras.

"We cannot allow the Americans to treat us in the way they dealt with the redskins," French director Bertrand Tavernier declared in a speech to the European Parliament.[4] This arch statement is bolstered by a 1989 European Community directive that requires member states to devote a majority proportion of television time to European programs *where possible*. Indeed, European culture figures, primarily French, fear that Europe's culture will be doomed by American cultural imperialism. They sound an alarm. To some the tone is chauvinistic; to others it is a reasoned response to mass-produced media products that have been amortized in the large American market and then sold to foreign broadcasters and distribution outlets at prices European producers cannot match.

The U.S. position is that subsidies and quotas, as proposed by the French, would distort the market for media products—a position that, of course, may well be influenced by the fact that media products are enormous export earners, second only to commercial aircraft in importance. One side views media as an economic product, not unlike agricultural and industrial products—rice and cars, for example. The other looks on the problem as one of "culture" and its preservation, thus justifying an economic nationalism.

This is difficult terrain to traverse. Fundamentally, the nature of taste is at issue, and whether it is constrained or expanded is a matter of perspective. "DJ Disciple" Banks does his weekly "Mix Show" for the Brooklyn station WNYE-FM and is heard on three stations in Japan—not particularly impressive in terms of syndication but more a credit to the Japanese stations than not. DJ Disciple's program may be syndicated, but he sets himself off from other deejays among the New York club scene, sees himself playing music that others do not, taking risks, championing new artists and producers.[5] Interestingly enough, Banks' "Mix Show" is broadcast on a Brooklyn *community station,* which can be heard in a good part of the New York area, including Manhattan. He bypasses record companies by getting his musical material, usually in the form of cassettes, directly from producers. Banks uses two vari-speed tape decks (with pitch control) for the "Mix Show." The compromise is that he has to "play vinyl"—test pressings and new releases—because people want to hear music that, at least in part, they will actually be able to buy. Add in the Japanese stations that broadcast the "Mix Show" and you have an interesting case study for "cultural capitalism"—and a complicating case to the usual arguments. For one thing, a part of the "imperialistic culture industry"—the record companies and distributors—is cut out by going directly to producers and musicians. For another, the original "channel," WNYE, is not a commercial radio station.

In a different scenario, the New Zealand Broadcasting Act "preserves the interests of women, minorities, the disabled, and Maoris but not the interests of people who want to watch the best television [or listen to the best radio] programs from around the world. We miss tremendous stuff they see everywhere else—and little New Zealand at the bottom of the Pacific gets another segment about a disabled child in Timaru [a small seaport on South Island]."[6] And so you have another complicating example about the nature of choice: Friends of National Radio (New Zealand) lobbying for more quality overseas material, not less. Dr. Dennis Dutton, a member of Friends, believes that these same arguments apply to Radio New Zealand's programming.

If "little" New Zealand, with a population of about three million, feels conflict about programming, what must be the perception from nearby yet smaller island nations?

Although it may be easier for someone from the developed North to say, apprehensions regarding cultural capitalism are easily overstated in the abstract. The nature of programming and the availability of programming are separate issues, however, and need to be kept separate from taste for one or another sort of programming. For a program manager to make use of syndicated programs is not necessarily a moral lapse. Elitism with regard to these matters—BBC feeds in the case of some—cannot but leave all of us with a bit of mass culture lurking in the closet at some time or other, a Big Mac here, a visit to (Euro-) Disneyland there.

In a world of global mass communications, small and peripheral countries are no doubt vulnerable to media industries. But that vulnerability extends no less to the media audience in the developed North. If you are a parent, keeping "dinomania" and *Jurassic Park*–like blockbuster films and other products of global communications out of your children's lives proves even more difficult because of the nature of mass culture. Professor Stephen Jay Gould, while reviewing the "science" of Michael Crichton's novel favorably, sees a great danger in movies like *Jurassic Park* because of their larger "culture force."[7]

Gould's fear is not unlike the French fear, which is that the Euro-Disneyland theme park and other symbols of American power and influence endanger their culture. They see this in the much larger process of the globalization of media and, perhaps, culture too. As global markets spread, local and regional markets are absorbed, marginalized, and, often, destroyed. As a global economic product, media are no different from other global economic products. Globalization in communications—what in fonder times we might have called the spread of cosmopolitan culture and internationalism—moves beyond the scope of local media as taste and desire expand. This is a process which has been going on for a century or more. Whether we are menaced or entertained and informed is a debate which will not be settled by pointing out that Matt Groening's cartoon creation *The Simpsons,* a popular American television series, is shown on TV Blong Vanuatu Mondays at 6:57 P.M. *Sesame Street* in both French and English is also aired. So too are *Benny Hill* and *Cuisine de France.* But rather than focus on one sort of programming over another, or even the dominance of one media giant over another, what is really of interest here are the boundaries of choice.

Syndication and nonlocal programming are not, however, a reflection on personal taste but on media culture and choice—in one example, on the penetration of canned music programming. Where cultural experiences are varied, the issue is not of particular concern: just turn the dial. But in the Pacific, choice is more constrained by what is accessible locally and by the fact that there usually is only one place on the dial to select—unless you resort to shortwave radio. Indeed, the slogan of the one-kilowatt FM station in Majuro, capital of the Marshall Islands, is

ONE NATION . . . ONE STATION, V99.9 FM.

The slogan may be mere wishful thinking on the part of this single commercial station because of the mixture of government, religious, and private noncommercial stations in the Marshalls.

In the Solomons, however, only one station serves the entire nation country. (A competing FM commercial station has begun to serve the capital of Honiara.) SIBC's Dykes Angiki, news director, indicated there was a good reason why Junior Adifaka played some foreign cuts on his Saturday morning request program but also a good deal of music from Solomon Islands and nearby Melanesia: at the time, the station could not afford to install CD players in the control room; records were starting to go out of production, and even if they were not, budget constraints would not allow for more records or CDs.

Choice Constrained

In the Pacific, media choices can be constrained even more fundamentally, on the level of personal income. For example, in the United States 95 percent of all automobiles is equipped with a radio. To be sure, there are more radios than there are people in the United States, a pattern that is true in most of the developed world, but that figure does not hold in low- and medium-income nations. In the Cook Islands, the population is about 19,000, and the number of radio sets is estimated at 10,000. Or take the case of Kiribati: population 83,400, radio sets somewhere over 10,000. If you ask a general manager of a Pacific island station what the actual per capita radio ownership figures are, he will admit uncertainty despite the UNESCO statistics. In most cases, funds for an audience survey are lacking. The figures are, by and large, crude estimates. But they do give a flavor of the situation in those countries. The figures for Kiribati at one per 0.13 of the population seem low, and the figures for the Cook Islands are about average for the Pacific—roughly one radio for every two people. But what these gross figures also do is obscure important details such as the distribution within the populations.

In general, people in the capital or the urban areas have higher incomes than those in highland or outlying islands. What radio means in terms of personal income, personal choice, is important. The radio which sits in your kitchen or which you plug into your ears and walk around with represents nowhere near the percentage of yearly income it does for an average Pacific islander. Two cases illustrate the point. In Nuku'alofa the cheapest AM/FM radio costs about 8.90 Tongan pa'anga, the national currency. But to operate this radio, you need two AA batteries at 40 Tongan cents apiece, which might keep it running for perhaps ten or fewer hours depending on how loud you turn up the volume and what bandwidth you listen to. Total cost: T$9.70. If you were to buy a Gold Star AM/FM radio with two shortwave bands, the cost is T$56. In addition, you need three batteries, at 65 Tongan cents apiece. Don't forget to add tax.

In downtown Port Vila, a citizen from Vanuatu can buy an AM/FM radio for around 2,500–3,600 vatu. The very cheapest AM radio, produced in China, might be as low as 1,000 vatu. Four AA batteries are 160 vatu. If you were to buy a National shortwave, longwave, AM/FM radio, the cost is 32,000 vatu. Again, remember that batteries have to be factored into the equation because in some outlying areas there may be no electricity.

Think, then, in terms of yearly income. In the case of Tonga, the average yearly income is a bit over US$1,000; in Vanuatu it is slightly over US$800. In both cases, the cost of a small AM/FM radio represents 10–20 percent of yearly income, assuming the purchase of batteries for use over the course of a year. To acquire a shortwave radio, which would allow for reception of stations outside the country, the cost rises to 30–38 percent of income, again assuming the acquisition of a year's supply of batteries. The batteries alone could run 14–34 percent of yearly per capita income, depending on the kind of radio and the length of time and the conditions under which the radio is used. These hypothetical figures highlight the differences between the high-income North and the lower-income South.[8] In higher-income countries, the problem is information overload—how to avoid media and how to reduce the costs of information abundance and choice. In lower-income countries, the problems are significantly different as these figures indicate. And in the Pacific, it is not only personal budgets that are constrained.

Public service radio stations in the Pacific are under terrific financial pressure as well. Not unlike the United States, nearly all the small Pacific island nations have sizable trade imbalances. Foreign aid is important to their economies but is declining as developed nations cut back. So these governments are in turn squeezing their radio stations, insisting that they begin to provide money to alleviate government support. Stations are being privatized or corporatized, and general managers now seek additional domestic sources of revenue wherever possible.

The result is a move toward commercialization, while leaving the stations in more or less the same political structure as before: privatization, with strings attached in the form of subventions for public service. But commercial professional know-how is in scarce supply in government-controlled and subsidized public service and national stations. This lack of professionalism is a problem—where to get it if you want to be on air and, if you are the GM, where to find it and how to employ it. Turning a civil servant into a freewheeling commercial-message producer is no mean task. In any event, many stations have personnel shortages because they cannot afford to pay people. Switching to commercialization is not easy.

Furthermore, most stations and nations in the Pacific do not have codes regulating advertising.[9] In Britain a clear distinction between programs and advertisements must be maintained, and all developed nations have duration and interval rules concerning the playing of advertising spots. Claims of advertising copy have to be substantiated. To fill this need, the Pacific Islands Broadcasting Association has held training sessions for station personnel and workshops to help the stations develop standards. Consultants, brought in to teach basic skills and awareness, help the stations create commercial staff.

On Radio Vanuatu's FM service, FM 98 Nambawan, you can now hear commercial programming. The logo, Nambawan (number one), is an effect of the training in commercial awareness. FM 98 uses a commercial block of time—four hours a day—rather than scattering advertisements throughout the day's program schedule. In effect, this segregates the commercial sector from the public service portion of the station. Most of the commercials are for local advertisers and produced locally.

Commercialization is a compromise with a national system of public service broadcasting. Whether this compromise can be maintained over the long term remains to be seen. Where funds are in short supply, it is easy to see four hours of programming being expanded to five, and from five to six, and so on. Commercial radio is a business. The norms, styles, values, and production codes of national service media are, by necessity, different from those of a commercial station. Even though there are many variations on a public system, commercial service is widely at odds with national services, which must also further social and economic development goals. That means providing programs about agricultural improvement, family planning, and public health. Local Top 40 radio becomes only one among many competing formats and programs for air time on a national service. Nonetheless, other Pacific island stations are beginning to turn to commercialization for survival too. Whether commercialization of public service radio can ever provide sufficient funds to support the stations is debatable.

Outside the United States, few broadcasters depend on advertising revenue for their entire budget. Budgets may be supplemented but even so probably cannot support entire stations. In the Pacific, conditions are such that possibilities for advertising are limited by demographics such as the size of the audience (small) and its income level (low). The consumer purchasing power needed to sustain commercial broadcasting may simply not exist, or the audience may be too meager in absolute numbers or dispersed over a vast area.

In low-income countries around the world, station-support formulas tend to look something like this: government plus advertising; government plus license fees; or advertising only.[10] Where there is advertising, on average it rarely supplies 100 percent of revenue. There is no reason to believe that the Pacific will turn out to be different.

But there is one source of advertising revenue that many Pacific island stations have effectively tapped into: personal listener-service announcements. For a small fee, listeners can have personal messages read on air. This would be illegal in the United States under Federal Communications Commission rules, in Japan, and in most developed nations. But Pacific stations do a thriving business in service announcements—particularly as radio messages serve as a vital link from one island to another where other means of communication are lacking or involve long delays. For SI$15 (about US$6), SIBC will broadcast from its Honiara studios up to twenty words of your personal message, and it will reach the entire country of 401,100, north to Malaita and as far east as Temotu. The rate rises for the number of words; 36–50 words would cost SI$45. In recent years, service messages have been the largest generator of station revenue. In fact, over 60 percent of Radio Happy Isles' revenue now comes from this source.

In the Kingdom of Tonga too, Radio Tonga, AZ3, broadcasts personal messages. If the message is a service announcement—personal message—the rate for twenty words is T$2.50 (US$1.85) and ten seniti (10 Tongan cents) for each additional word. AZ3 also takes spot announcements. For fifty words the rate is a reasonable T$6.

Service announcements represent quite a range of messages. Someone who puts a parcel on the ferry MV *'Olovaha* for relatives on the outlying islands of Ha'apai, Vava'u, or Niuas may pay for a message to be played on the air so that the ship will be met when it gets to port. Tongans, like other Pacific islanders, resort to radio because there may be no other way to get a message out; the outer islands may not have telephones, or their relatives may not. Even if you miss the message when it is read over the air, someone in your neighborhood is sure to hear and alert you. An employer may send a message to an errant employee:

> TAVAKE, I GAVE YOU TWO WEEKS' VACATION BUT YOU HAVE BEEN AWAY FOR FOUR; IF YOU DON'T COME TO WORK BY NEXT FRIDAY, YOU ARE FIRED.

(26 words; US$2.30 on AZ3.) Less ominous are congratulatory messages. When school kids graduate or receive examination results, friends and relatives often take out a service message. On any one day, the messages run into the hundreds on Radio Tonga. But on Mother's Day, the station has to run overtime to get all the messages read. There may be as many as three to four thousand messages. The bulk of the messages are read on the air in the late afternoon and early evening, when the majority of the audience is listening in.

With the push to commercialize, SIBC requires that the prime minister and other government agencies, as well as churches, pay for their air time as well. At first the churches in Honiara refused, and the station left them off the air. After some months an agreement was reached and churches now pay for the Sunday live-worship broadcasts; these broadcasts are alternated among the various denominations—Church of Melanesia (Anglican), Roman Catholic, South Seas Evangelical Church, United Church (Methodist), Seventh Day Adventist Church, and others. But note, the fee is *not* a commercial rate.

The Solomons, like most of the Pacific, is devout, and most of Sunday is set aside for religious programming. This too is common in the Pacific where stations observe Sunday-for-sermons formats. Even on weekdays there are broadcasts of morning and evening devotions on SIBC. That SIBC charges the churches for air time should not be surprising; a number of commercial stations in the United States have turned to religious formats and they are *big* moneymakers.

Radio Tonga also broadcasts religious devotions, but the station shuts down early on Sunday afternoon. In Tonga, an electronic church is no substitute for sitting in a pew. You don't have the God Squad and fast-paced moral messages interspersed with rock 'n' roll. Religious music in Tonga is strongly devotional, not simply "spiritual" or humanistic in character, and church choirs are truly moving.

As a public service broadcaster, even the BBC sells advertising in its profit-oriented enterprises like commercial publishing. Pacific stations have similarly turned to other sources of funding. Radio Tonga's additional source of revenue is the Radio Store on Taufa'ahau Road in downtown Nuku'alofa. It commands the Sanyo distributorship and a few others as well. You can buy AM/FM radios, VCRs, Walkman-type receivers, and other appliances there, and if the merchandise breaks, the engineers at the station will attempt to repair the equipment for you at a nominal fee, usually the price of the parts. In fact, if you visit the station, the soldering iron is hot, and the workbench is piled high with tape recorders, radios, and other electronics which the technical service people are poring over in an attempt to bring back to life. It is something they do in addition to keeping AZ3 on the air.

The station also runs a "hire purchase scheme" in which government employees and those from independent statutory authorities in the Kingdom can obtain the goods and have the price deducted from their salary monthly. If the Radio Store does not have the product you want, they can get it from another store. Radio Tonga gets a small cut on the transaction. Refrigerators, video cassette recorders, gas ranges, of course radios, furniture, and even washing machines can be obtained by this means.

Although the station does not receive a direct subvention from the government, it does indirectly in the sense that it charges government agencies for public announcements and for programs. Through these various means, Radio Tonga supports itself. Money is money, and Pacific stations do what they can to stay on the air in the face of declining revenue from their own governments.

So the stations of the Pacific are not like those of the North, the North of the North/South divide, which most of us hear. Of course, on Pacific stations in the small island nations that dot the region, you can hear canned programs and feeds from other places too: Voice of America, Radio Australia, Radio New Zealand, BBC, and Deutsches Welle. Most often it is news; sometimes it is programs about health and agricultural development; other times it is so-called cultural programs such as music and, less often, drama. These are not the kind of expensive canned programs produced in Los Angeles, syndicated, and aired in Eugene, Oregon, and Yokohama, Japan, that most of us know. By and large the stations cannot afford these "sophisticated," syndicated programs. Their budgets are precarious, and in many cases overseas development assistance has had to provide the facilities and a lot of the personnel training too. Nonetheless, the result is a lot more local programming, occasional dead air, and once in a while some not very professional announcing. Fast-food radio it is not.

Listening to Local Music

Without doubt, you can hear some of the most popular music groups from the United States, Australia, and the United Kingdom on stations in the Pacific. And if you ask Junior Adifaka, the deejay on the SIBC Saturday morning "Top International 40" request show, about station guidelines regarding local content, he will tell you, sure there are guidelines—two-thirds local, one-third foreign. If you ask him what the station really plays, the answer is, about one-third local and two-thirds foreign. Supposing the true figure is anywhere near this, the achievement is remarkable if we recall that from a much larger nation, New Zealand, radio broadcasts a little less than 30 percent local music. (In Tonga, the station personnel report that they do maintain a three-to-one balance in favor of local music, but the figure does not seem possible. According to Jack Lang, France's former minister of culture, even in Europe about a third of the music played is American.[11] Lang is probably thinking about music played in France.) But music from outside the country doesn't necessarily mean Western. There are string bands as well as other sounds from all over the Pacific. The music scene is local to the Pacific, and it is thriving. The importance is that who speaks—in this case who sings—is a regional voice identifiable as such.

Some of the most popular groups in the Pacific, groups that get big air play and also do live performances in the region, are from Papua New Guinea (PNG). (There is a thriving music scene in Fiji too.) The PNG music groups are professionally produced and popular throughout Melanesia. Tune in Radio Vanuatu and chances are you'll hear a PNG band. Similarly in the Solomon Islands, where a lot of the requests on SIBC are for PNG musicians like Lista Laka, John Wong, Basil Greg, Dika Dai, Telek, Steve Lahui, Henry Kuskus, Nokondi Nama, and Variki. You might also hear Unisound, RYO, Iron Juice, Jana, and Sisirikiti from the Solomon Islands. There is a good chance too that the sound of didgeridoos would come over the air as Yothu Yindi, an Aboriginal band from Australia's coastal communities of northeast Arnhem Land, is played.[12]

Not so surprising when you think about it: broadcasting regional music groups made up of members of the same generation as much of the audience.

The median age in the Solomons is 15.8 years. In Vanuatu it is 17.6 years. The population of the Pacific is young. The *tok pisin* songs—songs in regional dialect—concern local matters, are the concerns of local kids. The themes run to women, love, religion, growing up, local and national identity, and belonging.[13] According to David Palapu, program manager for SIBC, lyrics also frequently deal with special occasions—something that happened at a particular time in the musician's life.[14] The lyrics may be about a specific place where people have lived before coming to the capital—a boat that sails from home on the island of Isabel, for example. It is difficult to get a copy of the lyrics because they are not written down and may change from performance to performance. But these are lyrics and vocabulary from a local pen—an echo of a theme of modern desires experienced from the contradictions of a traditional society.

Not untypical are lyrics to a song called "You and Me and the Band," by a Papua New Guinea group called Brukim Bus.[15]

Mi bin tingting bek bipo	*I was thinking of the past*
Long taim yumi bin go long Hagen Taun	*Of the time we went to Hagen Town*
Ol manki i bin amamas tru	*All the boys were extremely happy*
Long lukim Hailans	*To see the Highlands*

This song, which deals in particular with regional identity, is a reminiscence about the rock band's tour around the country.

Concerning local and regional themes, one group from the Solomon Islands, RYO, stands out because of its tempo—local, instruments—regional, themes—intrinsic, and beat—reggae. (RYO, which stands for Rural Youth Orchestra, is from the island of Malaita, but the group resides in the capital on Guadalcanal.) Group members have studied in Australia and New Zealand, but their lyrics focus on local life and deal with the transition from rural living to modern life. RYO performs in clubs at night. Music doesn't support most musicians full-time.

Popular music of the metropolitan North is often pointed to as the bane of local traditions, promoting universal values and taste, an orientation to a mass, homogeneous culture and audience. And perhaps it does induce such change where the media are a global product. But in the Pacific, control and ownership of the local cassette music is decentralized. Don Niles, editor of a series of volumes on music in Papua New Guinea, writes that most

Dear Announcer

Radio Happy Lagoon, a 10-watt medium-wave station in Gizo—a city and island in the New Georgia islands of the Solomon Islands, north, near the border with Papua New Guinea—was on air only a few hours a day, in the late afternoon, weekdays. Because of further budget cutbacks at the Solomon Islands Broadcasting Corporation in the latter 1990s, local Gizo broadcasting was forced off air. At the station, one person had performed all the duties related to keeping the station on air. That included programming, gathering local news, announcing, acting as deejay, collecting money for service announcements, and so on. The station was particularly important to Solomon Islands residents in the Western Province because the main SIBC station in Honiara could not always be heard this far north, and often the reception was not clear. Mostly "island music" was broadcast, defined by the announcer/deejay as music from the Pacific—which included Solomon Islands, Papua New Guinea, Cooks, Tonga, and Samoa. Sign-off was at sunset.

The following letter is from a listener on a nearby island to the north and west of Gizo and was addressed to Radio Happy Lagoon, Gizo, Solomon Islands, 945 kHz.

> Ranonga Island, Western Province
>
> Dear Announcer:
>
> I'm very happy. Could you kindly play a song from Junior Kopex. The song is called, "Lisim Yu." This song was mainly played for the following girls and boys like! Miss Joyce Lina, Miss Cathrine Vailo, Miss Carlyn Tanu Gu, Miss Luisa Tanzia, Miss Leroly Denmark, Miss Jena Besa, Mr. Bendick Sasa . . . Mr. Jimmy Reves. All young girls and boys from Rava Village, Ranonga Island, Western Province and all of them at Alomana Village, Rendova Island.
>
> And lastly to Miss Vermia Bruce, and at Ringi Cover, Kolombanara Island, and lastly myself, the writer, Henry Sianapitu.

cassettes containing Papua New Guinea music were released by local companies—almost 92 percent.[16] Indeed, PNG bands also produce their own video clips, which supplement a robust local cassette commerce.

In Vanuatu as well, Vanuata Productions produces and distributes a wide variety of local bands. In the Chew General Store in downtown Port Vila, several glass display cases contain stacks of cassettes by local groups. According to the liner notes to "Vanuatu in the Blue Pacific," by the Efate group Saratokowia, "Vanuatu local string band is a type of music created by ni-Vanuatu several years after the settlement of the first European in the country. It had played a major part in the music industry developing itself and [at] the same time maintaining the original principles of local music." These locally produced cassettes cost 750–800 vatu—about US$7–8.

In the fragmented Pacific market, diversity, which caters to localized communities, flourishes. Nor is this situation unique around the world.[17] Musicians may understand the rules of their genre and the histories of the music they play, but they also place high value on originality and self-expression, on expressing in music a unique identity—a Pacific sound. Because much of the music is also performed live, a musician has to "connect" with the community in order to succeed in popularity. But to be popular is not necessarily to be in opposition to cultural values. A more useful view might be to understand the music as giving the musicians a place culturally, perhaps politically and historically, in a complex system of their own symbolic meaning.

Lest one get sentimental, this is not global youth "drop out" culture sounded out on a panpipe to the tune of naïveté. Culture North to South could not be more different than it is within the Pacific itself. The music is *local* and the appeal is to *local* culture, confirmation of its own protagonism. And you buy the tapes—not CDs—at the *local* general store. There is no mass consumer market to attract chains like Tower and Virgin Records. Current cassette technology does, however, permit a thriving local music scene.[18] The nice thing is that if you ask the clerk behind the counter, he will play you some excerpts of the tape you are thinking of buying and talk to you about the groups and the songs. That too is not universal.

Don't expect down-tempo hip hop. Even so, you will encounter three surprises. One is what you could call reggae. An example is a song by the Solomon Islands group Sisirikiti, "Buala Reggae"—Buala being on the island of Isabel. Another is what you might call Pacific West African *soca* with a little *mbaqanga* (Zulu pop) thrown in. Locally it is simply called calypso, according to SIBC program manager Palapu. The third you could only describe as Pacific country and western, a real shock when you first hear it, but the ballad-like quality is unmistakable. Vocals are in a mixture of Pidgin and English but heavy on the Pidgin or other local language. Instruments are what you would expect these days—electric guitars, keyboards, rhythm, bass, drums. They are of course imported and expensive. You can imagine that setting up a band is beyond the means of most musicians. The instruments are made in Japan and the United States, the duty runs to 70 percent, and the VAT is 10 percent more.

At one shop in Port Vila, Vanuatu, a drum set with cymbals cost 110,000 vatu—about US$970. An electric guitar with an amp and one speaker runs about US$1,130. Throw in a conga drum for another US$255 and you haven't even managed to outfit the band, but already you are at US$2,355. Keep in mind too that the average income is a little over US$800 per year.[19] If you want to make music you can make do with less, but a regular string guitar still costs US$75–$105, and even a ukulele is US$35.

There are panpipe groups in the Solomons, and SIBC has even produced a solo tape "Are'Are," by the panpipe musician Emmanuel Sabati, under its own label, the Hapi Isles Super Sound. The Pacific Islands Broadcasting Association also offers an annual Song and Music Production competition to encourage local music. In 1993, Tiani Noa of Radio Tuvalu won both the first and third prizes. First prize was for the melody of the "Voice of Tuvalu," the third prize for "Music of the Tuvaluan Ancestors"—both in Tuvaluan language. So you *can* find groups that use traditional instruments and play music rooted in local culture and custom, but it is not quite the sound that kids always want to hear or play.

Assuming you get your act together, get the instruments, even get a reasonable local following, where do you record your music to get anything like a professional sound? In the Solomon Islands there are only two places, neither with digital studio equipment. One local musician has a studio, which approximates a professional setup, that he uses to record his own music. The other choice is the studios of SIBC, studios donated by overseas development assistance from the government of Japan. For SI$56 an hour (US$18.50) you can rent the studio from the station. Mixing costs SI$23 per hour (US$7.60), and you can probably even get some help from the station personnel.

These days, relatively inexpensive recording equipment, cheap considering what it used to cost, is now available. Digital studios are not entirely out of reason. In the Marshall Islands, for example, local groups can go to a digital recording studio set up by a local entrepreneur on Majuro. Steve Whitehead of Hitkicker Studios will produce, edit, and mix the music, customizing "a recording to fit everybody's needs and budget."[20] Groups from as far away as Kiribati and Pohnpei have also used the studio. Hitkicker is probably the only fully digital recording studio in Micronesia, with the exception of Guam. As the cost of this recording technology declines, one should expect a wider distribution.

Nonetheless, inequality in income shapes musical outcomes. Lack of talent or dedication is not the only factor that impedes young musicians; a paucity of material resources can prove a large stumbling block. Mixing or remixing, for one thing, is beyond the means of most Pacific island musicians. If it is done at a local public service radio station, the activity has to compete with the necessity to do regular programming and now commercials too. And it has to be paid for. Practice space and public performance space are at a premium as well.

SIBC program manager Palapu encourages local groups, telling them that they do not have to rely on imported instruments, that a local sound is valid and interesting. But convincing young musicians of this is an uphill battle. Why, is a difficult question. Perhaps the imagery of the music, while local and at the heart of society, fits more comfortably in the technology of modern instruments, more comfortably than in the traditional ones that evoke rural life—sounds of wind and rain, insects, animals, wood on wood, stone against stone. If their music is evidence, the musicians believe modern instruments convey the imagery best.

Electronics produce the sounds of modern life, which can be loud and earsplitting—metal on metal, sirens against horns, pounding on concrete. Music must convey musically as well as textually. It is these sounds, the sounds of modernization, that are at a basic level of experience and provide a context for the music. In general, urbanization is a recent phenomenon. In much of Melanesia, significant urbanization has only been present since the sixties when urban permanency became a contemporary change from circular migration.[21] The sound world of Pacific islanders is transforming itself as rapidly as other aspects of their lives, and it would seem that part of the modernization in these island states includes the music environment and what it represents.

This is not at all unusual. Modern Western artists have long had specific modernist cultural associations that they mapped to color, sound, texture, and shape. Consider the Russian composer Aleksandr Scriabin, who associated materialism with the color green and the musical note A. He formulated a whole color-music code.[22]

But there is no such thing as a *universal cultural sound,* and the instruments that musicians use can be looked at as freeing the human spirit as much as imprisoning it in some modern alienated form. The negative aspects are easy enough to point to. Yet there is a balance here, and in that balance it should not be forgotten that local music also provides an awareness of ideas and local culture in general. The loss in the equation may be in terms of insularity and traditional cohesiveness.

Technology is a force to be contended with, and no less for musical technology. The strength is noncoercive but is clearly present as part of the musicians' larger social imagery in their center of self-understanding. Music technology produces a technological frame in which musicians seek and find a solution in the form of performance and music. But it would also be a mistake to assume that these musicians were somehow like the poet in Jean Cocteau's *Orpheus,* who transcribes his poetry from the car radio. These musicians find their way creatively through the context of modern instruments. That the technology has artificial limits goes without saying. The program manager is no doubt right to provide advice and caution, to be concerned about the consequences for local culture where traditional musical traditions are abandoned. His caution points to an imposition of imagery from outside and the reading of an "alien" media text into local music. Yet in the very troupes of the "traditional" music and dance championed by Palapu, troupes that also earn a living by playing to tourists in hotels, you can see rubber slippers used as percussive devices to pound bamboo pipes—and the sound is not bad.

Musical technology and instrumental innovation may help to create an alien presence, and more importantly, they do suggest a loss in core cultural values of illusions evoked by local instruments. This is a loss with which societies large and small must grapple; it is not a dictate of technology and control.[23] Here the loss is specific and is evidenced in a decline of traditional folk performance in the face of the local cassette music industry and other mass media. But it is not at all clear the choice which the program manager urges and which musicians resist is a failure of cultural will. Culture is not fixed in time. And these young musicians too are working with the meanings, ideas, traditions, and symbols of their age in an effort to make sense of their times. In a modern world, media are the carriers of a large part of our national and cultural identity.[24] The imagery of media is electronics, not stick and stone.

The radio station alone has changed the orientation of the program manager's society; for returning to some sort of independent narrative of cultural purpose, a romantic fiction in itself, is inconceivable. The Solomons is, after all, a country of more than eighty indigenous languages, compressed into the broadcast vernacular of SIBC: Pidgin and English. In any event, local popular music is not a sort of *agitprop* in which a political message, or a cultural one, acts as instructor for the masses on a specific theme. For that, one must move out of the Pacific to listen to Radio Myanmar at 8:40 A.M. (and at other times too) for "Slogans" and "Music Now to Nine"—solemn affirmations of the proletariat, marching tunes, and *arbeitervolkslieder.* A functional attitude toward the music—media linked to agitation or cultural purpose—is outside the greater current relevance which musicians might intend.

We can, nonetheless, appreciate the program manager's sense of regret: the Solomon Islands is culturally rich and complex, if exasperatingly so.[25] Still, not all crews demand low funk guitar loops and heavy scratch attacks. There remains a lively world of string bands, panpipe groups, and other indigenous Pacific musical forms. This is not to suggest a passive presence of tradition amid modern media, but neither is it cause for complacency in the face of the asymmetrical relationships that quite obviously exist in small island states.

Because of their small populations, you can imagine that it would not be easy for Pacific nations to program anything near three-to-one or two-to-one local music to foreign music, despite the wealth of live music in the area. Even so, these governmental guidelines themselves serve to confirm the intent of explicit policies—that is, to control the nature of media exposure within national boundaries. In some substantial sense, they do no worse than Europeans or even their nearby neighbor New Zealand. This is no mean feat in societies so small.

Not all stations attempt this balance, nor do they want to. The private FM station, "Magik 98 FM," in Apia, Samoa, started as an all-music station in 1989. The playlist is mostly soft rock with some heavy metal, much of it from the personal collection of the station manager, Corey Keil. Keil, an attractive guy with a braid tattoo encircling his left biceps, owns the station with his father; about 10 percent is owned by uncles and other relations. The station is modest. "We have ten staff, eleven with the sweeper."

Keil plays "foreign" music, he says, because that is what he likes. He reads deejay magazines and keeps close track of listener requests. He does the music programming, and he also serves as a deejay. Why no local music? Keil's answer: his choice, his CD collection, and his belief that local bands in Samoa do not have enough "local" sound. "Too many local musicians are just doing Elton John translated into Samoan with a few changes here and there as cover." Were it not for his Magik 98, Keil laughs, the government station "would be playing the Beatles until the year 2000. Them or Frank Sinatra or Nelson Riddle." And it's true: if you tune in, you can hear "My Way" sung in Samoan.

Although Keil does not program Pacific music on his station, it is not because he dislikes it. In fact he complains about the *lack* of Pacific sound in the music available in Samoa. Music from the Cook Islands, he thinks, has an authentic ring to it.

Magik 98 FM has a unique on-air signature. When there is a quiet moment in a song, or a pause, the station inserts a breathy, almost whispered voice-over

MAGIK.

and sometimes

MAGIK 98 FM.

Keil calls this a "stamp." He adds his stamp to deter piracy. If someone were to pull his music off the station's stereo transmissions, the stamp would clearly indicate where the music originated. As Magik 98 grew in popularity, Keil believes his music was re-recorded, somehow finding its way back onto the air in Samoa. Some songs on the government-run station, he noted ironically, would stop abruptly, just before the "Magik."

In Palau, the government-run station also programs mostly foreign music, very little Pacific music, and a modest amount of local music.

In Kosrae, Federated States of Micronesia, foreign rock music is heard too.

Not all of the music of Oceania is popular music—Tonga has remarkable religious choirs—and most of it is not recorded, but an amazing variety is available on cassette. Not all of the recordings—religious or popular—are of professional quality: recording studios are scarce and, relative to the local economy, cost a great deal. Sometimes the liner notes appear to have been produced on colored paper on a copy machine, cut to size, and inserted in the tape case. But professionalism is not really the point. The syndicated programs we hear on radio in New York or Tokyo are very professionally produced. Price is not the issue either. If you want to hear a Western group, you can buy a pirated tape in your price range. Change and choice are the issue.

Local Choice

One argument concerning choice is that the low-income countries in the South are exporters of raw materials to the developed North and importers of cultural goods that in turn corrupt and dominate. Liberal conscience tells us this is "Bad," "Dangerous," and "Off the Wall"—now more than ever. The problem with such views is that they are gross overstatements and imply a globalization of culture that is, in fact, if one listens, not to be heard. Using electrical instruments and choosing reggae as a musical form imply no necessary common history or bond with other musicians elsewhere, save in a superficial sense.

An analogy, comparable in its falseness, resides in laughter, as if we expect laughter to be universal when we know it is not. In Japan and other societies too, laughter can as easily suggest embarrassment as shared humor. We simply do not laugh at the same things. Roland Barthes provides another example of the misreading of assumptions of universalism in his examination of the photographs in *The Family of Man.* History, he finds, is suppressed in a sentimental appeal to nature over ethnic peculiarity.[26] Similarly, musical universalism or globalism is a misreading. The cultural context always conditions the media text, which encompasses music as well as other media forms. While media imperialism may not be in evidence in the Pacific, there are other matters of concern.

The spontaneous nature of local popular music, though rooted on the spot, is all well and good. A particular technology and commodification, with all they portend, are what music and musicians organize around. That locals have hold of the larger part of the techno-economic lever only obscures the fact that other means of cultural expression may be marginalized—shifted to performances in hotels, regional meetings, and gatherings. When you make a tape and you hear yourself on local radio or see your cassettes in the local general store, a decisive and perceptible shift in the social and cultural locus has taken place: modern meaning is marked off from traditional and is articulated through a mass-mediated style and conveyed through the communication structure. Music is separated from family and traditional life in the rationalizing process of modernity. This is a loss and a change, however we choose to view it. Reactions to this shift in the cultural locus range from the traditionalists, who decry that customary cultural values are lost to a newfound modernism, to the hegemonists, who bemoan the outside imposition of cultural imperialism. The fact that the form is tapes and radio and not newspapers and television or PCs and multimedia is of interest but not fundamental to the issue. More to the point, traditional culture survives but may in time be marginalized or moved to the realm of tourist-hula as dance in Hawaii once was before its renaissance in the late sixties. How to view these changes is subject to debate.[27]

Well to remember, the Pacific is a small fish in a large media lake—peripheral to the core of alleged media imperialism. It benefits us little to generalize or to romanticize the life there. Consider, for one thing, that the population of all the Pacific island nations together is less than that of Tokyo. Suva, capital of Fiji, is one of the larger cities among the low- and medium-income countries in the Pacific, but the mid-year 1997 population projection for the whole country of Fiji, with a land area of 18,272 square kilometers spread over 330 islands, is only 779,200.[28] Global culture born of modern global capitalism requires a market. There are about 2,100 people on Niue, 1,500 on Tokelau, and Pitcairn, home to the descendants of the *Bounty* mutineers, could count an entire population of 47 at the last census.

Pacific markets are small—in terms of total population as well as market segments. Pundits may express concern with corporate marketing and manipulation of audiences in the Third World, the South of low-income countries. But in the low-income Pacific, television is not so common, many newspapers are weeklies or bi-weeklies, and radio is the most important medium. The media experience of Pacific islanders is distinguishable from the continental experience in that the islands' small populations continue to be isolated from their Oceanic, as well as continental, neighbors.

Further, the media experience takes place against a specific background: living standards are not comparable to Western levels. The countries are poor with all the dimensions that poverty implies: large underage populations, low income levels with high dependency ratios, and short population-doubling intervals. Their economies are not fully commercialized, they remain in a stage of postcolonial transition, urbanization is recent, nation building is new, as is mass migration.

For nearly a century now the expansion of commercial entertainment, first through film and then radio, has encroached on the leisure activities of the general public. Small island states enter this media process in its maturity. But radio is the means by which the outside world is brought to the attention of a sizable section of the Pacific island populations. Radio is not simply the medium of relaxation and entertainment it is for most in the developed North; it is the primary source of news. Radio is the permeable boundary around the larger realm of social action, one locus where Oceanic people begin to describe themselves in sound.

Saturday morning "International Top 40" on Radio Happy Isles with Junior Adifaka, as in similar programs on other island nation stations, is a delightfully complicated affair where the imagination of social time and space is played out on live air, a mediascape of aurality in a larger world of text and image. Radio captures the social and cultural sphere because it is not just bedroom radio or car radio or kitchen radio or even office radio of Western developed nations.[29] Pacific radio is not marginal to other forms of mass communications. You would have to be deaf not to hear the pervasive sound. Of course, this sound is scattered, scattered across expanses of ocean, fleeting, fragmented, mediating, not at all the same from place to place. Radio is an eclectic mixture of packaged mass-consumption programs and of local culture too, but the sound is assembled around the memories, symbols, myths, and traditions of listeners, Pacific listeners.

It's an idea that we've got, I suppose—distantly—
from the BBC and the way the Brits ran things,
which filtered its way through various stages
of colonialism.
—Ian Johnstone, *Radio New Zealand International*

2

Distantly from the BBC

Pacific Broadcasting Models

A few years back it was not uncommon for radio professionals in the Pacific to refer to the organizational structure and operational style of their stations as "BBC-like." The characterization crops up particularly in former British colonies or protectorates. What this phrase brings to mind, what this reference in fact means, is national public service broadcasting, a model forged and consolidated by the British Broadcasting Corporation over a period of years since the granting of a Royal Charter in 1927. At the time, the charter granted the BBC the right to be sole provider of British broadcasting. Directed by a board of governors and administered by a director-general, BBC has been reasonably free of government supervision despite a few government attacks on it.

"Auntie Beeb," as it was less than affectionately known, is largely financed by an annual license fee tied to the retail price index.[1] Additional sources of revenue derive from books and from media products such as records, videocassettes, and programs that are sold to broadcasters outside the United Kingdom. Popular BBC series have been aired on American television, and in the Pacific, radio programs are broadcast. There is no commercial advertising carried over the air.

This model of broadcasting is quite unlike the American model of commercial and noncommercial broadcasting, where the source of broadcast funding is either advertising or listener contributions, private foundations, and religious bodies.[2] The commercial system is not without some public service or, more appropriately, public affairs programming. Within the variations of this system, governments may set limits on the amount of commercialization that extends into programming and may establish requirements for various forms of public service, such as mandates to provide air time for candidates for public office. In the commercial system, noncommercial broadcasters are seen as a complement to their commercial counterparts, providing cultural and public affairs programming.

In contrast, the ideal of a national public service model is an institution independent of political party and commercial interest, an institution with responsibility to inform citizens with impartiality and balance and to let them be heard. Theoretically, by the creation of an independent entity to oversee broadcasting, elected officials are kept from interfering with programming decisions. This is known as the "arm's length principle." A reverse protection is provided as well. That is, if the programming arouses public opposition, politicians are in turn shielded because the decisions are taken by a body independent of them. In theory, that's the way things are supposed to work.

Another difference between the two systems concerns the source of funds to maintain service. Commercial broadcasters, as the name implies, receive money from advertisers who sponsor programs. Public service broadcasters receive their funds through a variety of means, which include government subventions and user fees. In this respect, some Pacific stations are financially inventive. Radio Tonga runs the Radio Store, which sells electric appliances. Other stations provide studio time and repair electronics. As the costs of programming rise and as government revenue falls, pressures for commercialization and privatization increase. In the first instance, stations retain their character as national public broadcasters but seek commercial activities to maintain viability. In the second case, public service broadcast units are sold, privatized. In both cases, stations must respond to commercial programming standards. A fallout of these trends toward commercialization and privatization is that programming begins to have similar characteristics no matter what the broadcasting system is. The practical result is that public information and communication services begin to erode.

Objectives of public service broadcasting systems vary considerably from country to country. In addition, broadcasting is currently undergoing widespread reordering as the monopoly-like hold of public broadcasting gives way to more hybrid forms. In most of the Pacific countries, the emphasis is on a national public service, although some broadcasters provide regional or local public service broadcasts. For example, in Papua New Guinea, a country of great linguistic diversity, the National Broadcasting Corporation (NBC) has three services: Kalang, which provides local commercial FM broadcasting; Karai, which is a provincial shortwave service; and Kundu, which is an AM (medium wave) system. NBC also has a national system of shortwave broadcasts.

Broadcast mandates differ from Pacific country to country, but often there are references to the promotion of the nation as a whole as well as development and industry—in part because these nations are recent creations and all are among a grouping of so-called South or less-developed states. Their mandates, however, are not so different from those of their North counterparts in public service broadcasting, who are often charged to exhibit fairness and diversity, particularly in the area of current affairs programs.[3]

In the beginning, the BBC's mission as a public service broadcaster was "to educate, to entertain, and to inform." A wide variety of programming, from gardening tips to drama, of the sort we have come to expect of public service broadcasting, was inaugurated as a service to the nation.

Interestingly, news or independent political information was not originally part of the BBC mission. John Reith, the first director-general, seems to have expected listeners to get their news from the morning papers, not from Broadcasting House. (That attitude would hardly work in the Pacific; as Frank Morgan, professor of communication and media arts, University of Newcastle, notes, "The bulk of media in the Pacific is broadcast media.") In fact, early on the BBC got its news from wire services. But owing to an evolution in purpose, by the end of World War II, for many the BBC was established as the standard in the independent reporting of news and political opinion.[4]

The BBC, in its inception, was also enjoined to maintain balanced coverage of events in the nation. Conflict between social groups and institutions was to be reported with strict impartiality. That was the ideal. An unstated political ideology—that of liberalism and the value of individual freedoms—was clearly at work in the very notion of this model. The notion of balance implies that in a forum of national debate, broadcasters are to steer a middle course, which is well and good where the social climate admits of a settled social compact or where, at the least, the possibility for dialogue exists.

But even in Britain, postwar changes put a strain on the model, and the BBC found it difficult to give coherence to multiethnic, regional, gender, and class points of view. V. S. Naipaul notes that thirty years ago, before his publishing success, he was relegated to broadcasts for the shortwave BBC

Caribbean Service. His Oxonian accent was apparently acceptable for the external service but not for an audience at home. In an interview looking back at that "hard and mean" period, he mused how, when he asked to broadcast feature pieces for the home service, "they laughed. I remember them laughing to this day. It was too absurd in the 1950s, for an Asiatic from the Caribbean. All this has been forgotten now, because they can't find enough half-witted people to represent these communities. But it was different then."[5] Surrounded by a haze of rhetoric and illusory principles, the model still shows strains.

Nonetheless, the overall concept of broadcasting for public service, developed in Britain through the years, spread and resides today in many spots around the globe. In the Pacific, the model has undergone regional variation as even broadcasters in the Commonwealth nations of New Zealand and Australia demonstrate. In New Zealand, the minister of broadcasting specifies government policy for national radio: deliver "a nationwide, noncommercial service providing programming of the highest quality to as many New Zealanders as possible."[6] The ministerial directive specifically calls for programs for Maori audiences. And in what is by now a ritual incantation, the minister asks that there be "comprehensive, independent and impartial national and international news services as well as current affairs programs." In both Australia and New Zealand, however, the years between the inception of radio and the present have left broadcasters a lot closer to the cost consciousness of Lady Thatcher than to the ideals of Lord Reith, BBC's founder. Stations are squeezed for revenue. Thus one of the distinguishing characteristics between public service and commercial broadcasters, source of revenue, begins to blur as more and more public service stations turn to some form of commercial activity to sustain themselves.

Most Pacific island broadcasters that follow the public service model also have a social purpose, variously defined.[7] In addition to a particular approach to programming and to journalism's fundamentals of accuracy, balance, and clarity, the centralized models of national communications found in the metropolitan powers of Britain and France are the pattern of most stations of the South Pacific. The island broadcaster's usual institutional charge is similar but somewhat different from that of either metropolitan power, providing for the development of the country, specifically for information, education, and, last, entertainment.

An example was the rather explicit charge in the objectives of the Cook Islands Broadcasting Corporation, established in 1989. The objectives, in part, are "to communicate useful information to all those engaged in industries or developing and harvesting the country's natural resources and economies; to create an awareness of new developments within a whole sphere of interests; and to present musical, documentary, magazines, and other types of programs in a manner which interests all sections of the community."[8]

The intent of the objectives is a radio of consequence to the public and to the state. In this definition of purpose, note that if media were to exist as entertainment, such a role would have to be secondary to development. Note, too, that there is a concern with the way in which information is presented—that the information will be "useful" to a stated purpose and will be prepared with an eye to public service. Any notion of information or entertainment as a product of market forces is absent. For everything that is broadcast, there is an unstated responsibility and obligation. Further, it bears repeating that the larger social good rather than individual or specific rights is the implicit reference in "all sections of the community" and the "country's natural resources and economies." These are objectives of a national broadcaster.

In the early 1990s from its six-person station, you could hear Cook Islands Broadcasting Corporation (CIBC) on two frequencies—one medium-wave station, one shortwave station, serving the national population of a little over 19,000. CIBC was on air eighteen hours a day in two languages—English and Cook Islands Maori. The broadcasting range includes the southern group of Cook Islands, with the volcanic island Rarotonga, which is the capital, and continues to the Cooks' northern reaches of Penrhyn Island in the Manihiki group, a stretch of over 2,500 kilometers (1,600 miles). In Rarotonga, there are two commercial FM stations broadcasting in stereo at one kilowatt each—luxurious by the standards of some of the smaller Pacific nations. Rarotonga, the largest of the islands, even has a modest daily newspaper, and the *New Zealand Herald* can usually be found in hotels. Until it was privatized, CIBC also supported local television. The outer islands received taped material previously shown in Rarotonga and flown in from the capital for local viewing. As with other parts of the Pacific, the Cooks is in a state of transformation. As a representative from the radio station noted at the 1997 Pacific Islands Broadcasting Association meeting, "Our situation is fluid." The general manager was doing his own engineering. With a further note of gloom, he added, "Radio is doing its best to deliver. But I am not a broadcaster if I merely transmit material from elsewhere." CIBC is to be privatized. What will happen to broadcasting objectives is unclear.

In Honolulu, by way of contrast, there are over fifty radio stations, nine or ten television stations in addition to cable channels, and a rich harvest of print media to cater to the needs of 836,000 people.

Two Broad Patterns

If we think of the world of radio broadcasting as represented by two broad patterns—one, the public service model, and the other, the commercial model, composed primarily of commercial stations with some public or non-commercial broadcasters thrown in for good measure, as in the United States—then radio stations in the nearly twenty small Pacific nations, territories, and dependencies divide roughly as follows: 30 percent has stations public or governmentally controlled, following a public service model; about 15 percent, a commercial/noncommercial system; and 55 percent, a mix of the two categories.[9]

Within the category "public service broadcasters," I include government stations, that is, stations owned and operated by the state, as well as those that are statutory authorities such as broadcasting commissions. Often, whether the station is government- or commission-owned is of little consequence. Governments regularly interfere in station policy, particularly with regard to editorial policy, personnel, and other operating procedures. What the figures indicate, then, is a significant proportion of Pacific radio that is not of a commercial character as known in the United States, where radio is licensed by government and, for the most part, under private ownership.

One view of these rough statistics is a nod toward the lingering legacy of empire. It would be naive to ignore the fact that the 15 percent commercial/noncommercial pattern lies primarily in the central Pacific, an area of U.S. influence, and that the majority of the public service media lies in the South Pacific, where metropolitan powers such as Britain (or surrogates, Australia and New Zealand) and France held sway. The patterns are clear. Far more interesting than this prevailing view, however, are the details and variations concealed within these patterns. An observer would be wise to consider the details with care, lest the mediascape be seen as a function of what was given to the Pacific rather than what is taken. The assumption that Western institutional forms move in one direction to impose themselves on other cultures is not only facile, it is a trap. National (or local) custom acts to inform contemporary institutions too.[10]

First of all, the content of Pacific radio, whether public service or commercial, tends to be local in origin. (Television, however, does not follow this pattern in the least. In the late 1990s there are twelve or more countries with some form of television. Most rely extensively on foreign programming, in which TV New Zealand and other outside programmers appear prominently.) And obviously, there are fewer "programs-for-profit" on public service stations than one would ordinarily find on privately owned and operated commercial systems that rely on advertisers for revenue. But beyond this, among Pacific radio broadcasters, there is a noticeable trend for public service radio broadcasters to turn to commercial advertisers as well as "noncommercial" (public and institutional) advertising for some part of their broadcast day. This trend is dubbed commercialization, sometimes corporatization, where the structure of the station purportedly changes. As the trend accelerates, the dichotomy between noncommercial public broadcasters that carry advertising and their commercial competitors begins to dissolve.

Ephraim Tammy, general manager of NBC, the national broadcaster of Papua New Guinea, describes corporatization as a "system which is eating the Pacific." NBC, an extensive service with five hundred employees (but being trimmed) and nineteen stations (if there is no equipment failure), broadcasting in ten different languages, was for a time one of the few Pacific island statutory radio authorities not moving in this direction. Corporatization, however, seems to be in the offing. Meanwhile, NBC's FM Kalang service does accept commercials, putting NBC in the category of public service radio broadcasters that turn to commercial, public, and institutional advertising. But Tammy is not unmindful of the difficulties or the costs of running a public, government-funded station. At the 1994 Pacific Islands Broadcasting Association General Assembly in Apia, Samoa, Tammy reported that NBC, in an effort to improve the productivity of senior managers and to "break the civil service mentality," recategorized their positions from civil service to a contract basis.

Another large broadcasting system in the Pacific, Radio Fiji, joined the corporatizing, privatizing movement in 1997.

Whether public or private, most Pacific stations accept money from individuals to broadcast private messages, the so-called service announcements discussed in an earlier chapter, and public funds for noncommercial messages.

Categories may be blurring, but between the two models of broadcasting, there remains one significant difference. Even where commercials are introduced by public service broadcasters, there is not necessarily a move to privatize. Control of the stations rests largely in the hands of public authorities and governments through one or a number of means. Indeed, a number of the broadcast units are not independent statutory authorities at all. Radio

Tonga is. But others, such as the government station in Palau, V6AK on Chuuk in the Federated States of Micronesia, and Radio Marshall Islands (V7AB), are organized as departments within the government. True of Nauru as well. One (perhaps positive) result is that stations must often operate under written guidelines which speak to community values and with development broadcasting goals which further the aims of the state, rather than simply the bottom line.

Increasingly, national public service ideals are being appended to a quasi-commercial model of broadcasting without private ownership. How this trend will realize itself is difficult to say and can only be assessed in the long term, but Ephraim Tammy's observation seems apt: one station after another "eaten" by corporatization and now privatization. In such an appending of broadcast models, an issue that has arisen widely in the Pacific, there are glaring practical and philosophical contradictions.

So the change is ongoing. In Fiji, for example, not only did the Fiji Broadcasting Commission become corporatized, but the general manager of the FBC had to effect this change with anticipated new and competing private stations as well. With the passage of a public enterprise bill, FBC became privatized in 1997. The government is expected to provide a FJ$600,000 subvention per year to maintain public service broadcasting. So Radio Fiji has been privatized, yes, but is not free of government by any means. Any inventory of Pacific stations, then, captures sound in a moment of time.

Among the public service broadcasters, which constitute the majority, Channel 1 and Channel 2AP, both medium-wave radio broadcasts on Upolu Island, Samoa, are managed by the Samoa Broadcasting Service, a governmental agency, from the capital in Apia. The government station, known as 2AP, is funded by advertising. Studios, transmitter, and antennae are located on Mulinu'u Peninsula, just up the road from the Fono, the Samoan parliament. In back of the station building, facing Apia harbor, papaya and bananas trees grow along the fringe. Advertising revenue goes to the government and, as the late Tupai Brown, the general manager, explained, 2AP has then to submit a budget request for funding. The fiftieth year of radio broadcasting in Samoa was marked in 1997—a year of "financial difficulties and drastic cuts."

Radio Kiribati is overseen by the Broadcasting and Publications Authority, a government unit. Radio Kiribati is corporatizing too. Radio Vanuatu, on the other hand, is overseen by the Vanuatu Broadcasting TV Corporation

(VBTC), a statutory authority. Radio Vanuatu's FM 98 has been corporatized, an example of a public service broadcaster that has turned to commercialization for revenue to maintain service. The general manager reports that even with commercial advertising, the station is "living hand-to-mouth." And the only station in the Republic of Nauru, population 11,200, where the single, valuable economic resource is phosphate, is, as with most things, government-run. (In 1997, however, the station was off the air for six weeks because of equipment problems, and there was no one in Nauru, according to Briar-Rose Nagaya, director of the Nauru Media Bureau, who could get the station back on air.)

All the stations mentioned above are examples of the public service model of broadcasting taken in the broadest sense. Let me stress that they are national public broadcasters, some as government departments, others as statutory bodies of one sort or another.

Radio broadcasting in Guam, a U.S. territory, follows the commercial model with some noncommercial stations thrown in. That is, in addition to several commercial broadcasters, such as KGUM in Agana, a number of the stations are noncommercial, owned and managed by religious organizations. There is also a noncommercial FM station licensed to the Guam Educational Radio Foundation that follows an American pattern of universities running radio stations.[11] American Samoa, also a U.S. territory, has two private commercial stations, WVUV Pago Pago and KSBS-FM, owned by Samoa Technologies. Northern Mariana Islands, a U.S. Commonwealth, follows the same pattern.

In the Federated States of Micronesia (FSM), there are stations in each of the four states—Kosrae, Pohnpei, Chuuk, and Yap—loosely associated through the FSM Broadcasting Association established in 1991. These stations are government-owned through public information and broadcasting departments and run by each state in the federation. In effect, they are the government radio stations, with programming focused on the political boundaries and language groups within each state. For example, V6AJ Radio in Tofol, the administrative center of Kosrae, advertises itself as the "Voice of Kosrae." The station call letters are read in English, but the announcement is made in native Kosraean.

PAINGE STATION V6AJ, FWIN AN KOSRAE.

Likewise, programs are broadcast to the population, over 7,000, many of whom continue to rely on subsistence farming and fishing for a living, in English and Kosraean. In addition, FSM has two religious stations: a medium-wave station run by the Evangelical Church in Chuuk and an FM station run by the Calvary Baptist Church on Pohnpei. The pattern in FSM, then, falls within the 55 percent mix of public service and commercial/noncommercial. That is, the mix is government-run and noncommercial religious stations.

In the Republic of the Marshall Islands, formerly a part of the UN Trust Territory of the Pacific Islands and now an independent republic in Compact of Free Association with the United States, there is also a mixed broadcasting system. A government commission oversees the 25-kilowatt medium-wave station, Radio Majuro, which broadcasts from the capital on Majuro Atoll. The thirteen-member staff keeps the station on air eighteen hours a day. Sometimes their broadcasts can be heard as far away as Hawaii on 1098 kHz. The mostly music FM V99.9 broadcasts in English. Radio V7AA, 96 FM, is a religious station. Because of insufficient revenue, "Micronesian Heatwave," a commercial music station, was forced to close down.

Complicating the picture is the presence of U.S. military radio at Kwajalein, a large atoll within the Marshall Islands. The U.S. Army Kwajalein Atoll command (USAKA) oversees the Kwajalein Missile Range. Intercontinental ballistic missiles (ICBMs) are fired from California, 7,800 kilometers distant (about 4,200 nautical miles), and splash down within the confines of the 2,850,000-square-kilometer Kwajalein lagoon (1,100 square miles). Two stations run by the U.S. military's Central Pacific Network, one medium wave, the other FM, provide radio coverage for military personnel stationed here as well as for civilian contract workers and their families. FM programming is provided by automated satellite feeds from the United States. An FM station on Ebeye islet, run by the Kwajalein Atoll Development Authority, is on the air sporadically, and there have been plans to incorporate it into the government-controlled broadcasting commission. The station is private, noncommercial, serving the Marshallese who crowd onto Ebeye and are moved by boat to work locations within the missile range.

The case of the Marshall Islands provides an interesting hybrid because, while there is a national broadcaster on its soil, there is also an agency of a foreign government controlling two stations; commercial broadcasters; and private, noncommercial stations. So the Republic of the Marshall Islands can be said to exemplify all patterns.

The Republic of Palau, whose southwest border reaches almost as far as Indonesia, has a mixed system as well. WSZB is government-run from Malakal Island, broadcasting in English and Palauan with relays from Voice of America and other overseas services. KHBN, on the other hand, is a private, noncommercial religious station, transmitting from the nearby island of Koror. The station broadcasts on six frequencies from two transmitters of 100 kilowatts each, for an audience primarily outside the region.

The situation with the government station on Palau is interesting because it shows that broadcast policy, as far as categories go, may be semi-permeable. WSZB, a ten-person station that was once owned by the government, was later attached to the telecommunications authority. More recently, however, radio was split off to become again part of the government when it was discovered that private radio was ineligible for overseas development assistance (ODA). In terms of actual broadcast policy, little changed as these switches were made.

The stations mentioned here are illustrative of the three general patterns found in Pacific radio. Public service, the largest category, may admit of some commercialization, but the stations are publicly held and run, sometimes by government, at other times by statutory authorities. Commercial/noncommercial may include private enterprises that program for profit or noncommercial stations held by not-for-profit organizations such as churches and universities. And last, a hybrid variation of all forms is exemplified by the broadcasters of the Republic of the Marshall Islands.

Clandestine Radio

One notable radio transmission has existed outside these categories. Bougainville, the principal island of the North Solomons Province, has been the site of an insurgency movement directed against the government of Papua New Guinea. Hostilities, centering on issues over an open-pit copper mine on the island, began in 1988 and quickly escalated. If one grants legitimacy to the insurgency, then the clandestine radio of the Bougainville Revolutionary Army (BRA), which broadcast for the Republic of Bougainville Interim Government, might be considered a "public service" broadcaster in that it has been run by a government, albeit provisional. The government of Papua New Guinea has not viewed the broadcasts in such light, it would be safe to say. It has claimed the BRA transmitter to be illegal and seditious, and it has attempted by force of arms to get it off the air.

Radio Free Bougainville, on air intermittently since January 1992, has endeavored to broadcast on a shortwave frequency of 3870 kHz, but from no fixed broadcast site. The BRA has had to keep its portable transmitter on the move, going from place to place in the bush, a step ahead of the PNG Defense Forces. When able to broadcast, Radio Free Bougainville has been on air from seven until nine in the evening. Primarily, the substance of the broadcasts has been announcements from the interim government about areas gained control of, particularly in the central and southern portion of Bougainville Island. There have also been service messages from people in BRA-controlled areas, messages that run the gamut of personal concerns, from letting loved ones know of their plight or their needs to assuring family members, both inside and out the BRA-controlled areas, that BRA operatives are safe. Sometimes there have been requests: soap or clothing. Occasionally there has been music, including popular Papua New Guinea bands and Pacific songs. There might be pop or country-style music and religious music too.

The generators that have run Radio Free Bougainville are reported to have been fueled not with diesel oil but with coconut oil. BRA forces in some areas have been responsible for the production of so many liters of coconut oil in the course of a certain period. After the oil is extracted from the coconut, the product is further heated to drive off water and then put to broadcast use. It is a primitive, labor-intensive task, but essential to the cause and necessary to circumvent the blockade of the island imposed by the PNG Defense Forces. Supplies of oil and other goods might not easily get through to the insurgents, but Bougainville has no want of coconuts.

Running generators with coconut oil to keep radio on air has the ring of revolutionary myth making, but the story was corroborated, with reasonable consistency, by four different sources, all associated with the BRA or the Bougainville Interim Government. Whether the story is true or part of a propaganda effort, what is undeniable is that the station has been maintained with tremendous difficulty and at great risk to life and has been critical to the revolutionary effort.

Radio Free Bougainville, however, has not been the only voice of that conflict heard throughout the region. At one time Radio United Bougainville, an "unregistered" station, could be heard on 3880 MHz, and was purported to be under the control of (or an organ of) the PNG Defense Forces, a claim the Defense Forces denies. It maintains instead that Radio United Bougainville was run by Bougainvilleans who lived within government-controlled areas known as "care centers." These care centers were set up by PNG in 1990, ostensibly to create a safe haven for noncombatants fleeing the BRA. Reports, however, describe Bougainvilleans who had been forcibly removed from their villages and interned in the care centers—which the BRA refers to as "occupied areas."[12]

From Loloho in the southeast, near Arawa town, where the ore ships for the Panguna open pit copper mine used to harbor, Radio United Bougainville went on air in January 1994. The nature of its broadcasts, called a "hearts-and-minds campaign," was clearly designed as a counter to the broadcasts of Radio Free Bougainville.

WE ARE CONSCIOUS OF THE CONTINUED THREATS BY
CRIMINALS TO MUTUAL COEXISTENCE, TO HARMONY AND
TO ENGAGEMENT IN PROSPEROUS ENDEAVORS . . .

People were urged to come to the care centers. At the time there were pro–Defense Forces announcements, some music programming, and material relayed from the national service. The station broadcast three hours a day, overlapping Radio Free Bougainville from 7 to 9 P.M. and extending an additional hour until 10. One of the details that locals note in commenting on the two stations is that the transmitter of the Defense Forces station is a German make, while Radio Free Bougainville's is Japanese.

One additional station has been reported to be run by the Defense Forces on the island of Buka, situated across a narrow strait from Bougainville. Broadcasting on 3877 MHz, this station likewise has offered news and messages with a pro-government, pro-military point of view. As with the other stations mentioned here, Radio Free and Radio United Bougainville, this station falls outside usual categories. It is not clandestine but neither does it fall within the category of public service broadcaster with the rest of Papua New Guinea's National Broadcasting Corporation stations.

Also on Buka is a station run legitimately under the national authority, the NBC, as part of the Karai service. The station is called Maus Bilong San Kam-ap, which means, literally, "voice belonging sun come up," a reference to the fact of Buka's location at the eastern end of Papua New Guinea. Because of the political and military complications of the Bougainville insurgency, the station has had difficulty staying on air.

Clandestine radio, or "freedom radio" as it is sometimes called, exists even in the United States, and in other countries too. In California you can sometimes listen to San Francisco Liberation Radio or in Berkeley to 88.1 FM, free-form "people's radio." These are broadcasts that fall outside the usual categories but not outside the interest of the U.S. Federal Communications

Radio Tanafo

Clandestine radio is not new to the Pacific. Perhaps the most spectacular instance occurred during the transition of New Hebrides from colonial dependency, under Condominium rule of France and Britain, to nationhood as Vanuatu, a long, complicated period that stretched from the 1950s to the early 1980s. French settlers on the island of Espiritu Santo were attempting to move their agricultural pursuits away from coconut and other tree crops, which were a volatile market, and into cattle, less labor intensive but requiring more land. Expanding their operations into higher inland areas, they began clearing and fencing off custom land, ownership of which had been contested under traditional Melanesian land occupation traditions. This touched off a string of bitter confrontations with certain local interests that culminated in 1965 with the founding of the Nagriamel movement.

The symbol of the movement was two leaves from the foliage of *nagria* and *namele,* plants endemic to the islands. The names were combined to form Nagriamel, symbolic on one hand of people and on the other of custom law. Nagriamel was spearheaded by Jimmy Stephens, a charismatic local leader. Stephens joined forces with Paul Buluk, a traditional *(kastom)* chief, and together they issued a series of manifestos that became known as the Act of the Dark Bush.[1] These manifestos mark the beginnings of Nagriamel as a movement. The Act of the Dark Bush forbade settlers from moving into the interior and from extending their cattle operations, and it demanded that custom land be returned "entirely to the Santo Bushmen's descendants from this time onwards."

Not far from Luganville, on Espiritu Santo, in an area claimed by custom rights, Chief Buluk then set up a village by the name of Tanafo. Tanafo was a parcel in a vast piece of property also claimed by the French company Société Française des Nouvelles-Hébrides, and Tanafo through the years became the site of land disputes, protest, and finally rebellion. During this period, Radio Tanafo was born. A 125-watt transmitter was supplied through private American business and a right-wing foundation.[2] Later, supporters provided a second transmitter that permitted routine contact overseas. American technicians operated the clandestine radio.

Radio Tanafo broadcast threats not only to the French and British settlers but also to ni-Vanuatu (native-born Melanesian) immigrants, who had arrived from other islands in the New Hebrides as laborers for the colonialists and who were not supporters of Stephen's Nagriamel movement. The ni-Vanuatu immigrants aligned themselves instead with the Vanua'aku Pati (Vanuatu Party), which had been set up by English-educated, primarily Presbyterian and Anglican groups. The Vanua'aku Pati had grown out of a cultural association that also stood for the preservation of indigenous rights to land and local custom. The Anglican priest and later prime minister, Father Walter Lini, was a member of this alliance.

The presence of these ni-Vanuatu immigrants had shifted the numbers of eligible voters on Espiritu Santo, and in the 1979 election for the Representative Assembly the Vanua'aku Pati scored a narrow electoral victory. Joined by other traditional leaders and now some French settlers and officials, Jimmy Stephens refused to accept the election results. And Radio Tanafo broadcast his challenge. After the broadcasts, there was turmoil. People fled the island, helped by the British who used the British Residency vessel to get those in danger out.

The transition to nationhood in Vanuatu, achieved a year after this election, was less than smooth. Jimmy Stephens, who had seemed to change his alliances at will, led a secessionist attempt—dubbed the "Coconut War" by international observers—throwing the newly independent country into chaos. Father Lini, then chief minister, went to the South Pacific Forum meeting held in Kiribati in 1980 and sought regional support in putting down the secession. He found a willing ear in Papua New Guinea prime minister Sir Julius Chan, who saw the matter in a larger geopolitical setting where outside influences were manipulating island states.[3] (Local French officials and expatriates had supported Stephens for a time—at least against the British—when it suited them.) Chan dispatched four hundred fifty PNG Defense Force troops, who alongside members of the Vanuatu Mobile Force landed on Espiritu Santo with Australian logistics and communications support. The Santo rebellion was crushed, Stephens and others were jailed, foreign—primarily French—nationals supporting the rebellion arrested and deported. Throughout this turbulent period, Radio Tanafo was the voice of Stephens' Nagriamel militants.

---

1. Stephen Henningham, *France and the South Pacific* (Honolulu: University of Hawai'i Press, 1992), 28–30, 40.

2. Howard van Trease, *The Politics of Land in Vanuatu* (Suva: University of the South Pacific, 1987), 152.

3. Henningham, *France and the South Pacific*, 197.

Commission. The FCC has fined Stephen Dunifer, who is reported to run Radio Free Berkeley from a 12-volt battery with a hand-built transmitter. Dunifer's idea is that radio can be a sort of "electronic democracy," giving voice to the people.

There is other free radio as well, such as Black Liberation Radio in Springfield, Illinois. While the station has only about a one-mile broadcast radius, in 1994 it had been running for about seven years—also to the displeasure of the FCC. Black Liberation Radio was originally set up by Mbanna Kantako to provide coverage of concerns at the Springfield public housing project, site of the one-kilowatt transmitter. The transmissions step outside the official, commercial channels of communication, which Kantako sees as irrelevant and biased against the Black Liberation Radio's micro audience.

Europe has a number of clandestine radio stations and even some pirate TV stations. Indeed, one former head of state, François Mitterand, has been involved in "free radio." His speeches could be heard on Radio Riposte.

Japan has seen a "mini-FM boom," with more than a hundred low-watt free "stations."[13]

But I need not exaggerate the contrast to American, Japanese, or European radio to underscore the fact that Radio Free Bougainville is not micro radio, any more than Radio Tanafo was in Vanuatu. To do so would trivialize mortal combat. Radio Free Bougainville's audience, furthermore, has been larger even than the insurgents on Bougainville, Buka, and nearby islands in the Solomons. The BRA's portable shortwave transmitter broadcasts to the world at large the conditions that Bougainvilleans must live under. Victories have been proclaimed, and even their losses, that would otherwise go unreported, unless publicized by the will of the Papua New Guinea government.

It goes without saying that the news from the National Broadcasting Commission of Papua New Guinea has reflected the government position on the matter of Bougainville. But should a journalist from the NBC, let alone an outside journalist, have wished to report directly from the Bougainville, it would have been difficult to obtain permission. In the past it was impossible.

Big Media—Kilowatts and Frequencies

Whether to call these stations that dot the Pacific big or little media is a difficult call.[14] The stations are big in the sense that to cover a vast ocean expanse, the wattage of the stations has to be reasonably strong. But in Kiribati, for example, T3K1, the one medium-wave station in the republic that broadcasts from Nanikaai, Tarawa Island, at 846 kHz, does so with only 10 kilowatts. Radio Kiribati, with its one-kilowatt shortwave transmitter at Betio, is a division of the government Broadcasting and Publications Authority. In a typical pattern, the country, with a modest population of 83,400, covers a vast ocean area, 2,131,000 square kilometers. It is doubtful that the signal of Radio Kiribati reaches the entire territory.

In other places in the world where the population is more concentrated, a station of from one to five kilowatts might suffice to reach an audience thirty to fifty kilometers (twenty to thirty miles) from the broadcast center. But in the Pacific, population densities vary from the least dense Melanesia, at an average of 9 people per square kilometer, to a denser Micronesia, at 128 people per square kilometer. Consider too the geographical extent of the islands. By contrast, the broadcast strength of the commercial station WQEQ-AM, a twenty-four-hour pop and standards station in New York City, is 50 kilowatts. Think how much wider an audience those 50 kilowatts reach in a country more dense than Papua New Guinea, where there are only 8 people per square kilometer.

So by international standards these Pacific stations are not big media. If you are a microradio operator—"pirate radio" to the FCC—you might purchase your 5–10-kilowatt station and be on air for US$300–$500. Microradio revolutionary Stephen Dunifer of Radio Free Berkeley reportedly sells one-kilowatt handheld transmitters for US$45. But you cannot supply a country with a hand transmitter. A 100-watt station costs something on the order of US$50,000. Recently, however, some low-watt FM transmitters have come onto the market for about $10,000. (These prices are for transmission equipment alone and do not include the additional materials required to go on air.) Despite the comparatively low wattage of Pacific radio, within their own realm they are big media in terms of the impact on their target audiences.

Most of the political units of the Pacific have medium-wave stations, a few have FM broadcasts, and an even smaller number have shortwave. Take the example of Radio Tuvalu. Thirteen staff maintain the government-run station, T2U2, broadcasting at 621 kHz from the coral atoll of Funafuti. This station, on the islet of Fongafale, the capital, is the country's only radio, serving a population of 10,900, most of them Polynesian. About 35–40 percent of the population resides in the capital, the rest scattered over the remaining eight inhabited atolls. The local T-shirt logo, "Tiny Island Nation," explains Tuvalu well. It is a thousand kilometers north of Fiji, consists of nine low-lying atolls, islands which rise to the height of a coconut tree and which, beyond the distance of a few kilometers, cannot be seen. Broadcasting House is situated at the government center at Vaiaku, where you can also buy postcards.

T2U2's transmitter has a strength of just 5 kilowatts and serves its audience with broadcasts in English and Tuvaluan, a Polynesian language related to Samoan. In 1993 Radio Tuvalu won two prizes in the PIBA competitions, although station personnel were unable to travel to Suva, Fiji, to accept their honors. One was for a radio documentary, "The Traditional Canoe Makers of Tuvalu," produced in the Tuvaluan language. The other was for an AIDS/STD campaign in a competition jointly sponsored by PIBA and the South Pacific Commission; Radio Tuvalu took first prize.

Tuvalu residents do not expect a newspaper on their doorstep in the morning. Nor are they in the habit of switching on the TV to check the weather. They are more accustomed to the fourteen-day pace of the *Nivaga II* as it makes its rounds, depending on tides and weather, with an hour's stop at various islands. The ship's northern leg, up from Funafuti to three of the island stops, takes about four days. The islanders' link to the outside world is radio. In fact, radio takes on a personal touch. The arrival of all visitors from outside, typically far fewer than a thousand a year, is broadcast over air. The station also announces the coming and going of remittance workers, travel by government officials, and names of students who are off to study. And probably each one of the estimated three thousand radios in this Commonwealth nation is tuned to T2U2

THIS IS RADIO TUVALU

for some portion of the broadcast day.

The most powerful transmitters in the Pacific, however, do not have Pacific populations as their primary target audience. These are the religious broadcasters in the Northern Mariana Islands, Guam, and Palau. Trans World Radio Pacific, in Guam, has four 100-kilowatt transmitters; Adventist World Radio—Asia, also broadcasting from Guam, has two 100-kilowatt transmitters. In addition to English, these stations beam their programs in Burmese, Cantonese, Cebuano, Indonesian, Ilongo, Malay, Marathi, Russian and other languages of the former Soviet republics, Tagalog, Tamil, Telugu, Hakka,

Japanese, Twi, Mandarin, Korean, Hindi, and so on. Adventist World Radio does broadcast in Fijian although the station address is Hong Kong.

In the U.S. Commonwealth, Northern Mariana Islands, Monitor Radio International broadcasts to various areas around the world from two 100-kilowatt transmitters. The target audience is Asia, Australia, New Zealand, and other Pacific nations. Monitor Radio is a broadcast service of the Christian Science Monitor, which is headquartered in Boston. The broadcast facilities, purchased in 1987 and upgraded, began operating under the new call letters KHBI, which stand for Herald Broadcasting International, in 1989. Programs sent by satellite to the Saipan transmitters originate in Boston and are easily heard in Tokyo.

The religious station KFBS, run by the Far East Broadcasting Company on Saipan, has four 100-kilowatt transmitters for its shortwave broadcasts. Far East Broadcasting similarly transmits its programs in a wide variety of languages—Bugis, Hausa, Osetin, Kazakh, Kyrgyz, Mongolian, and more. KFBS is, in addition, a "home service," providing a 10-kilowatt medium-wave transmission in English for the local audience in the Northern Mariana Islands.

In the Republic of Palau, a self-governing Micronesian island group in the Western Pacific, KHBN is a shortwave station with two 100-kilowatt transmitters which also provides religious programming.

The only other station that matches these religious broadcasters in transmission strength can be found in Papua New Guinea. The National Broadcasting Commission of Papua New Guinea has a 100-kilowatt transmitter in the capital Port Moresby, the shortwave station P2T4, located at 4890 MHz on the 60-meter band. Because Papua New Guinea is not only large but also encompasses rough terrain and remote corners like the Star Mountains in the far west, shortwave is necessary for full national coverage. If the weather conditions are right—a cold night in winter, for example, when the ionospheric conditions happen to be optimal—you can hear the national service of this Papua New Guinea station from quite a distance outside the country, although you might have to endure a good bit of static.

NBC has been in existence for more than twenty years, but during this time the national radio service has not extended to the entire country. In 1994, NBC upgraded its service, going to high-frequency transmissions in an attempt to extend coverage. Much of the equipment is obsolete, and Papua New Guinea, like other Pacific stations, must appeal to various foreign funding agencies for grants for equipment and for training. Nonetheless, for a "middle income" developing nation, Papua New Guinea can boast of an extensive radio network. The range is the 100-kilowatt Port Moresby shortwave transmitter to the two-kilowatt medium-wave station at Lae, memorable as the spot where Amelia Earhart took off for Howland Island in her twin-engined Lockheed Electra on July 2, 1937. In addition, Papua New Guinea has several stations of less than one kilowatt that serve the Kalang network.

No other Pacific country has a radio service that matches the signal strength of Papua New Guinea's P2T4. Most radio transmitters are medium-wave stations in the 10-kilowatt range. But in some areas, there is no radio at all. Important is what is *not* heard—ocean expanses of no sound—as much as what is.

For example, a Paul Gauguin or a Herman Melville of today, if he can get to Nuku Hiva in the Marquesas Islands, could leave his stockbroker position or his life as a writer-sailor behind and live out his Pacific fantasy amid the smell of lemons and oranges. He might have to contend with the *no-no,* a gnat with an unpleasant bite, but he would be free of local radio entirely. But such a person's concerns would be inconsequential in any case. Pacific radio is not the voice of outsiders but of local folk, although the French-speaking part of the Pacific is an exception to this rule.

In the Marquesas, for example, Société Nationale de Radiodiffusion Française d'Outre Mer (RFO), the French broadcasting authority, maintains no radio for the seven thousand or so people who reside in these remote islands. RFO activities concentrate in New Caledonia, notable for its reserves of nickel, and in Polynesia—Tahiti and islands nearby. RFO is the voice of the French metropolis in the Pacific, sometimes sounded in a local voice. And on Mata-Utu, a volcanic island, there is also a medium-wave transmitter.

BONJOUR, VOUS ÊTES SUR RFO WALLIS ET FUTUNA

is heard from the French Overseas Territory, Wallis and Futuna, about an hour and fifteen minutes by 737, east-northeast of Fiji's international airport at Nadi.

There are, however, many communities in the Pacific that are out of the broadcast range of what one might think of as local radio and sometimes even national or metropolitan radio. Certainly this grouping includes the Pitcairn islanders. The December 1996 census recorded 47 people. Videocassette recorders have, at last, come to Pitcairn but not local radio or TV. The connection to the outside world is the few passing ships, ship-to-shore radio, and a satellite telephone, answered by the islander—invariably Christian, Warren, or Young, by name—who happens to be on satellite-station duty. Dial Pitcairn Island at 011-872-144-5372, but don't expect that a conversation with a descendant of the *Bounty* mutineers through satellite telephone will have economy rates.

Broadcasting Trends and Government Interest

Government subventions for public broadcasters have declined in the Pacific, but with that decline and with the subsequent move toward commercialization and privatization, a concomitant decline of government control in broadcasting policy has not necessarily followed.

Addressing Pacific broadcasters at a PIBA assembly, Lois Baird, of the Australian Film TV and Radio School, sounds a note of financial inevitability: "Commercialism, meaning the ability to make revenue from radio advertising, is something we, as broadcasters, will all have to face . . . as governments insist that those stations start to make some money to relieve the expensive government support they have grown used to over the years."[15] But there seems little unavoidable about what is going on—isn't this a policy choice, politically made?—and besides, doesn't Baird load the dice with the throwaway line "expensive government support"? Changing public service broadcasting into a public commercial service and even selling the broadcast facilities are, clearly, a trend among this group of broadcasters, and Professor Baird is paid as a consultant to help it along. How successful this change will prove to be is another matter.

The FM 98 station of the Vanuatu Broadcasting TV Corporation, for example, which has been commercialized, had difficulty meeting its payroll in 1993 and 1994. In addition, the station was occasionally off air because of cuts in service by the local power authority. It seems FM 98 was late in paying its electric bills.

Being the source of revenue is not the only point of access for government influence, however. One argument for commercialization of public stations is that radio will thereby be freed from government interference in their operations. But not so easily. Take the example of the Kingdom of Tonga, which was never a colony, although once a British protectorate. Tonga is a monarchy, led by King Taufa'ahau Tupou IV. Public radio is commercialized and successfully self-supporting. But inquire who sits on the "BBC-like" Tonga Broadcasting Commission board, and the answer is the prime minister, a titled peer, a baron, in fact, who acts as chair; the minister of finance; the chief cabinet secretary; the manager of the Tonga Telecommunications Commission; and three "listeners." "Listeners" here typically translates as retired civil servants or prominent businessmen. The general manager of the station is secretary to the board. In Tonga, as in a number of other Pacific states, the details defeat the BBC model.

The relationship between media and politics can be one of tension. Political (that is to say, governmental) or regime interests and those of an independent press do not necessarily coincide. To be sure, the independence of radio cannot be guaranteed where government has control, either directly or indirectly, over funding, personnel, programming, and content.

In the Pacific as elsewhere, government frequently is the news. But government in these economies is also often the main employer, and in the general nature of things, government officials tend toward media allergy. For media professionals, opportunities are scarce. Few staff jobs are available, even fewer top positions. A loss of employment has serious personal implications, and the possibility of such loss exerts pressures for censorship, or self-censorship, of the news.

SIBC: BBC-Like with a Melanesian Flavor

As described by station personnel at the Solomon Islands Broadcasting Corporation, radio in the Solomon Islands, once a British colony, also follows the BBC-like model. Indeed, before independence, the BBC ran the organization when it was known as the Solomon Islands Broadcasting Service. Today's SIBC may resemble its colonial model, but it has a distinctly Melanesian flavor. This is a condition one might reasonably expect: familiar names given to varying practices as the colonial model is projected forward.

SIBC is responsible for programming on its medium-wave station in the Solomons as well as its shortwave broadcast. Its radiocasts are the only nationwide news media. Following the majority pattern in the Pacific, SIBC is also the sole public service broadcaster in the country. A private FM station has been licensed, but the broadcast area is confined. The corporation is a member of PIBA—a body of public and private broadcasters. Former SIBC general manager Patteson Mae was once a member of PIBA's board of directors.

After the Solomons' independence from the British in 1978, SIBC existed under the Ministry of Transport, Works, and Communications. In the early 1980s, however, SIBC was made an independent statutory authority under the office of the prime minister. In this new administrative arrangement, there is a board of directors and a chair. The prime minister appoints members to this board for a term of three years. There is provision for a secretary to the board, but he serves under the general manager—at least in theory.

Except for appointing its members, the prime minister has no formal link to the SIBC board, and under the 1976 Broadcasting Act that established SIBC as a statutory body, the board sets all procedures and policy. But the Solomons is a small country in terms of population—401,100 people spread out over a land area of 27,556 square kilometers. Honiara, the capital, on the island of Guadalcanal, has a population of about 37,000. If you are the prime minister, it is not difficult to make your views known. Your office is just a few minutes down the road—literally and figuratively—from SIBC. And former prime minister Solomon S. Mamaloni made his views known explicitly.

Since Mamaloni came to power in 1989, government funding for SIBC has declined significantly. Government has demanded that radio become self-financing, but there is also the unspoken issue of policy differences. By the early nineties, government funding had been slashed by two-thirds, forcing SIBC to cease recruitment of staff and to reduce the number of hours of broadcasting on outlying islands. Radio received about SI$100,000 (US$32,000) from the government with an operational budget of about SI$1.5 million (US$482,000). (Later in the decade, the government subvention was withheld, forcing the closing of the two regional stations. One station official noted, "SIBC's public broadcasting status is severely jeopardized.")

To earn revenue, SIBC stations have commercialized. They now carry advertising and broadcast service messages. At one time, the commercial activity included the repair of electronic equipment and the selling of parts. Currently the station produces commercial tape recordings and rents out studio time.

The Solomon Islands government has a history of antagonism with the media, but one event seems to have triggered the slashing of the SIBC budget: live coverage of a race riot in 1990. The principal food market for the capital, Honiara, is the central market. It is dusty, unpaved, and uncovered in parts. Fruit and vegetables are sold—taro, corn, edu (a root similar to taro), yams, sweet potato, pomelo, sugarcane, breadfruit, papaya, coconuts, and bananas—as well as fresh fish. The produce comes from nearby villages as well as from outlying islands such as Savo, home of the megapode bird. You can also find betel nut, powdered lime, and the ofa leaf (which are chewed together), and coconut oil. The market is a swirl of cash exchange and barter, a gathering place, a center of commerce and gossip, especially on Saturday.

On one particular day, market goers were met with some graffiti painted on a wall: a curse against the Malaita. The "Malaita Mafia," as they are sometimes referred to, are the most prominent ethnic group in the Solomons. Malaita Island is part of a province of the same name, and its population, primarily Melanesian, as is most of the Solomons, represents over 25 percent of the total national citizenry. The Malaita are also the conspicuous elite in commerce and politics.

The curse sparked isolated violence in the marketplace. One incident led to another, and the brawl escalated, with groups dividing into island and ethnic identities. SIBC, under current affairs director Johnson Honimae, rushed to the market to carry live radio coverage of the event. On the airwaves, the only source of broadcast media in the country, there for the entire nation to hear, was a full-scale race riot in the central market of the capital.

Officials were furious. They blamed the live radio coverage, which alerted the listeners to the event, for causing the ranks of rioters to swell. When, for uncertain reasons, the government awarded compensation to some participants of the riot in the amount of SI$200,000—at the time, something a little less than US$65,000, a considerable sum by local standards—the prime minister let it be known, according to James Kilua, then secretary to the SIBC board and later general manager, that funds for this compensation would come out of the station's annual allotment. Subsequently, the station experienced a sharp reduction in the government's subvention.

Current affairs director Honimae was held responsible for the decision to "go live." After a series of other run-ins with the general manager and complaints from the government over reporting-policy practices, Honimae was fired. On one occasion, Honimae reported that the Australian foreign minister, Gareth Evans, on a visit to the Solomon Islands, would not be received by the prime minister, although in normal diplomatic discourse, ministers of similar rank deal with each other. The effect of Honimae's story was to suggest that this was a snub of the Australian minister. On another occasion, Honimae failed to clear a story on the Bougainville crisis with the news director or the general manager, as station protocol required, before putting it on the air. Nevertheless, station personnel maintain that Honimae was fired primarily because of his freelance activities, which included the use of station resources during working hours.

The insurgency on the island of Bougainville, ongoing since 1988, has threatened to spill over into the Solomons, and the Solomon Islands government has been apprehensive about all SIBC reports on the inflammatory situation there.

In general, Solomon Islanders have been supportive of the secessionists on Bougainville, which they see as geographically and ethnically a part of Solomon Islands. The government, however, has had to be considerably more circumspect toward its larger armed neighbor, Papua New Guinea. Support for Bougainville, particularly from the Solomon's Shortland Islands and other islands close to the conflict, has strained relations with Papua New Guinea, and the government has had reason for alarm. Given the limits to their latitude for action—the Solomons has only a police force—local politicians have also, no doubt, been concerned about how they appear to stand in the eyes of their constituents.

As tensions between Solomons and PNG have risen, government pressure has mounted, leading Patteson Mae, then SIBC general manager, to require that all politically sensitive stories be submitted for review prior to broadcast. But after the Honimae firing, Mae was roundly criticized by journalists in the region for editorial interference. Some called it outright censorship.

It is the responsibility and a duty of a general manager to set standards for a station, but the stakes here have been higher than personality conflicts with reporters or the political correctness of stylebooks, guides for usage in newsrooms. The concern has not been a lack of awareness of barbed words or ill stereotypes; it has been a clash between the responsibility of an independent journalism on the one hand and what the government viewed as "national interest" on the other. There is legitimate disagreement over judgment calls in what is often a subjective business, but Pacific journalists viewed Mae as bowing too deeply to pressure from the government regarding the substance of news broadcasts.

The issues may not have been as clear-cut as imagined. Johnson Honimae did not challenge his termination under Solomon Islands labor grievance procedures, choosing instead to accept a position as senior journalist with the *Solomon Islands Voice,* a bi-weekly newspaper. And Patteson Mae did not stand for reelection to the board of the Pacific Islands Broadcasting Association, as it seemed unlikely that regional professionals would support his candidacy. Moreover, Mae was not asked to stay on at SIBC at the end of his contract; he subsequently ran—unsuccessfully—for a seat in the legislature.

For all the difficulties that Pacific news and other media professionals face, professional standards and journalistic autonomy remain highly esteemed. Journalists may not be reformers in their societies, but responsible journalism, however defined, is seen as an essential part of the practice of the profession. One's reputation among peers throughout the Pacific is of great importance in this regard. As for former SIBC general manager Mae, media professionals observed that he was not a journalist and his background was in "programming or presenting," suggesting that he lacked adequate understanding of the fundamental issues of freedom of the press. Censorship in the newsroom was a violation of professional norms, especially when so fine a line may exist between it and responsible editorial control.

Journalists have been known to refer to their superiors in pejorative and ironic terms—the "heavenly one," chief, boss, the brass, the chairman, "our precious possession," and much worse—indicative of the power their superiors have over them. But authority is not the point. Autonomy, a precious commodity in the media, is. In the Pacific, autonomy of media and media personnel is always tied to financing, and what is illustrated here is that outright censorship is but one means of controlling media. Nor is legislation essential to institute restraints upon it. Where the media are national media and where funding is tied to the government's pleasure, restraint necessarily follows. Journalists call it self-censorship.

The SIBC case shows too the delicate nature of media intertwined in a political and bureaucratic system. "Sometimes and in some places unscrupulous politicians will manipulate these otherwise sensible rules [of broadcast responsibility] to their own advantage, on the basis that since they fund the national broadcaster from general revenue then they have a right to expect something in return," University of Southern Queensland's Malcolm Philpott thought to remind regional broadcasters at a PIBA assembly.[16] It was hardly a reminder they needed to hear.

In the area of political opinion, people are apt to differ. A reporter may see a fact; others see opinions and untruths, or vice versa. But the issue may be even wider ranging: "Sometimes you feel like you are split right down the middle of your core being on a daily basis," one radio news reporter stated. "Of course you feel professionally obligated to report stories which are sometimes critical of the government. But ours is a small country. We are reporting about our neighbors, friends, and often our extended family."

In the Pacific, professional media activity often takes place in an overlay of a kin society where opposition is muted or nonexistent.[17] News gets reported, just as it does elsewhere. If there is a misfocusing of a story, it may not be for ownership or commercial bias, at least not in the usual sense. The misfocusing, where it occurs, tends to arise where social and traditional values come into play. It is a view echoed throughout the region. "The sanctity of culture, more often than not, deprives the region's journalists the strongest use of their pens."[18]

In small Pacific countries and dependencies, radio is not so much "mass communications," in some abstract sense of the term, as local and familiar. Consider the effect of the following service messages:

> THE FOUNG CHEW FAMILY WISH TO CONVEY THEIR MOST SINCERE GRATITUDE TO ALL RELATIVES, FRIENDS IN FIJI AND ABROAD FOR THEIR MESSAGES OF CONDOLENCES, PRAYERS, FLOWERS, PERSONAL ASSISTANCE AND WORDS OF COMFORT DURING THE SAD LOSS OF THEIR BELOVED HUSBAND, FATHER, UNCLE, FATHER-IN-LAW AND GRANDFATHER MR TAURI FOUNG CHEW WHO WAS CALLED TO REST.

> HAPPY 1ST BIRTHDAY LEWA. MAY GOD BLESS YOU AND GRANT YOU MANY MORE HAPPY DAYS LIKE THIS. LOVE FROM ALL YOUR RELATIVES, YACA IN LAUTOKA AND A SPECIAL ONE FROM TA AND NA AT HOME.

The "mass" nature of communications has been replaced, quite literally, with shared personal histories, giving radio the feeling of a multiparty telephone line. It is not an impersonal voice in communications space, not simply a one-on-many communications model. It partakes, because of the intimacy of the form, of the social relationships of the broadcast audience, thereby setting up an antagonism when professional values and broadcast models clash with social and traditional values.

There is of course a self-enforcing corrective to misfocused news, no different in the South Pacific than elsewhere: the closer the reporting—so-called local reporting—the greater our skepticism of, first, the accuracy and, then, fairness.[19] We doubt news stories that are close to us. The news may come out of the air booth, but it holds little more magic than what is gathered on the street, at the church social, in the market, or at work. In the Pacific, the word-of-mouth network is called the "coconut wireless" or "radio 32," an allusion to the number of teeth in the human mouth. Interestingly, both these phrases use the metaphor of radio, as radio remains the most popular mass medium. But even though the news so close to home might be unreliable, the manipulation of news on the radio is difficult to justify.

The specific issues at SIBC are not exotic to the Solomon Islands. They are common to other island nations in the region. What governments see as licentious and capricious media acts and others see as the reportage of fact and the responsibilities of journalism both become unstable standards on which to base media freedoms and permissible political expression over the air waves. Institutional forms, represented here by models of broadcasting, are often honored in the breach. In any event, the jury in such matters is public opinion, to which governments are not prone to give full rein, particularly when they perceive reportage as libelous and identify their politics with truth. In the case of Johnson Honimae's coverage of the race riot, the prime minister of the Solomon Islands heard irresponsible reporting, while Honimae believed he was being a responsible reporter. Prime Minister Solomon Mamaloni had hold of the purse strings; reporter Honimae was fired.

In a twist of fate, after the Mamaloni government fell, Johnson Honimae was appointed director of information for the new government of Prime Minister Billy Hilly. Honimae sat on the board of directors of SIBC.

Radio is the sound salvation.
Radio is cleaning up the nation.
They say you'd better listen to the
voice of reason.
But they don't give you any choice
'cause they think that it's treason.
So you had better do as you were told.
You'd better listen to the radio.
—Elvis Costello, *"Radio, Radio"*

3

Fax in Exile

The Intervention of a Coup d'État

One afternoon, not long after the Pacific News Service (PACNEWS) moved to Port Vila, Vanuatu, to join the activities of its parent association, senior editor Shiu Singh received a distressing phone call from his wife. This was in May 1994. The police were interrogating a prisoner, and from the Singh apartment, just above the police station on the slope that rises from Vila harbor, the sounds of the interrogation could be heard clearly. To Singh, listening to his wife's alarm was enough to bring back vivid memories of the coup d'état he had experienced seven years earlier in Suva, the capital of Fiji.

The coup was launched when soldiers, wearing gas masks, stormed the parliament in Victoria Parade, downtown Suva. Led by the Hon., then Lt. Col. (later Maj. Gen.) Sitiveni L. Rabuka, now prime minister of Fiji, the soldiers joined forces on Southern Cross Road and proceeded to the government buildings, where they rounded up parliamentarians at gunpoint.

In 1987, when what would be the first of two coups took place, Singh was deputy editor at Radio Fiji. Among his responsibilities was the preparation of news stories in English. Radio Fiji broadcasts in three languages—English, Fijian, and Hindi—and typically, stories written in English are then translated into the other two languages.

Shiu Singh remembers how he was removed under force of arms from the first floor news offices of Radio Fiji, located behind the government buildings, and taken to prison. After questioning, he was released, but subsequently, on two occasions, his house was surrounded by soldiers who had come for him. Singh had by then started editing news for PACNEWS, the Pacific Islands Broadcasting Association's news exchange, and was not at home. His wife and children were there alone. It was not a situation he could rest easy about. These events are etched indelibly in his memory.

To this day, third-generation Singh does not know why he was detained by the military forces, except for the fact that he is Indian Fijian and that he worked in a position of media responsibility. Nor does he understand why he was released unharmed, nor why the soldiers offered to drop him off at his house, although he did not regard it as a consolation at the time.

Shiu Singh was interned at the Central Police Station and at Fiji Military Forces Headquarters, Queen Elizabeth Barracks, on Mead Road, not far from his house in Tamavua. He was not tortured. He remembers hearing people being tortured. Reports of the period confirm that there was torture and other abuses on the part of the military and that in the aftermath of the coup Fijians of Indian ancestry were victims of systematic intimidation. As Singh listened, seven years later, to his wife's alarm at the sounds of the prisoner's interrogation, memories of this nightmarish period came flooding back. It was a period that also happens to be closely intertwined with the history of PACNEWS.

In April 1987 a general election brought a coalition of the Labor Party and the National Federation Party (NFP) to power in Fiji. Labor was a racially mixed party headed by Dr. Timoci Bavadra, an ethnic Fijian. The NFP was supported in large part by Indian Fijians who had come to comprise a plurality of the country's population of 744,000.[1] After one month in office, however, there came the first coup d'état led by then Lt. Col. Sitiveni Rabuka, and the coalition government was overthrown.

On Thursday, May 17, 1987, at 10 o'clock in the morning, Lt. Col. Rabuka, army third-in-command at the time, flanked by ten soldiers brandishing pistols and wearing gas masks and camouflage jackets for disguise, stormed the House of Representatives.[2] The civilian parliamentary democracy was toppled in minutes, an act justified by the Colonel as necessary to ensure that ethnic Fijians did not relinquish control of the nation. The military did not get around to imposing media censorship until the next night, when soldiers entered Radio Fiji with their guns drawn.

After the coup, control of the country was handed over to Ratu Sir Penaia Ganilau, who was governor-general and later became president of the newly proclaimed republic. Rabuka, however, felt compelled to stage a second coup at the end of September 1987 when it appeared that Sir Penaia Ganilau would form a government that shared power with Indian Fijians. On this occasion the military knew what to do and wasted no time getting to the radio station. Media censorship was imposed immediately—again, guns in the station, guns in the newsroom, news read at gunpoint.

Of the ensuing coups, news stories that originated outside the Pacific often focused on what was termed "ethnic chauvinism." Stories generally followed the line of this Associated Press dispatch: "The election also led to violence between Fiji's two ethnic halves—Indians and native Fijians. The [Labor Party and National Federation Party] coalition is generally supported by Indians, and the more conservative Alliance Party by ethnic Fijians."[3] Even as late as December 1987, news article leads continued in a similar vein: "Racially torn Fiji returned to civilian rule Saturday after seven months of military leadership as coup leader, later promoted to Brig. Gen., Sitiveni Rabuka handed over power to the man he hand-picked as the nation's first president."[4]

Beyond their difference in ethnic composition, the two governments held strongly divergent points of view. Under Ratu Sir Kamisese Mara, the Alliance Party had been pro-Western in orientation, and visits by warships from the United Kingdom, United States, and Australia had been widely permitted. In contrast, the Labor Party proposed a nonaligned foreign policy. It advocated a ban on nuclear-capable warships, but not on warships in general.

The Labor Party was also prolabor and gained support from trade unions.

Other differences between the parties centered on sensitive issues of land tenure and education.

Of Pacific island nations, Fiji is the most prosperous. The economy derives a large percentage of revenue from tourism. Its main exports include sugar and molasses, gold, fish, copra (dried coconut meat), lumber, and biscuits. At the time of the first 1987 coup, the main export destinations were the United Kingdom (34 percent), Australia (17 percent), other Pacific islands (13 percent), New Zealand (6 percent), the United States (5 percent), Japan (3 percent), and other (22 percent). But after the two coups, the United Kingdom's share dropped to 25 percent, even as Japan's trade receipts increased to 7 percent.[5]

Overall the effect of the coups on the economy was disastrous. An Associated Press headline on June 3, 1987, summed up the situation: "Sugar,

Tourism Industries Languish Following Coup." Exports stagnated. Against most major currencies, the Fijian dollar tumbled. Inflation rose in the year following to almost 12 percent and continued the next year at a little over 6 percent. Tourism declined. Emigration of the skilled and educated increased, leaving an acute problem in a country where both are in short supply.[6] Private investment stalled. Capital flight was serious enough to require emergency measures to protect foreign exchange reserves. The government deficit rose to US$5.2 million as the real gross domestic product fell by an estimated 6 percent—from US$1,290 million in 1986 to US$1,142 million. General growth was negative—at one point the Fijian dollar was devalued by 33 percent—and the economy languished for several years after the coups.

During the period of military control, press freedom was curtailed in the name of public security: "Military authorities closed down newspapers, while the local radio station was taken over and surrounded by government troops. Early this morning troops with guns drawn burst into the hotel rooms of at least eight foreign reporters and seized notebooks, photographs, negatives and cassette tape recordings."[7]

Reporters were detained at local police headquarters. In addition, the *Washington Post* reported, "Despite signs that an end to the takeover was in sight, the military throughout the day continued to tighten its crackdown on foreign journalists." Trevor Watson of Radio Australia was expelled. A reporter from the BBC, who was filing a story from his hotel room when troops burst in, was frisked and locked in the bathroom while his room was scoured for notes and tape recordings. "Several reporters had their hotel rooms ransacked throughout the day. An employee at the telephone company said that 12 soldiers had been dispatched to monitor all outgoing international calls."[8]

Soldiers didn't find everything. Three staff from Radio Fiji drove to the residence of the president with a reel-to-reel tape recorder. Strangely enough, soldiers let them through the gates. One of the three remembers taping the president's "half-hearted appeal for the troops to return to barracks." Somehow, the staff member related with a smile, the tape found its way to FM 96 and was broadcast over the private station—even though there was timidity at Radio Fiji. Another copy found its way to a foreign reporter, who concealed it on his body and managed to get the tape out of the country where it was broadcast over Radio Australia's shortwave Pacific service.

From their offices in Suva, PACNEWS, the fledgling news service created by Pacific island broadcasters, where Shiu Singh later became full-time news editor, reported on the second coup and the interim military regime as part of its routine activities. But their activities, no less than the doings of foreign correspondents, came under the notice of coup authorities. Fijian security forces investigated the offices of this regional news service and "paid the PACNEWS coordinator a visit"—which did not bode well for the long-term survival of PACNEWS in Fiji.[9] During the post-coup period, military authorities demanded that PACNEWS submit to the police the news bulletins that PIBA issued twice a day for broadcasters. PACNEWS was forced to comply. Hendrik Bussiek took copies of the bulletin to the police station to avert further visits. Bussiek recalls that he "advised [the police] that they could get the stuff from Radio Fiji and to leave us in peace; so they did."[10]

In *The South Pacific,* Ron Crocombe is even stronger in his assessment of the time: "When the PACBROAD programme (which disseminates island news between island states from a base in Fiji) passed news to other islands which the military government did not wish broadcast, it sent troops, issued threats and otherwise intimidated, to ensure that its interests were preserved."[11] At the time, the region depended on Fiji for news. In the best of times, the perspective of this news carried Fiji's viewpoint. The repressive side of the coup now posed the potential for distortion of the news.

The Stirrings of a News Exchange

The events of the coups, however, throw the realization of PACNEWS as a Pacific regional news exchange out of sequence. The news exchange grew out of an organization for training in all spheres of broadcasting. While the training organization had its beginnings in 1985, history goes back even farther in the evolution of Pacific radio broadcasting cooperation.

The idea of a news exchange had been floating around the Asia-Pacific Broadcasting Union (ABU), a regional organization, for more than a decade starting in the early 1970s. Broadcasters from the area had discussed the idea at great length, but implementation was far in the distance.

In their minds, the aim was clear: provide a professional, reliable news service to fill the information gap, which could be wide, among the Pacific islands and furnish timely information about key events in the region, events which went unreported by news organizations in North countries. Events such as a coup in a country as regionally important as Fiji did get reported by international news organizations, but often events of significance within the Pacific did not. From a news point of view the idea of a news exchange was important because there had never been expeditious, comprehensive coverage over the range of the Pacific, certainly not for the smaller of the island nations. If a news exchange could be achieved, radio audiences for the first time would be linked on a daily basis and informed about major happenings in their own world neighborhood. Equally important, the news would not be an echo of empire.

The means to this end was a simple concept: Public service broadcast organizations would daily supply the main stories from their countries. The stories would be edited, supplemented, rewritten where necessary, and redistributed by facsimile (fax) back to these Pacific radio stations.

In the early 1980s Radio Australia and the Solomon Islands Broadcasting Corporation launched a study on implementation of such a news exchange, but various governments and information ministers were cool to the idea. It was one thing to have aid donors fund engineering departments of the island stations or provide equipment and maintenance, but news was another matter entirely. There was reluctance to give up control, particularly among government broadcasters who had management roles and who felt a proprietary need to "oversee" the news. Indeed, several of the broadcasters who met at regional gatherings were, if not in name in fact, representatives of their government inasmuch as many of the radio stations were government-owned and operated.

An offer of AU$200,000 was made by the Australian government to start a Pacific news exchange. Representatives involved in discussions of this offer remember a week of fighting. Even before there was any agreement on the idea of an exchange, there was disagreement about who would become editor. At least four participants wanted the post and began arguing over salary and a car. This was not the Pacific way at its best. To add to the chaos, the representative from Samoa threatened to withdraw if a news exchange was created. Eventually it became apparent that no agreement could be reached, and the money was returned.

So there were studies and proposals—by Pacific governments, media nongovernmental organizations (NGOs), UNESCO and other organizations, and out-of-region governments—for a news exchange and broadcast training, but agreement was elusive. One study established a fact-finding mission composed of participants from the Asia-Pacific Institute for Broadcasting Development (AIBD), UNESCO, and Friedrich-Ebert-Stiftung (FES), a German not-for-profit political foundation engaged in development projects throughout the Third World. The mission objective was to investigate the training needs of Pacific broadcasters. This was one report that did see results.

In March 1985, UNESCO made a start-up grant of US$100,000, based in part on the mission report, specifically for broadcast training. The effort was also supported by a grant of US$900,000 from FES. While there had been ad hoc training activities in the Pacific and such organizations as the Media Center of the South Pacific Commission had been active in the Pacific for several years, no formal broadcast training institution existed. Seizing the opportunity provided by UNESCO and FES, thirteen South Pacific radio networks joined forces, and the Pacific Broadcasting Training and Development Project (which became known as PACBROAD) came into being. Its founding meeting was held September 17–25, 1985, in Apia, Samoa.

One of the first acts of PACBROAD was the establishment of three media training sites: in Fiji, Papua New Guinea, and Samoa, where UNESCO maintained an office. UNESCO funded, among other activities, a media trainer, situating him in Samoa. FES set up a studio at 2AP, Samoa's government-run station, and similarly outfitted rooms at the Telecommunications Training Center in Suva. Fiji, where the government had early on expressed cooperation, was selected because of its central location in the Pacific and its existing telecommunications training center. Media facilities also existed in Papua New Guinea, so it became a logical site for training in Melanesia. Trainers provided a variety of in-country courses as well, traveling to local radio stations to train personnel. In some cases, these courses represented the first professional training that participants had ever received.

The technical training involved transmitter and studio techniques as well as other broadcast basics. Most of the training, however, focused on a variety of topics including station management, newswriting, basics of (radio) magazine programs, interview techniques, introduction to broadcasting, reporting techniques, writing for radio, news and current affairs, radio journalism, and documentary production.

The support that PACBROAD received for this training came from funds initially granted by UNESCO and FES, as well as from membership dues. When the initial three-year UNESCO funding ended, Deutsche Gesellschaft für Technische Zusammenarbeit (GTZ), the German technical aid association which receives its funding from the German Ministry for Economic Cooperation, stepped forward. Its grant to PACBROAD was to assist stations with urgent needs for equipment, spare parts, technical advice, and training.

As regards the next step, the creation of a news exchange, UNESCO was as much a part of the problem as it was the solution. Because of the nature of its charter, UNESCO must necessarily deal only through international organizations and through governments. Acknowledging this bureaucratic stricture, Peter Higginson, chief of the UNESCO Office for the Pacific States, sent a written welcome address to the second PACBROAD meeting in 1986 in which he strongly cautioned members that activities were "limited to training." The phrase was underlined.[12]

Various governments in the region were also part of the problem. While governments were not direct participants in PACBROAD, there was nervousness about media and of the role a news exchange would play in their own country. Reports from the same 1986 meeting in Rarotonga indicate a lack of understanding, criticism, and suspicion from some governments about PACBROAD's activities.

In a typically bureaucratic response to issues raised, the UNESCO-supported trainer Richard Henderson recommended that departments of foreign affairs be informed and that they be given all the correspondence between PACBROAD and member broadcast organizations. A number of stations, however, were seeking their own independence, no less than their recently decolonized states had sought theirs. Reporting to a unit of government would have surely defeated any notion of independent media.

The UNESCO representative also stipulated that his agency would support the idea of a news exchange only when it became the wish of all *governments* participating in PACBROAD.[13] Coming from an organization that had fought a controversial battle for the free flow of information, this caution came as a surprise to some PACBROAD members, who were quick to express their dismay. Among other things, the UNESCO response revealed a startling naïveté of internal considerations, among which was a lack of understanding of the jurisdictional murkiness owing to the fact that some broadcasters were from independent statutory authorities while others were from government-run stations.

Pacific broadcasters, because of their close connection to government, could agree on technical matters and on training even if they could not agree on a news exchange. And this, despite other basic disagreements, allowed PACBROAD to go on. The annual meetings attracted general managers, several of whom had journalism backgrounds and interests. UNESCO continued its bureaucratic hedging, and some members continued their veiled opposition, but PACBROAD had now become a convenient venue for discussing a regional news exchange.[14]

It was Tavake Fusimalohi, director of Radio Tonga, who first raised this idea of a news exchange. The item was not officially on the agenda at the second PACBROAD technical meeting in Rarotonga, Cook Islands, in 1986. Even so, Fusimalohi was able to speak to the issue, and there was discussion.

In a 1994 interview at PACNEWS offices, Fusimalohi recounts how the now deceased Tupai Joe Brown, the representative from Samoa, objected to the inclusion in the minutes of any reference to the discussion of a news exchange. The objection was procedural, Fusimalohi says. Brown maintained that the purpose of PACBROAD was to address the technical concerns of radio, specifically training; a news exchange was not part of PACBROAD's charge, and furthermore, it was not on the agenda. But, of course, there was a contest of wills being waged beneath the surface.

Fusimalohi wanted to get discussion of a news exchange into the minutes so that funding agencies, such as FES and even UNESCO, would be alerted to the regional interest and need. If the matter were "officially" raised, these organizations might be moved to provide funding, and the effort might then have a chance to get off the ground. Brown's objection was sustained by the chair, P. Vaine Rere, general manager of the Cook Islands Broadcasting Corporation, Fusimalohi remembers. Fusimalohi walked out in protest.

The matter did not end there, however. The official report of the Rarotonga meeting, it appears, does in fact contain a reference to a working session where a discussion concerning a *training* project for a news exchange took place.[15] The report includes as well a carefully worded reference to a more detailed proposal by Hendrik Bussiek for a news exchange *training* project. Bussiek was the PACBROAD coordinator and, incidentally, a representative of FES. In the breach, the stricture about training was honored. Participants agreed that as a training project, the idea could proceed. With that, the camel's nose was under PACBROAD's tent—to use a metaphor from another part of the world.

Bussiek, in his dual role, was apparently in a position to see that the final report did contain a reference to the news exchange dressed up as training.

He was able as well to ensure that the discussion was reported in his communications with FES headquarters in Bonn.[16] FES quickly provided the funds for the news exchange training. So the ability of the FES representative to act in a private capacity for his foundation, a nongovernmental organization not bound by state-to-state relations, was critical in moving events along. FES supports not only technical activities for media development but addresses concerns with production, presentation, and programming as well as press freedom. UNESCO, constrained by international agreements and procedures, could not and would not have acted as flexibly and boldly.

Pacific journalists—the people in the newsrooms—had long recognized the need for a news exchange. Politicians contended that there was no news in the Pacific. The Pacific was peaceful—why would anyone want a Pacific news service? At the time, people in the Pacific knew more about London, New York, and Paris than they did about neighboring island nations.

One of the most widely circulated regional news publications was the *Pacific Islands Monthly,* which carried the more important regional issues compressed into a monthly magazine.[17] But even here the problem was, as a number of journalists recall, one had to wait a month to hear about some important event on an adjacent island. The major news services, or the stringers working for Radio Australia, might or might not pick up a news development in a smaller country. Broadcasts from Radio Australia or Broadcasting Corporation New Zealand might or might not carry one or two items that dealt with *all* the smaller Pacific countries and territories combined. Most newsrooms in these small countries did not subscribe to a wire service—nor can they afford to do so now—and, if they had, there was scant news about the Pacific.

One news editor remembers that before PACNEWS, to obtain the day's news for his Pacific station, he listened to the BBC overseas broadcasts and transcribed the bulletins. He translated the bulletins, then read them on the air for the local audience.

In the late 1970s and early 1980s, there was another source of Pacific regional news available, mainly to broadcasters who were members of the Commonwealth Broadcasting Association in the Pacific. It was a radio program called "Pacific Link."

On a weekly basis, stations in the association would send tapes to the Wellington offices of Broadcasting Corporation New Zealand (BCNZ), now called Radio New Zealand International.[18] BCNZ's Rudi Hill, whose idea it was to start this interisland communication in 1980, would then edit the individual submissions into a tape redistributed under the title "Pacific Link." This enterprise went on for some time, arousing a great deal of interest because the voices on the tapes were local. That is to say, even if you were in Tonga, you heard the news read by someone from Fiji or the Solomon Islands or Niue. This unique feature, a local voice, was an important part of the appeal and interest in Hill's program.

"Pacific Link," of course, was only as good as the tapes that Rudi Hill received. Broadcasters recall that some of the segments were interesting, and some were not. It depended on what came in the mail to BCNZ in any week's time. Hill remembers that some stations were more regular in their submissions than others. Ashley Wickham, then at Solomon Islands Broadcasting, was a systematic contributor, as was Bob Makin in Vanuatu. Tonga, Fiji, and Kiribati were also regular contributors of reports. Samoa, Cook Islands, Niue, and Nauru were the "worst performers." In the case of Samoa, "Brown's contribution from 2AP was never more than lip service."[19]

In the initial phase, the other problem was the unreliability of the mails and the length of time involved to distribute the program. Tapes would have to come from all over the Pacific to Wellington, be assembled into a coherent program, and then mailed back for transmission. By the time they were broadcast, the stories would be a week or more stale. In some places, that would be history, not news. Hill later set up a collect-call facility for the island stations. The process was referred to as "feeding down the line." Incoming calls were recorded in Wellington studios and then sent to Hill for editing.

With the telephone link, stations such as those in Fiji, Samoa, and the Cook Islands received their tapes twenty-four hours after production. The weekly program was rushed to Air New Zealand for delivery. Despite the change, some stations, such as Kiribati and Tuvalu, still got their tapes a week or so later.

Recall that getting information about developments in neighboring states and territories in the Pacific, even in the early 1980s, was not an easy undertaking. An election would occur and, if it were in a smaller country, the results would not be known for weeks. Cabinets changed; that too went unnoticed by regional neighbors. To some small extent, "Pacific Link" was a remedy because each island station contributed its local news, and the program broke new ground in interisland communication. Yet, getting the region's news into a half-hour program once a week had limits. Indeed, Hill sometimes could not produce enough stories to last thirty minutes—sufficient stories did not arrive—and the weekly program was considerably shorter.

There have been other news exchanges in the Pacific. American authorities set up a telex news exchange in the trust territories in the Northern Pacific.[20] Items from the telex were sometimes used by papers in Guam to cover that part of Micronesia. Regional broadcasters have even resorted to newspaper rings, that is, waiting for newspapers from neighboring countries to arrive and then using stories from the papers for the news. But the newspapers came by mail, and the mail did not arrive so often, air traffic then less frequent. As with the tapes for "Pacific Link," by the time the paper arrived, the value of these newspapers was an uncertain proposition.

Before one can get the news to disseminate, someone has to want news as part of their broadcasts. That would seem to be a given, but in the Pacific the general manager of a radio station sometimes has priorities other than news. Sometimes he will have arrived at his position through a career path quite different from a journalist's—in Samoa, for example, Tupai Brown was the station's chief engineer before becoming GM. Others might have been civil servants or government appointees.

One general manager, when asked how he kept his position through a succession of governments, replied, "I was related to the first prime minister, but I worked my way up from accounting to general manager. And my wife is related to the current prime minister so I retained my job as GM." A Pacific island observer dubbed the survivorship of a colleague who opposed the creation of a Pacific news exchange as a remarkable course of "remaining the government's boy—any government will do." Some general managers, through "bobbing, weaving, and ducking"—their own words—have managed to hold on to their positions through a succession of governments. In any case, a free exchange of news and a spotlight on activities in their country were the last thing some general managers, or the political figures at whose pleasure they served, wanted. The dissimulation of news would be a more apt characterization of their attitude.

Although the idea for a news exchange was raised on a number of occasions, regional agreement could not be reached until several years after broadcast training cooperation had been under way. Chief among the proponents of the idea were Kedea Uru, chair of the PNG National Broadcasting

Corporation, and Tavake Fusimalohi, general manager of Radio Tonga, who had been responsible for initiating discussion of the news exchange at the second PACBROAD meeting.

On the other hand, there was the late Tupai Brown of station 2AP, Samoa, who was at first hostile. That is one view of the situation offered by a participant at the PACBROAD meetings. A kinder view suggests that Brown did not want the training cooperation diluted or endangered by something as controversial as a news exchange. But the more common perception participants had at the time is that Brown attempted to scuttle the news exchange. Indeed, after the news exchange was up and running, Brown sent a message to the exchange's offices telling them not to waste his station's fax paper by sending dispatches, whether news or sports. News bulletins broadcast from the station Brown managed reflect this particular predisposition. But Brown was a singular minority.

At the Pacific Islands Broadcasting Association Assembly in Samoa in 1994, Brown made reference to "Western media powers" in his opening remarks. He was the only one heard to do so. Brown did not elaborate, and no one else took up the theme.

For a good part of this meeting, however, Brown was seen conferring with officials from TV New Zealand. Apparently, most of the programming on Samoa's TV station originated in New Zealand, and it was Brown's role as general manager of both the TV station and the radio station in Samoa to arrange for the "media domination" of his audience. Given his views, the choice of TV New Zealand, on the one hand, and his rejection of the regional news exchange that is a Pacific voice, on the other, Brown was, to say the least, idiosyncratic.

What Brown applied to radio goes for TV as well. Samoa has, apparently, a long history of media control. A story submitted to PACNEWS by Mark Kneubuhl from American Samoa, carried in PACNEWS editions on July 25, 1994, and in an extended bulletin on Radio New Zealand International on the same date, reported the Samoa practice of not allowing the political opposition on the air. Tuiatua Tupa Tamisese Efi, an opposition leader in the Fono, the parliament, would be kept off the government-owned television station, the report indicates, for suggesting that Samoa's prime minister was "incompetent." The story went on to report that anyone who attacked a controversial law dealing with a goods and services tax would be deemed to have "disturbed the peace."

As a footnote, the opposition leader once did nearly appear on television.

The prime minister indicated a willingness to "allow television to do an interview with Tuiatua and himself but instructed that the interview with the opposition be aired first so that he could reply to it." In the end, however, the opposition leader's statement was not aired—a decision, according to the prime minister, made by the head of television, Tupai Brown.[21]

Before the 1994 assembly, Brown's station had been delinquent in its dues to PIBA for some time. To smooth over the appearance of difficulty between broadcasters and to keep Samoa officially in the organization, Radio Tonga and Radio Fiji paid the Samoa station's dues for the 1991–1992 period. At the 1994 PIBA Assembly, the seventh annual meeting, however, Brown indicated that he was "pleased to be back in the fold." The station later paid its dues, including arrears. He also promised that 2AP would begin sending stories to PACNEWS, a promise not yet delivered on. PACNEWS editors seek Samoan news through other channels.

In early discussions of the news exchange, broadcasting officials in the region were not as vociferous as Brown. There had been much talk at meetings such as the Asia-Pacific Broadcasting Union and the Commonwealth Broadcasting Association, but prior to the late 1970s, no action. Many were indifferent. In July 1987, however, in a meeting in Kiribati of the Pacific Group of the Commonwealth Broadcasting Association (CBA), the tenor changed. In attendance were the general managers of radio stations from the Commonwealth countries as well as UNESCO's Dik Henderson and the FES representative, Hendrik Bussiek. The issue of a regional news exchange was raised, and a heated debate erupted with Henderson strongly in opposition and Bussiek strongly in favor. Bussiek remembers that, privately, the managers present encouraged him to proceed regardless of consequences.[22] He did.

But it was not general managers who created the news exchange, even though a number of them created the conditions for its coming into being. Clearly it would have been impossible to establish an exchange without the participation of key station officials. In the end it was a very well planned PACBROAD workshop, with all the necessary equipment in place prior to it, that got things started. News editors and broadcast journalists present at the workshop took the next step in fine tuning the system that would be put in place. The recollection of one of the editors present was that the training exercise transformed into a news exchange out of exasperation: "Let's not talk about it any more; let's just do it." And they did. The feeling was that if the editors waited for their various governments or their general managers to act, it would never happen. The same observer noted, "Pacific governments don't particularly like the idea of an independent news service." It was at this editors' workshop run by Hendrik Bussiek in September 1987, in Fiji, held under the auspices of PACBROAD, that participants simply agreed that two news editors would stay on in Fiji to begin the work on the Monday immediately after the workshop.

Thus was the news exchange born, dubbed PACNEWS for Pacific News Service, to exist in tandem with PACBROAD, the broadcast training effort. Details about the incipient news exchange were to be hammered out later, rather anticlimactically.

FES, which had continued funding PACBROAD after the start-up initiative two years earlier, funded the news exchange project on a three-month trial basis. Again, because the German foundation is a nongovernmental organization, it could flexibly provide the crucial support needed to get the project off the ground.

The timing of this action was both good and bad. On the one hand, PACBROAD members were scheduled to meet about three months later. They would be in a position to ratify the activity and to provide organizational support. On the other hand, a coup in Fiji would intervene within days of PACNEWS's beginning.

Because of the political turmoil in Fiji, PACBROAD broadcasters chose to meet in Tonga rather than Fiji. At the meeting, they were faced with a fait accompli: PACNEWS had begun its work as a news exchange, and news was flowing to their stations. It was the first time that contemporaneous, region-wide news had been available to any news organization in the Pacific, and what local audiences were hearing over the air was exciting to them. Some PACBROAD members who had been opposed to the news exchange "suddenly had a change of heart." There was discussion, and then PACBROAD members agreed to ask FES to fund PACNEWS for a longer term.

It was at this time that the idea of an umbrella organization surfaced. With two projects running there was need for a coordinating body. Members thus agreed to create the Pacific Islands Broadcasting Association, PIBA, which would be responsible for the training effort, called PACBROAD, and now the news exchange, called PACNEWS. A constitutional committee, composed of broadcast representatives from Tonga, Fiji, and Papua New Guinea, was named. The committee met three times during the course of the year to work out a proposed constitution in consultation with the FES representative. In 1988, PIBA was formally launched and with it, PACNEWS.[23]

PIBA Is Formed

Three years after broadcast training cooperation began under PACBROAD in the Pacific, PIBA was formed as a professional association of the national, publicly owned radio networks of thirteen independent Pacific island countries—Cook Islands, Federated States of Micronesia, Fiji, Kiribati, Marshall Islands, Niue, Papua New Guinea, Palau, Solomon Islands, Tonga, Tuvalu, Vanuatu, and Samoa—in addition to Australia and New Zealand. "Independent" is the operative word here, as many of the media institutions involved were from newly independent nations of the Pacific. Broadcasters were moving away from inherited media institutions and seeking to create their own.

Tavake Fusimalohi was the first chair of the association. Behind the scenes he had been a prime proponent of the news exchange, and he had been active in PACBROAD. There had been difficulties over the years. But as the director of Radio Tonga, Fusimalohi was in a position to understand the needs of regional broadcasters: Fusimalohi has an M.A. in communications from the University of Hawai'i and was a Jefferson Fellow at the East-West Center. He was also head of news at his station. As general manager, he had trained the news people at Radio Tonga.[24]

Membership in PIBA has shifted over time and now includes a variety of commercial radio stations as well as other organizations and members. At first, commercial stations were only granted associate member status. To some extent, the opening of membership categories is a result of the commercialization and privatization that are occurring apace in the Pacific. It is an attempt to make the organization more inclusive of Pacific media broadcasting needs and to make the association financially viable. One goal is to move away from dependence on aid. PIBA associate members, at one time or another, have included Hawaii Public Radio, Hawaii Public Television, Voice of America, and Communications Fiji (FM 96).

A general assembly of members, which meets annually, is the governing body of the Pacific Islands Broadcasting Association. The assembly reviews projects of the association, discusses reports of the chair and coordinators of the projects, and reviews the accounts. Between annual meetings, a PIBA governing board is responsible for running the association.

Briefly, PIBA has a variety of objectives and programs, the main objectives of which have been to provide a system of news and program exchange in the Pacific region; to provide a system of technical cooperation on telecommunications; to provide training for the staff of broadcasting organizations in all aspects of broadcasting; to promote cooperation of member news and broadcast organizations; to provide services for the coverage of special events of interest in the region; to promote development of broadcasting in the region; to establish relations with broadcasting associations and organizations outside the region such as UNESCO and the Asia-Pacific Broadcasting Union.[25]

Fax in Exile, Relocation of PACNEWS

The two editors who produced PACNEWS that first week of its existence were from Papua New Guinea and Tuvalu. According to the PACNEWS plan, two news editors from different stations in the Pacific would stay in Suva for two weeks to staff the news exchange. They would then be replaced by two others, and two others, and so on throughout the year.

One week after the news exchange began operations, however, this initial staffing plan had to be changed. The occasion of this change in plan was the second coup in Fiji. With telex and other international communications cut off, PACNEWS could not continue. Shiu Singh recalled being on the telephone to Kiribati to get a story on the reaction to the coup in that country: "They were saying that Kiribati will never support a coup when the line went dead. This happened several times. The army was listening in on our international calls." Given these sudden new circumstances, the first two PACNEWS editors returned home as quickly as they could. In the aftermath of the coup d'état, general managers were leery about sending their personnel to Fiji, so PACNEWS came to a halt.

But another difficulty was the impracticality of a short rotation period. Getting from one island to another, particularly from some of the remoter islands, often takes several days, so a two-week stint might involve an additional week of travel time. Cost was a factor too. It is expensive to travel the Pacific. Stations are chronically short of personnel, so if a staff member is out of the office, the remaining staff may have to double up on duties to cover all the requirements of running a station.

At the initiative of Hendrik Bussiek, the FES representative, PACNEWS restarted operations in Suva. He asked Shiu Singh, who was still officially the deputy editor of Radio Fiji, to begin the news exchange again. Singh's position at Radio Fiji was tenuous, given his race and the prevailing situation in Fiji. At the time, papers in Fiji were publishing stories indicating that various Pacific island nations would not welcome the Indian Fijians despite their professional qualifications—notwithstanding the sizable brain drain that Fiji felt as talented people fled the country. Singh accepted the offer of a PACNEWS editorship.

In any case, PACNEWS was back in business in Suva a week after it shut

Mise En Scène: Friedrich-Ebert-Stiftung

The main support for PIBA activities has been a foundation known by the initials FES. Friedrich-Ebert-Stiftung, the oldest political foundation in Germany, has media programs in Africa, Asia-Pacific, Latin America, and the Caribbean, as well as eastern Europe.[1] Founded in 1925 by private donations and donations from the German government, FES started by awarding scholarships to "young and able proletarians." In 1994, its total budget was DM210 million. All told, FES had a total of 650 staff, including more than 140 representatives in 76 countries, and had projects ongoing in 100 countries. In recent years, funding, staff, and projects have declined. Media funding is about 10 percent of the FES budget.

FES has also funded a wide variety of media projects outside the Pacific. But what first brought FES to the Pacific was a request by an official of Radio Fiji to fund a ten-year plan for the Fiji Broadcasting Commission.[2]

In the 1980s, Reinhard Keune, then head of the FES media department, was instrumental in assembling funding for the initial training project of PACBROAD. It was he who attempted to negotiate an unlikely cooperative agreement between FES and UNESCO in Paris. But because of the different nature of their charters—FES is a nongovernmental organization and UNESCO is an international organization that works through governments—each felt constrained to take a different path. Separately, both organizations did finally fund activities that fall under the PACBROAD description, but they had to proceed on the informal basis of an "understanding." This proved problematic, but it was not without success.[3]

Keune brought FES staff with him to the Pacific. The FES regional representative for the South Pacific was Karlheinz Renfordt, who contributed to the training effort. In addition, an FES coordinator was placed in the PIBA offices. To date, there have been four project coordinators: Hendrik Bussiek, Wolfgang Holler, Hartmut Hess, and H.-J. Esderts.

It is clear that FES representatives have played a key role in PIBA, not only in financial backing from a very early period when FES awarded scholarships to Pacific broadcasters but also in hands-on, practice-related activities. One regional journalist spoke fondly of "can-do Bussiek" and his antibureaucratic, action-oriented stance while he was the resident representative in the early days of PACBROAD. As an aid project, FES's Pacific media work surely has to be regarded as successful.

Germans have made their presence known in the Pacific before. In letters and essays published around the turn of the century, Scottish novelist and poet Robert Louis Stevenson, who was living in Samoa at the time, recounts a series of events in 1888–1889 involving the *Samoa Times and South Sea Advertiser.* "It is of course a tiny sheet; but I have often had occasion to wonder at the ability of its articles, and almost always at the decency of its tone."[4] German colonial powers, however, did not share this opinion. Stevenson was on the other side of their colonial dispute and was suspected of trying to sway public opinion. The *Times* may have treated the German officials "a little roughly, at times a little captiously, criticized," Stevenson concedes, but they received nothing more than what officials might suffer in England or the United States.

> Anglo-Saxons and Germans have been differently brought up. To our galled experience the paper appears moderate; to their untried sensations it seems violent. We think a public man fair game; we think it a part of his duty, and I am told he finds it a part of his reward, to be continually canvassed by the press. For the Germans, on the other hand, an official wears a certain sacredness; when he is called over the coals, they are shocked, and feel that Germany itself has been insulted.[5]

The Germans took steps to defend their position. They brought in another printer, giving him government work to help finance his activities. They fined the *Samoa Times* editor, Cusack, £20. Cusack, undeterred, kept up his "mountain of offenses" until the paper was suspended under martial law.

Sailors from that unhappy European power, "wild with offended patriotism" and out to punish the editor, stormed ashore. But a kind of justice prevailed that day in Apia. The German bluecoats demanded to know where the "English publisher" was. People pointed the way. Somehow, though, it was the wrong editor who received the blows of the sailors: Jones, the Germans' import, got stripes, not Cusack.

These days, the Germans, through FES, are on the other side, giving strong support to freedom of the media in the Pacific and elsewhere.

The dissemination of public information—in both the substance of the message and the technical means—is always a sensitive political matter, both domestically and internationally. At the first PACBROAD gathering in Apia in 1985 the FES regional representative, Renfordt, spoke to "the urgency to expand the Third World information systems so as to change the developing countries from being mere consumers to independent producers of information, and to eliminate the one-sided dependence on the industrialized countries in favor of an evenly-weighted partnership in a world-wide information exchange."[6] The statement should be considered in context of the rhetoric of the time, which was an attack by the South on the North's monopoly of media in the face of a largely silent South audience. But here was a representative of a North metropolitan power honoring the complaints of South nations, offering support to rectify the problem. The FES mission, since the beginning of its involvement in the Pacific, has been to invert this formula of North domination in broadcast news. While the global flow of news may not be balanced even now for Pacific microstates, FES has been significant in helping substantially to change the intraregional flow of Pacific information. In the wake of decolonization, the support of efforts such as PACNEWS helped to create a Pacific social space that is other than a mere geographical domain.

---

1. Ralf Siepmann, *Developing Media in the Third World: Project Examples* (Bonn: Friedrich-Ebert-Stiftung, 1990).

2. Interview, FES Offices, New York, February 1995. Reinhard Keune got FES to fund a project begun in late

1980 and concluded in 1981. There was a variety of findings in the report by the media consultant Burt Cowlan, one of which produced unexpected connections: At the time, Radio Fiji broadcast strength was generally weak, particularly outside the capital, Suva. To hear broadcasts, it was necessary to increase the volume on battery-powered radios. That meant that batteries lasted only 6–8 hours. Trade balances were affected because Fiji then had to import about US$1 million in batteries. Needless to say, it requires the export of quite a lot of sugarcane to pay for those batteries. All other things being equal, increasing signal strength extends battery life, battery imports decline, trade balance improves.

3. Reinhard Keune is very careful, one might say respectful, in his statements about FES's cooperation with UNESCO. Having in mind U.S. policy with regard to UNESCO, he argues, "If UNESCO didn't exist, it would have to be invented." (Note: The United States withdrew from UNESCO in 1984 on accusations by the Reagan administration that the organization was mismanaged under the direction of Amadou Mahtar M'Bow of Senegal. The administration also argued that UNESCO-sponsored initiatives under the New World Information and Communication Order sought to impose regulations on journalists and publishers that interfered with their freedom and independence.) On the other hand, UNESCO is state-oriented, with a complex and sometimes turf-oriented bureaucracy that required inventive skills to work around to make PACBROAD, later PIBA, succeed. (To Keune's credit, he did make the arrangement work.) At the same time, because of the project's involvement with media, UNESCO participation was important because it gave a veneer of legitimacy to an activity that was controversial to suspicious governments. This was a legitimacy that FES alone, as a nongovernmental organization, could not have provided.

4. Robert Louis Stevenson, *In the South Seas: A Foot-Note to History, Letters and Miscellanies* (New York: Charles Scribner's Sons, 1905), 533ff. The episode took place between December 1888 and March 1889. Stevenson died in Samoa in 1894.

5. Ibid.

6. PACBROAD, *General Meeting, Report,* September 17–25, 1985, Apia, Samoa, 10.

down. It has continued to operate since. In the reincarnated PACNEWS, Shiu Singh was appointed the full-time editor, assisted by others. Dykes Angiki, an editor from the newsroom at the Solomon Islands Broadcasting Corporation, came as a rotating editor during the first few weeks of PACNEWS's new existence. In fact, it was one of Angiki's stories that caused the military to visit Singh's home for a second time. Authorities thought Singh had written the story. He had not. It was a rare occasion when he was ill and the writing tasks had fallen to Angiki.

After the second coup in Fiji, in September 1987, media freedoms in Fiji deteriorated. And by mid-1989, the Fiji Telecommunications Training Center (TTC), PIBA's host in Fiji, had grown leery about their arrangement. The official reason was that while PACBROAD was a training activity, PACNEWS was not. The unofficial reason for the eventual request to relocate to another venue was that the TTC "was somehow afraid" of a news exchange on its premises. And so PIBA and its projects moved.

On Richards Road in Suva, PIBA House, as the new location was called, was for a year home to PACNEWS and PACBROAD. At the site of the former deputy prime minister's residence, PIBA House still stands, occupied today by the Fiji forestry ministry. But in relocating there from its first headquarters at the Fiji Telecommunications Training Center, PIBA had made major renovations, installing a studio for training, rooms for workshops, a lecture room, and editors' space, as well as other facilities. Renovation was underwritten by FES.

Hendrik Kettner, PACBROAD technical coordinator, who oversaw construction of the studio, remembers it as an "ideal situation" even though the building was old. If you walked on one end, your steps could be heard on the other. This was clearly unacceptable for a recording studio. So Kettner fashioned together a house-within-a-house, using thin concrete slabs to stabilize the sound room.

Acoustics were important too. The quality of sound is very different from place to place. One might even say that sound is culturally defined. If you ever listen to Radio Moscow on shortwave, it always sounds as if the broadcasting studio is in the middle of a hallway. The broadcasts are distinctive, as with other international services. Even before you hear the language, you can almost guess the broadcaster from the "sound." NHK, the Japanese broadcaster, has a very distinct sound signature as well—as if the broadcasting studio is in a broadcasting studio. This was the Pacific. What to do?

Sounds are softer. Sounds bounce off fiber, not off steel and concrete. Kettner decided to line the walls with split bamboo.

This decision was not without its problems. Bamboo is organic. Bugs like bamboo. Builders are not too pleased to handle buggy materials. So the bamboo had to be cut when the insects were in a state of relative inactivity, then dried and treated. It was hoped that the split bamboo would soften the reverberations and perhaps give the sound recorded in the studio a Pacific signature. But all of this was rendered academic when PIBA House, and the garden around it, had to be abandoned when the government voided the lease.

Matters worsened in Fiji, and as the "Two Hendriks" (as Bussiek and Kettner were known) were to be expelled, Shiu Singh and his colleagues made plans to move PACNEWS and other PIBA operations elsewhere.[26] PIBA left its site of operations in May 1990. Editor Singh left Suva on Sunday, May 13, 1990. A colleague from National Broadcasting Corporation of PNG continued PACNEWS while Shiu Singh prepared offices in Auckland. By Thursday, PACNEWS was operating from its new location in New Zealand. It was the same day that Bougainville declared its independence from Papua New Guinea.

Arrangements made with Radio New Zealand saw PACNEWS temporarily housed in leased offices in Takapuna, a suburb of Auckland. New Zealand had been chosen for reasons of expediency. RNZ had responded quickly to the emergency with work permits for the various personnel and customs exemptions for the equipment that would be moved. It offered office space, computers, telephones linked to RNZ's radio news computer, and other facilities. To the outside world, there was no interruption in service between the departure from Fiji and the arrival in New Zealand.

Controversy over the expulsion of Kettner and Bussiek erupted throughout the media community. PIBA chair Fusimalohi lodged an appeal with the Fiji Ministry of Information, asking the government to reconsider its position. The appeal was futile.

PIBA members, expressing fear of interference by the military government in its operations and in the substance of the news, determined to move all PIBA activities out of Fiji. Several Pacific nations, among them Papua New Guinea, Vanuatu, and Solomon Islands, immediately stepped forward to offer to host PACNEWS. Fusimalohi had hoped that PIBA and its operations would find a home in Tonga. Before an international organization can be invited into Tonga, cabinet-level approval is necessary, and Fusimalohi made the requisite governmental request. The government response, Fusimalohi recalls, was diplomatic: the Kingdom of Tonga would not stand against the applications of the other Pacific states. The response seems to have coincided with the visit of the minister of information of Fiji.

Gerard Sullivan and Victor Valbuena, media specialists from the Asian Media Information and Communication Centre, in an assessment of PACNEWS, have written that "the news exchange is careful not to offend the government [of Fiji]" and that reporting on the political situation in Fiji is calculatedly "moderate."[27] They suggest that the "visit" by the military had a chilling effect on objective reporting, despite purported government assurances to PACNEWS that the government would not interfere with editorial policy. Censorship, however, need not always be outright to achieve its end. At the time, 15 percent of stories carried over PACNEWS was rewritten press releases from official sources checked by editors against other sources.[28]

But the point that Sullivan and Valbuena miss, or perhaps felt that they could not make, is that responsibility for such "moderate"—or any—reporting does not rest with PACNEWS, which—if one need be reminded—is a news exchange. Most of the stories that are produced by PACNEWS do not originate with PACNEWS but come from its member radio stations. If reporting was "moderate," it was the "moderate" reporting of Radio Fiji, not from the editorial desk at PACNEWS. To that extent, PACNEWS is as good —or as free from censorship—as the reports it receives. (PIBA attempts to address such issues in training activities and media education for Pacific journalists—a formidable task because of prevailing economic, labor, and education conditions.) Moreover, for researchers to say that the news product that comes from Radio Fiji was affected by the coup is an understatement in the extreme.

The assessment by Sullivan and Valbuena also neglects a development in PACNEWS bulletins that creates more balanced reporting: Due to the difficulties that Radio Fiji faced in freely reporting the news, PACNEWS looked to the *Fiji Times* and an occasional stringer as alternative sources for stories. There have been complaints about this in PIBA assemblies by at least one Radio Fiji general manager, but the innovation stands.

Since the two coups, editors and news staff at Radio Fiji have had to operate under a variety of government controls. For example, subsequent to a story's being aired, an editor might get a call from the general manager of Radio Fiji or another in authority—a minister of information, say—with instructions to change the story or to kill it. On some occasions the admonitory call will come *before* the story is aired. At one point, news staff, suspecting the presence of a mole in the office, kept their eyes open. They discovered a junior editor making calls to higher-ups.

There have also been the peregrinations of one reporter whose position at the newsroom came through political "appointment." His work was so racist and biased that after the charge could not be denied—"we let him hang himself," news staff smiled—the reporter was fired.

As regards sources, editors now also worry about computer records of outgoing calls, originally used for determining which department to charge. Reporters believe that this same computerized record has been used by the government to trace news sources. Needless to say, the confidentiality of these sources was compromised, and news tips soon dried up.

One major effect of the transition from coup to civilian government is yet to be seen in full. In 1997, Radio Fiji was privatized, requiring the radio station to seek advertising and other forms of revenue to support itself. What kind of change will be effected by this? The government has promised to provide FJ$600,000 for public service functions. While this is not sufficient to sustain such a large system broadcasting on six or seven frequencies—yearly electrical costs are FJ$200,000 alone—it is a sizable lever over the station.

Francis Herman, named editor for news and current affairs at Radio Fiji in 1994, was optimistic at the time: "Nothing will change when we are corporatized. But at least the guidelines [for radio news] are more flexible than for TV1 [the state television station]." Even so, another problem Herman faces is that the staff at Radio Fiji is young, with no experience of a free press: "They think the [post-coup] situation is the way it should be or the way it is." To remedy that situation, the Fiji Islands Media Association (FIMA) is taking some steps to provide basic journalism training in the country.[29] Herman was quick to add he believed that, as more time passes, things will get better in the newsroom and that Radio Fiji will gain more credibility. (Three years later, in 1997, Herman's concerns were more with the financial crisis facing Radio Fiji as it privatized.)

After the coups, advertising revenue plummeted as news sources grew scarce. To say, then, that "things are getting better" in the newsroom may be to say not a great deal. But Herman does cite as evidence that as reporting grew more evenhanded, advertising revenues rose, which was due, in part, to the Indian Fijian business community. Further, with credibility came more information.

Back in 1987, the creation of this news exchange was a small event to the larger geopolitical churning of the time. Response to the coups took various turns. Tensions between India and Fiji escalated. The Fiji military government ordered the Indian embassy closed, complaining of the country's interference in internal affairs. India banned trade with Fiji and opposed Fiji's readmission to the British Commonwealth. Indeed, as a result of the coups, Fiji was expelled.

Sosuke Uno, Japan's foreign minister, announced Japan's recognition of the Fiji military government. Economic aid continued with hardly a beat.[30]

Australia, New Zealand, the United Kingdom, and the United States voiced outrage at the coups and demanded a return to the principles of a constitutional democracy. Aid was suspended. Later, after Fiji applied some "constitutional window dressing," these same nations quietly—perhaps more grudgingly on the part of Australia and New Zealand—normalized relations with Fiji.

By May 1990, with most of the turmoil receding, PIBA with the association's two projects, PACNEWS and PACBROAD, operated out of temporary quarters in Auckland. PACNEWS's fax machines whirred along in exile, undeterred.

In August 1990, at the third general meeting of PIBA in Port Vila, Vanuatu, participants deliberated on the permanent relocation of the association offices. Although PIBA was taking refuge in Auckland, Radio New Zealand did not bid for the projects, apparently based on the consideration that the identity of PACNEWS as a Pacific islands service should be preserved. After discussion, it was agreed that PIBA activities would be split between two countries. PACNEWS would relocate to Honiara, Solomon Islands. PACBROAD would relocate to Port Vila, Vanuatu, together with the main PIBA offices. The moves occurred in late 1990.

There are several ironies inherent in the effort to relocate PIBA. The response of most Pacific states to the coup d'état in Fiji was measured and cautious. There was no outright condemnation. Most Pacific states follow a policy of noninterference in the internal affairs of other Pacific states, and the crisis in Fiji was viewed as such an internal matter. Where there was regional press criticism, it centered on the undemocratic action of the coups. And in fact, these were the first coups that the Pacific islands had known in modern times.

On the other hand, Papua New Guinea, the Solomon Islands, and Vanuatu—which form the "Melanesian Spearhead Group" (MSG)—expressed support of the Fijian military takeover. For them the crux of the issue was political control by native islanders. Apparently, the majority presence of Indian Fijians, a nonnative Pacific people, overrode any other considerations.

In the case of Vanuatu, there was irony in the fact that the nonaligned foreign policy, as promulgated by the dominant Indian Fijian coalition government, was close to its own.

And there was perhaps a larger irony as regards something known as the New World Information and Communication Order. NWICO started several decades ago as a UNESCO debate over the proper role of media and communication systems in rectifying the imbalance of reporting. The more developed nations of the North were believed to enjoy a certain hegemony over news and communications, and South nations, such as in the Pacific, suffered in coverage and accuracy. The formation of PACNEWS came in the wake of these sentiments, and the initial funding that PACBROAD received from UNESCO arose out of NWICO.

Some of the NWICO-related initiatives have generated controversy in relations between North and South countries over government interference in media. The coups in Fiji, the not-so-veiled attempt to influence the press, and the subsequent expulsion of PIBA fit the worst-case scenario of those North nations, such as the United States, opposed to NWICO: fear of exclusion of reporters, censorship, editorial constraints, and limits on media agencies. During the Fiji coup, reporters were detained and expelled, and the news reports received by PACNEWS from Radio Fiji were carefully written so as not to offend the military regime.

Most developing nations, however, would argue for the need of some form of state control over media. Reasons for media curbs vary from the expedient to the necessary—invoking national security, ensuring public interests in general, and maintaining peace and order. In reality, most media North and South are subject to restriction and control of one sort or another.[31] PACNEWS exists in a world of politics and media, but at least it is the politics and media of the Pacific island nations. Depending on how you view the matter, you could say that PACNEWS was reasonably successful in sustaining a flow of alternative news from the Pacific—even in a period of crisis and even in face of its own expulsion. PACNEWS continues activities from its new base in Port Vila where it moved in early 1994, consolidating all PIBA media activities in one city.

Behind the Scenes in the Early Days

To say that behind the scenes the PACNEWS operation was an involved process is to overlook a more basic struggle. Member stations got their news, but getting it to them was another matter. At the beginning PACNEWS was an expensive enterprise, and communicating by telephone was not the easy reaching out that most of us imagine. Telephone was unreliable: you could not always get through. A station in a small country might not have many lines, and the journalists on assignment to PACNEWS in Suva would have to wait on an open line for several minutes while their colleagues were tracked down in the station. Shiu Singh remembers having to hold for ten minutes at a time while people yelled around for the news editor. Fax was uncommon and not widely distributed when PACNEWS began; computer networks were unknown.

If you wanted to call certain countries in the Pacific, you had to go through an operator. There was no direct dial. In Fiji, you called the operator, asked her to place the call, and then you hung up and waited for a call-back. When an international circuit was free, the operator would ring you back and then attempt to reach your party. In the case of Niue and a few other locations, that might be several days later, not minutes or hours. PACNEWS had arranged a schedule of calls with the telecommunications authorities, so all the news participants had to be ready at the convenience of the telephone system. They called this "polling" the stations.

Neither were there any telephone satellite downlinks. In the case of Tuvalu and Niue, the telephone was a "radio telephone." That means manual operations through an operator. It was a one-way link, which is to say that only one person talked at a time. You had to be quiet while the other party was speaking, and when he or she stopped, you could begin. At times the connection was so degraded—the sound of a voice so poor—that it was impossible to use for the news. Editors could not be sure that they had heard correctly enough to incorporate the message into a news dispatch.

Some locations in the Pacific still use radio telephones. The Banks Islands in Vanuatu and the Shortland Islands in the Solomons, up near the border with Bougainville, are two examples. Hendrik Kettner, who was trained as a sound engineer and holds a diploma in communications technology from Germany, had to relearn some of his training because the equipment he encountered was so dated. When he got to the Pacific in the summer of 1986, mechanical relays were the rule in telecommunications, not the exception. SFB, Radio Free Berlin, had been a bit different. In the intervening years, telecommunications in the Pacific have developed rapidly. You can direct dial most places in the Pacific these days—most places of size, that is.

Besides telephone, telex was the other means to receive news dispatches and the sole means to send news bulletins to various stations. To some destinations with particularly bad lines, however, it might take as long as forty-five minutes to transmit the equivalent of six pages by telex.

Telex was also used to coordinate arrangements. Shiu Singh recalls that when PACNEWS began, he used to "talk on telex." He would type a message to a colleague, wait for a response, and then send back the reply. It was fairly common practice, apparently:

FOR HENDRIK KETTNER FROM BOB MAKIN, [RADIO] VANUATU,
FOR HENDRIK BUSSIEK, . . . ARE YOU THERE HENDRIK????????
I'LL GET HIM FROM HIS WORKSHOP, IS HB AROUND?
YES, WE WOULD LIKE HENDRIK KETTNER TO RING HENDRIK
BUSSIEK HERE ON VILA 2996 NOW IF IT CAN BE DONE?
OK HE WILL CALL HB NOW. THKS.
THANKS OVER AND OUT.[32]

Not only were there many problems with the telex system, but there were no word processors. Editors actually used the telex as a kind of primitive word processor. And transmission was often spotty, degraded telephone lines producing garbled messages. In the PACNEWS archives one telex message received from abroad reads: "Lieber Herr Bussiek, von Ihrem gerade laufendem Telex ist die Seite 6/8 nicht klar."

Some telex messages were appeals for equipment aid.

TELEX FJ2252
ATTN: HENDRIK BUSSIEK, COORDINATOR PACBROAD
FM: TOMATI KEI TARAU, TARAWA [IN THE MICRONESIAN
REPUBLIC OF KIRIBATI]
RE: CASSETTE DECK FOR BROADCASTING PURPOSES
I WOULD LIKE TO PURCHASE A SONY CASSETTE DECK TC-K71
OR EQUIVALENT FOR OUR ON-AIR STUDIO AND HUMBLY ASK IF
YOU COULD FIND ONE IN SUVA AND ADVISE US COST INCLUD-
ING AIR FREIGHT. WE ARE PREPARED TO PAY UP TO AU$700.
TOMATI KEI TARAU, MANAGER.

TO: HENDRIK BUSSIEK PIBA HOUSE
FROM: HIMA DOUGLAS, [GM OF] BROADCASTING CORPORATION
OF NIUE [AND NOW CHAIRMAN OF PIBA]

SUBJECT: STUDIO EQUIPMENT

LIGHTNING STRIKE COMPLETELY DESTROYED ALL OUR ON-AIR STUDIO EQUIPMENT INCLUDING THE TWO BE CART MACHINES ACQUIRED UNDER AID FROM PACBROAD. WE HAVE BEEN RELUCTANT TO APPROACH PACBROAD AGAIN IN VIEW OF THE GENEROUS ASSISTANCE . . . WE WONDERED THEREFORE . . . KIND REGARDS TO ALL AT PIBA HOUSE.

Other communications were launched just to coordinate the details of polling the newsrooms for the day's news.

2252 PACNEWS FJ

FOR: SHIU SINGH [PACNEWS EDITOR]

FROM: BOB MAKIN [RADIO VANUATU]

DEAR SHIU, SORRY THERE WAS NO NEWS AT 12.15, YET AGAIN. IT IS NOW STANDING BY FOR YOU TO POLL. COULD WE CHANGE OUR TIME TO 1400 (NOW) (WE ARE ON DAYLIGHT SAVING SO OUR 1400 IS THE SAME AS YOURS) AND EXPERIMENT. WE WOULD THEN HAVE ALL MAIN STORIES TRANSLATED, AND YOU WOULDN'T NEED TO POLL AGAIN. THERE WOULD JUST BE THE ONE TIME EACH DAY—1400. WHAT DO YOU THINK? REGARDS, BOB.

To gather the news, PACNEWS used telephones and tape recorders. News editors at various stations in the region would anticipate a poll, a telephone call at a certain hour. When the call came, they would read their stories over the line. Two stories could be filed. Shiu Singh remembers the dedication of the news editors; their stories were always ready to go. Telephone charges were, in addition, very expensive, so that lent urgency to the call.

At the PACNEWS end, the editor would transcribe the stories that had been read over the line, edit them, assemble the lot into a bulletin, and hand the copy to an assistant, who would then type it out on the telex.

When a second telex arrived, a word processor was attached. This eased some of the burden of the work. Previously PACNEWS editors wrote out in longhand the stories read to them over the telephone for later transcription and editing. A tape recorder attached to the line permitted replay of the tape if it was necessary to verify certain points in a story.

Twice a day, in two editions, this was the work that was done.

The news stories, by necessity, were of a rip-and-read sort.[33] One reason was simply the expense of sending the PACNEWS editions. Another was that the writing was exclusively for reading over the air.

The early bulletins were terse:

(PACNEWS 2/4/88 INFLATION—RADIO FIJI)

FIJI'S INFLATION RATE IS CONTINUING TO RISE STEADILY.

RADIO FIJI SAYS THE RATE NOW STANDS AT NEARLY NINE PERCENT AS AGAINST ALMOST EIGHT PERCENT OF THE TWELVE MONTHS TO THE END OF MARCH.

THE CONSUMER PRICES INDEX ROSE BY ONE PERCENT IN APRIL WITH HIGHER PRICES BEING RECORDED FOR A RANGE OF GOODS AND SERVICES. . . . ENDS

(2ND EDITION ENDS)

What a story like this does not include, nor could it include in a rip-and-read format, is any explanation why Fiji's economy was doing so poorly. For that, you would have to look to the coup aftereffects. While coups clearly do not pay where the economy is concerned, radio news did not have the format to discuss it.

PACNEWS gradually shifted from away from the use of telex. With aid money from GTZ, the German Association for Technical Cooperation, every newsroom in the region was outfitted with a fax machine.[34] Radio Kiribati was the first, in the spring of 1988, to get one installed. There was an interim period when both telex and fax were used, but it was clear that the fax machine cut costs for transmitting messages and, more important, increased the speed, length, and quality of the messages transmitted back and forth.

With fax machines, however, new problems for the PACBROAD coordinator emerged.

APRIL 1989

FOR HENDRIK KETTNER, PACBROAD

FROM ARTHUR TARIPO, CIBNC [COOK ISLANDS]

RE: FAX MACHINE

OUR [BROKEN] FAX MACHINE IS BEING DISPATCHED TO YOU BY LOCAL FIRM AIR FREIGHT INTERNATIONAL LTD ON THURSDAY 20 APRIL (COOK ISLANDS TIME) VIA AUCKLAND. AIRWAY BILL 086–86302882 REFERS.

KIND REGARDS.

But there was always the news.

TO 2252 PACNEWS FJ

TWENTY-SIX CANDIDATES WILL CONTEND FOR THE REMAINING

ELEVEN SEATS IN THE TUVALU PARLIAMENT IN THE GENERAL ELECTIONS ON THURSDAY (29/9/89)

Over the years, PACNEWS's bulletins have changed in response to its changing audience. Currently, nearly 38 percent of subscribers is member radio stations. They were the initial recipients and correspondents of PACNEWS bulletins. Ten years after PACNEWS's founding, only 15.6 percent of subscribers is newspapers and magazines (Table 1). Bulletins have become fuller to attract print journalists.

PACNEWS has evolved over the years, but its original mission as a news exchange for the Pacific region remains. The service gathers and distributes news from member stations from a central news office. PACNEWS also covers stories from the French territories such as French Polynesia and New Caledonia, the former American trust territories and dependencies, and other countries that are of interest in the region. It initiates few stories and contin-

Table 1
PACNEWS Subscribers, 1994 and 1998, by Category (percent)

	1994	1998
Radio stations	30.2	37.8
Newspapers and magazines	22.6	15.6
News agencies	5.7	2.2
TV stations	1.9	2.2
Government-related—embassies, information services, defense ministries, etc.	24.5	22.2
Universities and libraries	5.7	8.9
Other recipients—private organizations and individuals	9.4	11.1
Total	100.0	100.0

Source: PACNEWS, Port Vila, Vanuatu

Note: Although PACNEWS has some of the widest coverage of issues in Pacific island countries, the service has fewer than 100 subscribers and will need to increase its audience substantially to achieve financial independence. E-mail has made it possible to download stories. As the service becomes easier and cheaper to use, it may move toward profitability.

ues to be dependent on its correspondent radio stations, which are the primary contributors and recipients of the service.

Kicked out of Fiji, accepted in exile into New Zealand, transferred from Honiara in the Solomon Islands to its current location in Port Vila, Vanuatu, PACNEWS produced news bulletins five days a week without missing an edition since the first week's interruption by the coup. Today there are three editions a day. That makes for a long day for three editors.

Although the newsroom is now computerized and the service accessible through electronic mail, PACNEWS's method of receiving and distributing stories by fax remains a particular feature of the news exchange. Even with computerization, most island newsrooms continue to receive their news bulletins by fax. Transition to the digital age will not be easy, given that a fair number of newsrooms still employ standard typewriters. Furthermore, additional technical assistance will be required to computerize the operation and radio facilities of PIBA members. (UNESCO has begun to provide that help here and there.)

Using telex, international telephone lines, and, later on, fax machines, Pacific radio stations have created a communications news network to meet the unique but common perspective of Pacific island member states. Most important is that PACNEWS reflects a perspective that is voice to the area, not without problems to be sure, but free of the cultural domination in information provided by foreign sources.

Sit in the PACNEWS offices adjacent to the yard of Vanuatu Broadcasting and Television Corporation. Tune in Radio Australia or Radio New Zealand on shortwave or Hawaii Public Radio's "Pacific Island News" on AM or FM. For any number of broadcasts, you can read the PACNEWS bulletin, pretty much word for word, that you hear on air.

The FES aid money set in motion PACNEWS, and Pacific islanders have worked to make it succeed.[35] Article 19 of the 1966 International Covenant on Civil and Political Rights states in part, "Everyone shall have the right to freedom of expression; this right shall include freedom to seek, receive, and impart information and ideas of all kinds, regardless of frontiers, either orally, in writing, or in print, in the form of art, or through any other media of his choice." In terms of content and distribution of news that speaks on behalf of the Pacific region, PACNEWS provides a remarkable contribution in honor of that covenant. But it is more easily said than done.

Chronology of Events Related to PACNEWS Formation

- Joint FES/UNESCO/AIBD mission on broadcast training in the Pacific, 1984.
- PACBROAD—Pacific Broadcasting Training and Development, General Meeting, Apia, Samoa, September 17–25, 1985. Initial planning meeting for training and a planning seminar supported by UNESCO and FES in cooperation with other regional bodies.
- PACBROAD, Second General Meeting, Rarotonga, Cook Islands, July 15–16, 1986.
- After elections in Fiji, Dr. Timoci Bavadra forms a new coalition government which contains a majority of Indian Fijian cabinet members, April 1987.
- First coup d'état in Fiji, led by Sitiveni L. Rabuka, May 1987.
- PACNEWS is begun as a three-month experiment after a PACBROAD editor's workshop in Suva, Fiji, September 14–18, 1987.
- Second coup d'état in Fiji, led by Sitiveni L. Rabuka, September 1987.
- PACBROAD, Third General Meeting, Nuku'alofa, Kingdom of Tonga, November 30–December 2, 1987. Members decide to form PIBA as a Pacific broadcasting association; a work group is appointed to draft a constitution. Decision made to continue PACNEWS.
- Coup leader Rabuka relinquishes military power to civilian rule, December 1987.
- Grant for fax machines and other technical equipment provided to PACBROAD member stations by Deutsche Gesellschaft für Technische Zusammenarbeit (GTZ), Spring 1988.
- PACBROAD, Fourth General Meeting (the Final Report lists the meeting as the Fourth General "meeting of leading representatives of national radio networks in the region of the Pacific"; strictly speaking, it is PACBROAD's fourth meeting at which PIBA is officially formed; it is considered PIBA's first meeting), Nuku'alofa, Kingdom of Tonga, October 17–19, 1988. Members decide to pursue PACNEWS as a permanent news service activity.

- Asian Media Information and Communication Centre, Singapore, conducts a review of PACNEWS activities, October 1988.
- PIBA Second General Assembly, Honiara, Solomon Islands, October 19–22, 1989.
- PACNEWS, PACBROAD, and PIBA offices temporarily relocate to New Zealand for seven months because of political conditions in Fiji, May 1990.
- PIBA Third General Assembly, Port Vila, Vanuatu, August 6–10, 1990. Members decide to move association activities to Vanuatu and Solomon Islands.
- PIBA and PACBROAD offices relocate from New Zealand to permanent quarters in Port Vila, Vanuatu, November 1990, and PACNEWS is moved to Honiara, Solomon Islands, December 1990.
- PIBA Fourth General Assembly, Auckland, New Zealand, October 1–5, 1991.
- PIBA Fifth General Assembly, Alofi, Niue, September 12–15, 1992.
- PIBA Sixth General Assembly, Suva, Fiji, 1993.
- PACNEWS moves from Solomon Islands to Port Vila, Vanuatu, to consolidate activities of PIBA, January 1994.
- PIBA Seventh General Assembly, Apia, Samoa, July 1994.
- Computer system installed (and functioning) in PACNEWS offices to download bulletins, 1995.
- PIBA Eighth General Assembly, Melbourne, Australia, August 1995. (PINA Meeting, Port Moresby, Papua New Guinea, June 26–29, 1995.)
- PIBA Ninth General Assembly, Nuku‘alofa, Tonga, August 1996.
- PIBA Tenth General Assembly, Port Vila, Vanuatu, July 1997.
- PIBA Eleventh General Assembly, Nadi, Fiji, March 1998.
- PIBA and PACNEWS relocate to Suva, Fiji, November 1998.

Raon long ol aelan blong yumi we ol i kavremap wan bigfela eria, stamba ples blong informesen em i Redio Vanuatu.

Throughout our scattered islands, Radio Vanuatu is the main source of information.

—*Vanuatu: 10 Yia Blong Independens*

Yet the common people for their part have scores if not hundreds of contemporary kith and kin about whom they endlessly "talk story"—tell the news. Now, news is not just anything about anybody; it is likewise a selective determination of what is significant according to canons of cultural value.

—Marshall Sahlins, *Islands of History*

4

News Sources—Mostly Radio

Radio Talk Story

In PACNEWS offices you can hear the news as it's coming in. The fax machine whirs continuously through the day, spewing out stories from sources around the region. The mechanical slice of the machine's automatic paper cutter thuds; curling pages drop, one after the other, into a cardboard box taped to the table. With an eye on the clock, the senior editor rises from his desk, retrieves the transmissions, sifts through this chimera of messages that will turn into news of the day. This is the data—these news stories, which are primarily radio narratives from the Pacific, the raw material out of which the PACNEWS bulletins will be formed. Rewrites are assigned, and editors transform words on paper into words that will be spoken, news on the air for an audience spread across the largest ocean on the face of the earth. In ten- and fifteen-minute bulletins, radio tells the news.

Most of the news stories that come to PACNEWS's offices in Port Vila, Vanuatu, are simply faxed from newsrooms of member stations. Selected stories are then edited for the morning, noon, and afternoon PACNEWS editions. PACNEWS morning edition is received in the eastern part of the

Pacific in time for a late afternoon or evening news broadcast. (Wednesday noon in Port Vila is three o'clock Tuesday in Rarotonga, Cook Islands.) In the Western Pacific, the same edition will be used for the noon broadcast. PACNEWS bulletins issued later in the day will be used for afternoon and evening broadcasts in the western part of the region, and on the other side of the international dateline, the same late afternoon edition will be featured in the morning news round-up. Considerable coordination, then, is required to assemble the daily bulletins and fax them out expeditiously. These bulletins must arrive at various destinations in time for local news editors to choose stories appropriate for the local audience and translate them into a vernacular language before air time.

For stories, PACNEWS editors also look to other sources. They survey the region's newspapers, and they monitor shortwave broadcasts, principally the daily feeds from RNZI (Radio New Zealand International), ABC (Australian Broadcasting Corporation), and NBC (National Broadcasting Corporation of Papua New Guinea).[1] It should be noted that both RNZI and ABC are recipients of PACNEWS bulletins, stories from which in turn appear periodically on RNZI and ABC broadcasts.

If PACNEWS editors discover a news hole from an area of the Pacific, they will "poll" their member stations. They will place occasional calls to local editors to check what the breaking stories are and decide if the stories have sufficient regionwide interest to be published. The calls have to be coordinated with the time differences and the routines of each of the stations. Of course, PACNEWS has its own deadlines to make, and because local broadcasters rely on PACNEWS bulletins, timing is critical. There is a good deal of pressure leading up to the dispatch of the thrice-daily bulletins, in no small part because the information has to be gathered from a wide number of sources by a remarkably small staff.

The news material, which filters into PACNEWS editorial offices from plural sources, is of uneven quality. All stories, regardless of their source, are edited to fit the day's editions. If the editors determine that a significant story has been carried by a member station, they may ask for specific supplemental material and detail useful in giving the story a broader angle. Often, the stories as received have not been written for regionwide consumption. Sometimes the stories are, to be charitable, rough:

> NAUTO TAKAIARA HAS BECOME THE FIRST I-KIRIBATI TO
> EARN A BLACK BELT IN AIKIDO, A JAPANESE MARTIAL ARTS.
> A REPORT FROM THE LOCAL AIKIDO SCHOOL AT TEAORAEREKE

SAYS NAUTO WAS PRESENTED WITH THE BELT EARLIER THIS WEEK AFTER FOUR YEARS OF TRAINING.

AIKIDO IS SIMILAR TO . . . JAPANESE MARTIAL ARTS SUCH AS KARATE AND KANFU, BUT IS LESS COMBATIVE. . . .

And so, under deadline, editors quickly rewrite, in radio format, for the broader PACNEWS audience:

KIRIBATI HAS REPORTED ITS FIRST NATIONAL . . .

Sometimes the stories are so self-circumscribed as to be incomprehensible to any but the particular local audience involved, as with this transmission (translated from a vernacular into English and sent by fax to PACNEWS):

THEY SAID THE BOARD HAD THOUGHT THE 130-MILLION HAD INCLUDED EVERYTHING IN THE BUILDING. DESPITE THIS CLAIMS, THE COMMISSIONER SAID . . .

Where necessary, PACNEWS editors alert their correspondents to interest in a story either by calling or faxing member stations. Clarifying copy is usually received back by fax; less often it is read over the telephone. PACNEWS editors have a short time to remake the tangled copy into something that is straightforward, has punch, is easy to listen to. They must think with their ears as well as their pens. And they are in a race with a clock and the needs of regional newsrooms waiting to go on air live.

Contributions to the daily bulletins from Pacific radio newsrooms vary considerably in frequency and geography. Obviously, larger broadcasting organizations in some of the larger countries, such as Fiji, Papua New Guinea, Solomon Islands, and Tonga, contribute more stories to PACNEWS bulletins than do some of their smaller counterparts. These larger countries comprise about 80 percent of the population in the Pacific, and they account for nearly half the stories in PACNEWS.

The overall pattern of contributions, however, is idiosyncratic. That is, quantity and quality have no direct correlation with size of country or level of development.[2] The reason for frequent and systematic contribution could simply be a person: a journalist may feel great dedication to PACNEWS, and he or she may see it as a professional duty to keep local news reported. On the other hand, a newsroom in a relatively large country could be small, and journalists there pressed for time. Contributions to PACNEWS could be irregular as a result. Very few stories are filed, for example, from the Samoa Broadcasting Corporation.

The role of a station's general manager is critical in this regard. If he encourages his staff to contribute stories, frequency and output will increase. Conversely, if the GM is less than supportive, stories will fall off. PACNEWS is therefore dependent on the goodwill of the general manager, as the news exchange relies on the resources of these contributions. Note that these contributions are without payment or charge. The return, the benefit locally, is PACNEWS's daily bulletins, no more but no less.

The training of news editors by PIBA will oftentimes result in an increase in contributions—both in quantity and quality—only to have them decline as personnel are promoted or move to other positions and are replaced by less dedicated, knowledgeable, or experienced personnel.

A specific event may lead to a series of stories about one or another country for a period of time, but as the event wanes, so will coverage. This is nothing unusual. Elections and regional conferences, for example, will be a focus of the news for a limited period. Similarly, "special events," such as labor unrest, disorders, natural disasters, emergency public health matters, racial conflict, balance of payment gains, sports achievements, and foreign policy decisions, are reported as they occur. In this sense, there is no period one could point to as representative of PACNEWS coverage as far as geography is concerned. And there is no comparable period in a year's time—or in several—to cast about for a pattern. One cannot say that certain contributions to PACNEWS bulletins are typical or that certain countries are typically in the news. And this is how it should be.

That is to say, one of the original objectives of PACNEWS was to provide balanced coverage of regional events and to inform the region of diverse events within the Pacific, without concern for size of country, economic importance, or international status.[3] An election in Niue, a tiny Pacific state, is not crowded out of the bulletins because of a plane crash in Papua New Guinea or Fiji, two of the larger and more economically dominant states—even though in a year's worth of bulletins there are, reasonably, more stories about larger states than about smaller states. In PACNEWS, bad news about the Pacific does not chase the good off the daily dispatches, as it does in stories about the Pacific that appear outside the region. To that extent, PACNEWS, as an intraregional exchange of news destined for Pacific audiences, has succeeded in decolonizing information. This flow of news provides not just an alternative to a determined North-to-South distribution of information; at times it is the *only* routine source of news about Pacific states, especially in the case of the microstates.

The working language of PACNEWS is English. Stories are faxed in English to PACNEWS offices from various sources, and stories are in turn dispatched by PACNEWS in English. In some cases English is the one language the correspondents have in common. When the respective radio stations broadcast stories taken from PACNEWS bulletins, though, they do so in a variety of languages other than English: Pidgin, Bislama, Hiri Motu, Samoan, Hindustani, Maori, Tongan, Fijian, Yapese, Trukese, Ponapean, Kosraean, Kiribati, Niuean, Palauan, French, and so on.

This rich multiplicity of languages in the Pacific divides, even within one country. English and French may be a remnant of the colonial period, but they serve to unite not only a country but the region as a whole. There are the eighty-plus indigenous languages in the Solomons alone (one language often unintelligible to a neighbor a few kilometers away), most from the Austronesian group. Papua New Guinea can count even more. This linguistic relatedness to a language family that extends from Southeast Asia as far east as Easter Island and north to Hawaii does not help in getting out the news. Within newsrooms, the pattern will vary, but in the Solomon Islands the news is written in English and translated into Pidgin when read over the air. Similarly in Fiji, stories are written in English for translation into Fijian and Hindi. In Vanuatu, on the other hand, the stories are generally first written in Bislama (Vanuatu Pidgin) and then translated into English and French for the airwaves.

Not all PIBA members join in the stream of messages arriving in Port Vila. Some countries are conspicuously absent. Member stations from the various Federated States of Micronesia have not filed stories for some time. The same is true of the Samoa Broadcasting Corporation, which was a founding member of PIBA but chose not to pay its dues for a period of several years. Other noncontributors include the Marshall Islands, Tokelau, Palau, Nauru, and the French territories of New Caledonia and French Polynesia. To be sure, until 1997 French Polynesia was not a member of PIBA. PACNEWS editors have extensive contacts in these noncontributing territories whom they will call when there is breaking news in that part of the Pacific.

The French-speaking part of the Pacific, which happens still to be

French-owned, was excluded from membership in PIBA at its inception but was warmly welcomed in 1997. The founders of the association may have wished for full Pacific participation in the news exchange but had agreed early on to a deliberate policy of keeping out the French public broadcasters. Asked the reason, Tavake Fusimalohi, former chair of PIBA, replied, "Well, they are not independent, are they?"

Fusimalohi's comment shows how strongly independence is felt in the Pacific, where decolonization is a phenomenon of only the last twenty years.[4] Particularly as regards media, there is fear of undue influence by metropolitan powers, in this case France, which retains colonial interests in the Pacific. New Caledonia and French Polynesia, as French dependencies, could not be expected to be free of French intervention in the news.

Distinctions of political independence or nonindependence in the Pacific are not so clear-cut, however. Vanuatu became independent in 1980, just as the UNESCO report by the MacBride Commission on the New World Information and Communication Order (NWICO) was issued.[5] Much of Micronesia did not obtain independence from the United States until 1986. Palau did not approve a Compact of Free Association with the United States until 1994. In December of the same year, Palau, the last UN trusteeship territory, became the 185th member of the United Nations, three years after the Marshall Islands and the Federated States of Micronesia, bringing the Pacific UN delegation of nations to ten. Even so, for PIBA the issue of political independence was not to be separated from independence in information and news.

Tavake Fusimalohi's comment concerning the lack of independence of the French Overseas Territories does not stand up to close examination if one simply divides the members of the organization into independent, dependent, and colonial categories. The political status of the various entities in the Pacific is less than easily described.[6] In the same way that attempts to impose uniform ethnological attributes have been dispelled by the varied social forms and religious practices in the Pacific, so too with political distinctions. Niue can hardly be considered a truly independent state in any real sense but is a voting member of PIBA and hosted the Fifth General Assembly in 1992. Hawaii, a state in the union of the United States, is not independent in a strict sense, but Hawaii Public Radio was not originally allowed a vote. The exceptions run on.

Nevertheless, this matter of classification was an important and difficult issue at the founding of the association, in part because of the emergence from colonial dependence, but also because of the imbalance in international communication. Empirical studies had shown how South nations were subject to imbalance and distorted news in North media, by stories that focused on "'negative' rather than 'developmental' news."[7] Political independence, cultural identity, and socioeconomic development—these were critical issues to Pacific leaders, and this larger complex debate found its way into the discussion and decisions required about PIBA as an association. As a practical matter, the founders needed to ensure that their organization would not be overwhelmed by voices outside their region, particularly the French.

So at the founding of PIBA, the Société Nationale de Radiodiffusion Television Française d'Outre Mer (RFO) was excluded. New Caledonia, Wallis and Futuna, and French Polynesia might have been within the Pacific map that the founders had drawn as qualification for eligibility, and the RFO might have been a public service broadcaster by definition, but membership into the association was excluded on grounds that the RFO was not a broadcaster of an independent Pacific state. It was, after all, owned and operated by a metropolitan power, France.

Yet, as Pacific circumstances changed and PIBA evolved, the requisite status of *independent* or *national* proved to be a larger stumbling block because it was excluding quite a number of other broadcast organizations from full membership—in particular, former national broadcasters that had privatized or corporatized. Pragmatism now rules. The cynical view suggests that as German support declines, the French, who could use some "good press" in the region, may be an alternate source of support. The less cynical view is that PIBA must sustain itself by opening membership to all broadcasters. Moreover, the welcoming of the French media may reflect a greater self-confidence in that the ten years since the founding of PIBA and PACNEWS has seen a sustained honoring of the obligation by regional broadcasters to move toward media independence. But without doubt, PACNEWS bulletins, with the contribution of the French, will be richer in regionwide news.

The observation—"Well, they are not independent, are they?"—of Fusimalohi, who comes from a Polynesian kingdom which was never a colony, pinpointed one of the influences that cuts across traditional cultural and physical boundaries. Colonial influences have affected patterns of communication, internally and externally, in the Pacific region, and they continue to do so.[8] It is a legacy that cannot be ignored, even as communication patterns also undergo great change. PIBA and PACNEWS are evidence of that.

If once communication patterns were primarily between the peripheral entity and a metropolitan government, that pattern is far more complicated now.[9]

PACNEWS Initiative

For South countries such as the Pacific island states, the issue of imbalance in the flow of world information still poses practical problems. For one, the amount of North-reported news about South countries, in terms of the overall flow circulating in multinational channels, remains relatively small. Take a practical example: the chair of the Alliance of Small Island States (AOSIS), Annette des Isles, ambassador from Trinidad and Tobago to the United Nations, heralded the Small Islands Summit in Barbados, April 1994, as a seminal event in "getting the voice of small islands heard and recognized" in the world community.[10] Be that as it may, even within AOSIS, short of a major disaster in the area any number of Pacific states remain unlikely to gain notice in international press reports.

On the international stage, for the most part it is the metropolitan press that covers such worldwide forums as the Barbados Small Islands Summit, the Global Environment Summit in Rio de Janeiro in 1992, and the International Conference on Population and Development in Cairo in 1994. All other things being equal, however, conference participants with greater leverage in world political terms get press attention.

Relative size and leverage may influence what enters wire service stories, but these factors do not determine a local audience's interest. It is well to know what prime ministers, presidents, and representatives of major nations have to say. But it is not unreasonable to ask that a local audience be able to hear what *their* representatives have to say on topics of worldwide dimension that affect them—population, for example, fisheries resources and other development issues, global warming and related environmental concerns, and security and disarmament.

To help rectify this imbalance, PACNEWS devised a means to have its own reporter present at major international events. Under a cooperative arrangement secured by Fusimalohi with the South Pacific Forum, forum information and publications officer Alfred Sasako was dispatched as a reporter to a number of international conferences.[11]

Keeping a Pacific perspective in mind, Sasako filed his stories, spotlighting the speeches and activities of Pacific representatives. Without his presence, it is safe to say that these speeches and activities would have been ignored by the media world. At the Cairo conference on population and development, Sasako wrote of an address to the assembly by Otinielu Tausi, the deputy prime minister of Tuvalu, population 10,900:

> TUVALU—ICPD: PACCAIRO, PACNEWS BULLETIN, SEPTEMBER 13, 1994.
> TUVALU HAS TOLD THE INTERNATIONAL CONFERENCE ON POPULATION AND DEVELOPMENT IN CAIRO THAT THE GOVERNMENT ON FUNAFUTI PLACES "THE HIGHEST PRIORITY" ON POPULATION ISSUES, A PACNEWS CORRESPONDENT REPORTED TUESDAY.
>
> THE COUNTRY'S DEPUTY PRIME MINISTER, OTINIELU TAUSI, WAS THE FIRST LEADER FROM THE PACIFIC ISLAND TO ADDRESS THE CONFERENCE SOON AFTER IT WAS OFFICIALLY OPENED ON MONDAY.
>
> MR. TAUSI SAID MANY PROBLEMS ASSOCIATED WITH POPULATION GROWTH WERE BEGINNING TO "IMPACT SEVERELY" ON TUVALU, BUT ADDED THAT IT WAS PLEASED THAT THE DOCUMENT BEFORE THE CONFERENCE RECOGNIZED POPULATION AS A MULTI-DIMENSIONAL ISSUE. "POPULATION, ENVIRONMENTAL AND DEVELOPMENT ISSUES ARE LINKED AND CANNOT BE SEPARATED," MR. TAUSI TOLD DELEGATES.

In the same PACNEWS bulletin, the remarks of the minister of economic and development and planning of Niue, population 2,100, were reported:

> NIUE—ICPD: PACCAIRO, SEPTEMBER 13, 1994.
> NIUE HAS TOLD THE INTERNATIONAL CONFERENCE ON POPULATION AND DEVELOPMENT THAT SEVENTY YEARS OF EXTERNAL RULE WITH IMPERIAL VALUES HAVE MADE THE PEOPLE OF THE COUNTRY DEPENDENT ON GOVERNMENT TO PROVIDE FOR THEIR EVERY NEED. . . .
>
> NIUE—PERHAPS THE ONLY COUNTRY IN THE WORLD WITH A DECREASING POPULATION AS A RESULT OF EMIGRATION—WAS ANNEXED BY GREAT BRITAIN IN 1900 AND A YEAR LATER WAS HANDED TO NEW ZEALAND TO ADMINISTER. [MINISTER OF ECONOMIC DEVELOPMENT AND PLANNING SANI] LAKATANI SAID THE ANNEXATION AND THE SUBSEQUENT ADMINISTRATION HAD TRANSPLANTED OUTSIDE VALUES WHICH THE PEOPLE OF NIUE HAD COME TO ACCEPT AS THEIR OWN.

Similarly, he reported the positions and comments of representatives from Fiji, Samoa, Federated States of Micronesia, Papua New Guinea, Cook Islands, Kiribati, and Tonga.

Needless to say, this reportage of statements by South delegates stood in marked contrast to coverage by press from the metropolitan North, which focused on the conflict between the United States and the Vatican regarding population issues. U.S. vice president Albert Gore's leg, in a cast, was also featured prominently. The *Atlanta Constitution* covered the opening of the conference this way: "Delegates to the UN population conference opening today sought to avert a clash pitting the Clinton administration against the Vatican and Islamic countries over the sensitive issues of abortion and birth control. A senior U.S. official said they were "very close" to an agreement."[12] The *Washington Post* presented the conference in terms of an alliance between the Vatican and Islamic fundamentalism, emphasizing the issue of sex: "Islamic leaders have begun to line up with the Vatican in condemning a landmark UN document on population and development, saying it condones extramarital sex, homosexuality, abortion and possibly prostitution."[13]

In these "bigger" story lines casting the secular state against the religious right, concerns of the Pacific and of most South countries went unreported. But let us be honest, if not so naïve. The stories about Niue and Tuvalu are unlikely to have caught our attention in the morning metropolitan edition even if a foreign desk editor had been so capricious as to include them. Without novelty, powerless countries rarely provide news dramatic enough to interest a global audience. But like his counterparts at the *Washington Post* and the *Atlanta Constitution,* Alfred Sasako was writing for the folks back home.

Following this pattern, journalists from member broadcasting organizations have been sent by PACNEWS to report regional conferences. The South Pacific Forum meetings are now routinely covered by a broadcast journalist within PIBA. Shiu Singh, former PACNEWS senior editor, recounts how officials and delegates at one Forum meeting actively sought out the daily PACNEWS bulletins because some of the news really was news, that is to say, not officially known.[14] PACNEWS has also managed to flash stories on news as it breaks. In one notable example, thirty minutes after his appointment, PACNEWS issued a special bulletin announcing that Sitiveni L. Rabuka was the new prime minister of Fiji, along with details of his support by the Labor Party. Some years earlier, the news might have taken days, even weeks, to filter across the Pacific.

Regional Conflict—Bougainville

Not all PACNEWS stories can be covered by a reporter on the spot. Source material may have to come from faxed press releases and other statements generously referred to as "handouts." Sometimes the traffic in such handouts can be heavy, particularly as concerns the insurgency on the island of Bougainville in Papua New Guinea. Reporting in any Third World insurgency is difficult at best, and Bougainville has presented special difficulties for any news agency reporter, Third World or not.

The Bougainville insurgency, begun in 1988, has continued for a decade. PNG troops have been deployed, and a blockade has been imposed on the island since April 1990. The insurgency has centered on a host of issues focusing on the second-largest open-pit copper mine in the world, Panguna. There has been severe environmental and social damage, and landowners have claimed inadequate compensation besides. Matters escalated to a political and military struggle for Bougainville's independence from Papua New Guinea—the central sticking point. In the protracted conflict, thousands have been killed and more have been displaced. In one of the more bizarre episodes, Prime Minister Sir Julius Chan signed an agreement with a London-based group to import mercenaries who were to train an elite PNG squad with the intent to eliminate the Bougainville Revolutionary Army leadership and supporters. In March 1997 news of the deal became known, nearly precipitating a coup d'état, and the country was sent headlong into a constitutional crisis.

Differences between the Bougainvilleans and the PNG government are not new: they appeared almost from the start of Papua New Guinea self-government in 1972. Shortly before PNG achieved independence from the trusteeship of Australia in 1975, Bougainville declared itself the North Solomons Republic, but in 1976 it agreed to accept provincial status as a part of PNG.

Ethnically, Bougainvilleans are more closely related to people in nearby Solomon Islands' Western Province than they are to PNG. Indeed, the border between Bougainville and Solomon Islands, an easily crossed line, is a classic colonial divide, an artificial border established by the British in 1886 and 1899 and perpetuated when Papua New Guinea gained its independence.

Of the estimated 160,000 inhabitants of Bougainville, some from the south of the island have relatives in the Solomons and, fleeing the violence, have sought refuge across the divide. In 1993 a series of border incursions into the Western Province by the PNG Defense Forces brought on rising tensions between the two countries. There have been skirmishes. The *Solomon Star,* a biweekly newspaper published in the capital, Honiara, reported Solomon nationals among the casualties—two adults killed and a child wounded in a night raid by the PNG Defense Forces. The territorial violations have occurred on Balalae airstrip in the Shortland Islands, near the border, and elsewhere.

News from this border area has been difficult to come by as the Solomon Islands government restricted travel there. Communication between the capital and outlying area is not easy to begin with—telecommunications are not well developed, distance is great, travel sporadic, arduous, and expensive. With hostilities, there has been real physical danger to anyone venturing into the area. According to Dykes Angiki, news director of the Solomon Islands Broadcasting Commission, officials advised journalists against going to the border area because safety cannot be assured. SIBC has, on occasion, gotten reporter George Tausiria, a former policeman, to the area by hitching a ride on a police launch. The stories SIBC files might then get faxed to PACNEWS for regional distribution. But most reports have not been on-the-scene coverage.

A good deal has come from handouts. But whether from official or unofficial organizations, they are routinely ignored by most journalists in major North media organizations. While this raw material arrives without charge, handouts are suspect because of potential bias, unverified information, and the lack of reportorial balance. PACNEWS editors, however, have not the luxury to simply disregard all the statements that are received, nor do their colleagues in other Pacific newsrooms. One consideration is, admittedly, financial: PACNEWS is not an affluent organization with paid journalists on budget, and so editors will filter through unsolicited material for information that may be newsworthy. Caution is exercised. If a handout raises an issue that editors determine has news value, they will get on the telephone to their colleagues across the Pacific for verification and supplemental information. They may request comment or response from an opposition party or group. Obviously, the news gathering has to be done by telephone and fax, because it is often physically impossible to get quickly to a location, even if there were funds and personnel for such travel, which there are not. This is not a happy compromise, but there is little choice. News is gathered through briefings and press packs, not by reporters wandering the bush in search of stories.

Faxed press releases may come from the press secretary of a government official, from an opposition party, from individuals and groups. An example of this sort of material is "Bougainville Today," a press release that has purported to be a "dispatch on daily events in Bougainville." The cover sheet that accompanies the transmission, however, has stated that "Bougainville Today" is a product of the Office of the Prime Minister of Papua New Guinea. Suffice it to say that the exercise of professional judgment is required when distinguishing between which sources are newsworthy and which are unreliable. Even so, PACNEWS will sometimes have to resort to qualifications—"statements cannot be immediately confirmed," "previous military statements have often proved inaccurate," and the like. While reporting constraints on Pacific journalists are greater than for their North counterparts, all journalists face similar problems of unverified claims and statements.[15]

"Bougainville Today" has been known to incorrectly—"prematurely"—announce the deaths of Bougainville insurgency leaders. And a typical statement may be the following: State Minister Responsible for Bougainville Affairs, Hon. Michael Ogio, said, "Public Servants are now being moved into Arawa [a port city] to serve the people, especially in Health and Education needs. He is now calling on the rebel elements to lay down their arms and work with the government."[16]

In the Bougainville conflict, the media battle for the hearts and minds of the people goes two ways. Press releases have also arrived at PACNEWS from the "Republic of Bougainville," that is to say, from the offices of the insurgents. Their refrain goes something like the following:

> BRA Kill 5 More PNG Soldiers in Central Bougainville
>
> BRA soldiers have reported that they have shot dead 5 more of PNG troops last week in Central Bougainville.
>
> Two of the PNG soldiers both believed to be from Rabaul in the East New Britain Province were shot dead at about 4 PM on Wednesday 17 March.[17]

A similar insurgent theme is this:

> PNG Troops Are Hit Harder by BRA Forces on Latest Developments in Bougainville
>
> "Members of the PNGDF and local resistance forces in Central and South Bougainville have been hit the hardest being forced to incur

heavy losses in latest developments in the battle front on Bougainville," the top BRA command reported this evening through Radio Free Bougainville.[18]

The number of deaths in any mounted operation has always been at odds and seems to be a focal point of these press releases. Depending on the reliability of the source, and subsequent to verification, PACNEWS publishes the story in its bulletins. This might then generate a new round of press releases. At times, the Office of the Prime Minister of Papua New Guinea weighs in with its own statement, such as this one issued directly by the press secretary:

> SITUATION BRIEF ON BOUGAINVILLE:
> FIVE MORE REBELS REPORTED KILLED IN BUIN
>
> North Solomons administrator Sam Tulo reported today that five rebels have been killed in Buin [a town in south Bougainville Island] this morning.
>
> Troops are reported to have ambushed rebels at Akku Community school 12 kilometers from Buin.
>
> The administrator reports that amongst those killed was rebel commander known as Sipping.[19]

Note how the press release is written in a rip-and-read style suitable for radio.

After BRA claims have been reported over Radio Bougainville, the clandestine station operated by insurgents in the bush on Bougainville Island, PACNEWS might ask for a PNG response. A counterclaim, this one faxed to PACNEWS by the chief of operations of the PNG Defense Forces, reads as follows:

> BLATANT AND INTENTIONAL MISREPORTING OF
> SECURITY FORCE MEMBERS DEATHS
>
> The office of the Commander of the PNGDF, Brigadier General Robert Dademo has rejected reports of recent killings of the members of the Security Forces on Bougainville as first degree propaganda by the BRA.
>
> Claims made by the BRA that they inflicted heavy casualties among the Papua New Guinea Security Forces in Central and South

Bougainville on Tuesday 24 March is nothing but bad yellow press reporting.[20]

But the Bougainville conflict is not *War and Peace in the Global Village.*[21] Anyone interested in the conflict is unlikely to *see* reportage of it on CNN, or any other television news network, or to *read* about it in a sustained fashion in any major North newspaper. (The chaos from the 1997 mercenary-contract affair was one exception, receiving wide coverage outside the Pacific as well as in.) Radio, local radio, is the medium of necessity here. And because of physical circumstances surrounding this long-running conflict, information sources from maladroit "public relations" have to be considered.

Experience and instinct—"a nose for what is news"—guide journalists in what to report and what not. Corroboration does exist in the number of body bags returned to Port Moresby, and people in a position to know suggest that both sides have been prone to exaggeration. Papua New Guinea underreports government casualties, the BRA overreports government casualties. There is no reliable data or means to estimate the death toll and suffering of BRA operatives. Nor do there seem to be evenhanded assessments of the suffering of Bougainville civilians, residents caught in a conflict where terrorism on both sides has been used to suppress or further the goal of secession. What evidence there is points to serious misery and rampant human rights violations as security forces have herded civilians into "protected" government villages. What is clear is that Bougainville has been an island of armed occupation and these press releases illustrated here are the sorts of material with which, perforce, PACNEWS must contend.

After ten years of strife and a battle for independence, the civil war on Bougainville has showed signs of being settled in 1998. Under the aegis of Australia and New Zealand, a truce has been brokered. A regional multinational group to monitor the truce has been put in place, to be followed by a United Nations–endorsed "special observing mission." The "Lincoln Agreement on Peace, Security and Development on Bougainville," which signified the cessation of armed violence, was signed at Lincoln University, Christchurch, New Zealand, on January 23, 1998, by all parties involved—the Papua New Guinea government, the Bougainville Transitional Government, the Bougainville Resistance Force, the Bougainville Interim Government, the Bougainville Revolutionary Army, and Bougainville leaders. If successful, the truce would become a cease-fire in the spring of 1998. The future political status of Bougainville remains for future discussion. Over the period of the conflict, the negative news of the civil strife has been carried in news stories outside of the region; the positive news of a permanent cease-fire has received scant coverage.

Like most of the hundred conflicts ongoing in the world at any one moment, Bougainville will seldom be encountered in the news of the metropolitan press. Interest in the conflict is, naturally, intense in the Pacific, and reportage, there as elsewhere, even under constraints, aspires to accuracy and credibility. Journalists must be careful about their sources, in this case especially those deemed "official."

Credibility, itself a complicated notion, is governed as much by propositions of belief on the part of the reader as it is by "objective" occurrences.[22] Nevertheless, it is a reporter's job is to find "facts," verify them as needed, and then report them. While most of the contributions about Bougainville have come from two Pacific broadcasters who are members of PIBA and participants in PACNEWS activities—the National Broadcasting Corporation of Papua New Guinea and the Solomon Islands Broadcasting Corporation—PACNEWS does contribute stories of its own to its daily bulletins, particularly when a variance in accounts demands explanation.

In such cases, a good deal of reporting effort can be spent corroborating statements. Often, professional and societal assumptions guide reporters as they identify an appropriate source of information and as they decide whether that information requires verification. Verification, as Gaye Tuchman observes in *Making News,* is typically geared to meet professional needs (deadlines, personal standards, credibility) as well as organizational needs (libel avoidance).[23] Responsibility for how the information is reported lies with the reporter, but clearly in most instances PACNEWS has not the time, resources, or staff to carry out this function at any high level of substantiation.

"Sources" here refers simply to providers of information in their capacity as representatives of organized and unorganized groups, official or unofficial. All sources are not equal, and journalists must exercise judgment as to the appropriateness of the source as well as of the information provided. Within such a framework, journalists follow what is known as the "two-source rule": if you need to verify, two sources, at least, are the rule. Even so, the matter is determined by the situation at hand and by professional evaluation of the reliability of the source.

In practice, the two-source rule means that when Papua New Guinea Defense Forces claim to have killed *x*-many BRA troops, PACNEWS faxes the information to a BRA office for confirmation and comment. Editors may also seek verification with sources in Papua New Guinea and in the Solomon Islands, across the border. The process works in reverse when the BRA makes a claim of *y*-many PNG Defense Forces killed.

To be sure, PNG government sources have been at an advantage because one knows where to find them. (Forces maintain a presence on Buka Island, near the northern tip of Bougainville, and make sea patrols from various bases in the area.) Sometimes reporters are kept waiting, as Sean Dorney of Radio Australia has complained of the PNG Bougainville Information Desk.[24] The insurgents, in hiding, are more difficult to reach. The BRA has been centered in the interior of Bougainville Island with headquarters believed to be near the Panguna copper mine. Their lines of communications have nothing of the bravura and sophistication of Mexico's Zapatista Subcomandante Marcos, who is reported to have a satellite telephone and who faxes his "postmodern revolutionary" media exchanges from Zapatistas' *territoria liberado.*[25] BRA lines of communication are fragile, and several days may pass before a response is gotten back from the bush. As technology has become more available, however, telephone contact with Bougainville leaders is sometimes possible—by satellite. A PACNEWS stringer occasionally interviews Francis Ona, but telephone charges are high—SI$300 for about a thirty-minute interview. These days, PACNEWS carries an occasional direct quote from some of the leadership on Bougainville in insurgent-held territory.

SPEAKING FROM BOUGAINVILLE, ONA SAID HE WAS NOT PLEASED WITH KABUA "SHORT CIRCUITING" THE RECONCILIATION PROCESS.

The importance of those two briefly quoted words originating from Bougainville must not be underestimated. They represent a process of transition to a regional, independent press—not one that is an echo of transnational media or a handmaiden of government.

But journalism runs on deadlines, and time and expense intervene. Without time, staff, and funds, PACNEWS will be of necessity limited in the information that can be acquired under pressure of the thrice-daily production process that is keyed to air time. Sources will tend to be what one can find, and even that information must be further winnowed to accommodate limited space.

The overwhelming percentage of stories that appear in PACNEWS bulletins originates in newsrooms of Pacific radio stations. PACNEWS editors have to trust that the news they receive from these news organizations has been subjected to journalistic standards and has undergone the process of verification. In a way, PACNEWS functions as a news dispatcher in a multi-production process which is largely outside its control. PACNEWS is, after all, a "news exchange" system. Within a locale, news is gathered and edited for local consumption. Stories are then selected for broader regional interest and, ideally, edited again for submission to PACNEWS via fax.

At PACNEWS, the editing process begins anew as stories are tailored to fit into the day's editions. Where stories have been taken from newspapers, the copy is edited for publication in a radio newscast, which in total rarely lasts more than ten to fifteen minutes a time slot. (An all-news radio station is unlikely in most Pacific island nations because radio fulfills multiple purposes and must serve a variety of listeners.) News stories, as stated earlier, are geared more to the "rip-and-read" headline approach rather than to in-depth coverage.

Page one of a PACNEWS edition usually contains two stories. Average word count per story—including caption, source, edition, and date—is 175 words. Other pages vary in word count as stories dictate. Occasionally, if deemed sufficiently newsworthy, or sensational, one story will cover the entire page one. For example, when a blanket ban of all programs or reportage on Bougainville was imposed on SIBC, the state radio, the story "Media Gag" filled page one of PACNEWS's second edition of the day.[26] While the cost of faxing larger stories can be an issue of financial concern, the primary consideration seems to be the necessity to meet radio stations' needs for a news format that can easily be scanned and read over the air.

Not simply a Pacific custom, during times of conflict governments will seek to deploy media in service of their own aims. It is at the margins of this relationship between government and media where stress is most evident and pressure brought to bear. In this sensitive area, journalists may contest news definitions dominated by state interests. But it is not simply the conception of news—development journalism, for example—that is at issue.[27] At a more fundamental level, governments will prefer that media seek "official" sources and will attempt to impose constraints on coverage.

In the case of Bougainville, if that practice had been followed, all information would flow from sources in Papua New Guinea—through the newsroom of the National Broadcasting Corporation of Papua New Guinea in Boroko; from the chief of operations speaking for the Office of the Commander of the PNG Defense Forces in Port Moresby; from the commander of the PNG Defense Forces in Bougainville; and from the press secretary in the Office of the Prime Minister of PNG at Moranta House. Indeed, that is where most of the information does originate.

But rarely has the "official" version been enough. While PNG claims of safety problems are indisputable, journalists as well as fact-finding missions of the Red Cross, Amnesty International, Pax Christi, the World Council of Churches, the International Commission of Jurists, and other humanitarian organizations have been denied unhindered access to Bougainville. A resolution of the UN Commission on Human Rights, Geneva, suspects human rights violations,[28] and Solomon Islands prime minister, Solomon S. Mamaloni, has officially charged "suppression of [Bougainvillean] civil liberty and rights, disruption to socioeconomic services and/or development activities. [Residents] have also been subjected to excessive brutalities, let alone hardship."[29]

Safety may not be the only reason PNG officials want outsiders kept away from the area. Bougainville, the "news story," would seem to have a larger tale than that which government has wished to tell.

Other Sources of Information: Clandestine Radio

One alternate source of information available to PACNEWS, besides official PNG or Solomon Islands government sources, has been an organization that calls itself the Bougainville Interim Government. Martin Miriori, known pejoratively in Papua New Guinea as the "black secessionist," was its representative and coordinator of the Bougainville Humanitarian Office in Honiara, which promotes secessionist interests.[30] But Miriori was forced to flee his home in Honiara when six masked men burned down his house. (Miriori sought and was granted asylum in The Netherlands in 1996.) The mere existence of this office in the Solomon Islands has represented provocation to PNG, as it suggests where the sympathies of Solomon Islanders might lie. Miriori is a quiet source of information about developments in the conflict, but most of the BRA press reports have since come from an office in Australia headed by Bougainville Interim Government spokesman Moses Havini.

Radio, in this case clandestine radio, has been critical to the insurgency.

In fact, because PNG Defense Forces have blockaded the island, radio may have been the sole source of information coming out of the area, with the exception of the intrepid few who slipped across the border and reported back. Radio Free Bougainville, the voice of the BRA, has had a mobile transmitter that broadcasts on the shortwave frequency 3870 kHz. PNG forces have tried to jam Radio Free Bougainville broadcasts, bomb the transmission locations, send in troops by airborne helicopters supplied by Australia. The broadcasts, with plenty of static and interference, have all been issued by BRA operatives in the bush.

In the beginning BRA operatives carted fuel into difficult terrain to keep generators running for the radio transmitter. Coconut oil, as stated earlier, was the reported source of energy. Miriori has also indicated that the BRA was able to harness solar power from funds supplied by a Sydney support group, which provided the BRA's Yaesu-Musen shortwave transmitting system as well.[31] While the use of solar power is a relatively simple operation, the panels, which are large, can be seen from the air and are difficult to move about. The details have been necessarily fuzzy because of security reasons.

Insurgency officials monitor BRA radio broadcasts. With information gathered from this and other sources, they have attempted to counter the censorship, and propaganda, of official PNG news through press releases that provide an alternative view of developments in the conflict.

These BRA press releases are faxed to several destinations: PACNEWS offices in Port Vila, Vanuatu; sixty outlets in Australia; another thirteen outlets in New Zealand; and so on. Some are sent to Europe. Many of these handouts are attributed to Havini, whose official title is Bougainville International Political Representative and Human Rights Advocate in Australia, but the route of his information is necessarily circuitous.

Typical PACNEWS stories about Bougainville might read as follows. The first concerns a response by Miriori to a change in government in Papua New Guinea. Radio Australia was PACNEWS's source for this story, which originated with reporter Sean Dorney, head of the Port Moresby office of Radio Australia/ABC.

> BOUG—CEASE-FIRE: RA, PACNEWS BULLETIN JULY 29, 1992.
> THE BOUGAINVILLE SECESSIONISTS HAVE CALLED FOR AN IMMEDIATE CEASE-FIRE SO THEY CAN RESUME TALKS WITH THE PAPUA NEW GUINEA GOVERNMENT ON THE FUTURE OF THE ISLAND.

THE SPOKESMAN FOR THE BOUGAINVILLE REVOLUTIONARY ARMY IN SOLOMON ISLANDS, MARTIN MIRIORI, SAID THE BRA WAS ENCOURAGED BY THE ATTITUDE SHOWN TO THE BOUGAINVILLE ISSUE BY PAPUA NEW GUINEA'S NEW PRIME MINISTER.

Radio Free Bougainville was the source of the following story, which was rewritten by a PACNEWS editor:

BOUG—FIGHTING: SOURCE IS PACNEWS, PACNEWS BULLETIN, JULY 6, 1994.

THE BOUGAINVILLE REVOLUTIONARY ARMY CLAIMS PAPUA NEW GUINEA DEFENSE FORCES HAVE STEPPED UP THEIR SEA PATROLS IN THE WATERS BETWEEN SOUTHERN BOUGAINVILLE AND THE SHORTLANDS GROUP IN SOLOMON ISLANDS.

RADIO FREE BOUGAINVILLE QUOTES THE BRA AS SAYING PNG SURVEILLANCE HAS BEEN MADE MORE EFFECTIVE WITH THE DEPLOYMENT OF THE PATROL BOAT DREGER WHICH IS EQUIPPED WITH RADAR WHICH THE REBELS CLAIM HAS A RANGE OF 25 NAUTICAL MILES.

THE DREGER IS BEING SUPPORTED BY TWO FAST CRAFT BASED AT TAURATO ISLAND CLOSE TO THE SEA BORDER.

HOWEVER, THE BRA CLAIMS THAT SMALL BOATS ARE STILL GETTING THROUGH THE PNG BLOCKADE WITH SUPPLIES FOR THE REBELS AND THAT PEOPLE IN THE REGION ARE CONTINUING TO MAKE TRADITIONAL CROSS-BORDER VISITS.

THE BRA SAYS THAT IN CLASHES DURING THE PAST WEEK, THREE PNG SOLDIERS AND A REBEL HAVE BEEN KILLED.

BRA GUERRILLAS ARE SAID TO BE CONTINUING THEIR HUNT FOR A SMALL GROUP OF PNG SOLDIERS BELIEVED TO BE HIDING IN THE BUSH NEAR PARUPARU, 20 KILOMETERS SOUTH-WEST OF THE DERELICT PANGUNA COPPER MINE.

THE REBEL RADIO SAID THEY WERE PART OF A FORCE OF PNG TROOPS WHICH LANDED IN THE AREA ON JUNE 20. THE REPORT CLAIMED THE TROOPS RAN INTO HEAVY OPPOSITION FROM THE REBELS AND WITHDREW NEXT MORNING, BUT SOME OF THEIR NUMBER WERE LEFT BEHIND.

Neither of these stories, it should be pointed out, was picked up by the international press outside the region.

The News Net

PACNEWS casts its news net wide, seeking Pacific stories appropriate for publication.[32] As metaphors go, the news net is reasonably useful as long as one is clear on its function.

A good deal of attention has been given to the deficiencies in the flow of news from one part of the world to another and, in particular, to the one-way flow of information from developed to developing nations. Now that the heat of the debate regarding the New World Information and Communication Order has settled somewhat, there is less criticism of the major world news agencies—Reuters, Associated Press, Agence France-Presse, or ITAR-Tass, the Russian news agency that is successor to Tass. Some of the criticism about the "structure of foreign news," such as the overemphasis on accidents, scandals, coup d'états, and weather, remains valid. On the other hand, a look at PACNEWS sources does not sustain this view of outside dominance (Table 2).

Collectively, the major news agencies employ thousands and have bureaus and offices in well over a hundred countries around the world. In the Pacific, they tend to be absent more than present, however.

Much of the empirical research that arose from the NWICO debate focused on negative reporting, the nature of communication, and cultural domination by the media of major economic and military powers. Although significant positive change emerged from that research, the ideological nature of the larger debate sometimes obscured important distinctions.

One question arising from that debate focused on news characterization: given its structure, how much does the media really tell us about the world, and how much is really contributed by a "preconceived" view of the world? To some, this question is important because of a desire to understand how professional activities influence the view of the world and because of a predisposition to treat "events" as conceptual or cultural issues rather than as the "facts-in-the-news." One view is that the "facts-in-the-news" are to be discovered by looking and seeing—by doing a reporter's job: "Sekove and Mosese Rauluni created history Monday when they became the first set of brothers to be halfbacks for the Fiji rugby team." But another view is that the "event," the index of the historical significance to rugby, is a conceptual matter and cannot necessarily be understood or addressed by the simple ratio of the total number of rugby players to related halfbacks. That would have to wait until the 1999 Rugby World Cup in Wales.

Table 2
News Sources of PACNEWS Daily Bulletins

Media name	Media type
ABC (Australian Broadcasting Corporation)	Radio Australia, shortwave service
BBC (British Broadcasting Corporation)	Radio, from rebroadcast on RNZI
BCN—Niue	Radio and TV
Cook Islands News	Radio and TV; also daily newspaper
Daily Post	Newspaper, daily; Fiji
The Dominion	Newspaper, daily; Wellington, NZ
Evening Post	Newspaper, daily; New Zealand
Fiji Times	Newspaper, daily
FM 96	Radio, private; Fiji
New Zealand Herald	Newspaper, daily
Hawaii Public Radio	Radio
NBC-Papua New Guinea	Radio
PACNEWS (Pacific News Service)	PACNEWS-originated stories, including stringers on special arrangements for news coverage for events of topical interest to Pacific stations
Post Courier	Newspaper, daily; PNG
Radio Fiji	Radio
Radio Kiribati	Radio
Radio Tonga	Radio
Radio Tuvalu	Radio
Radio Vanuatu	Radio
RNZI (Radio New Zealand International)	Radio, shortwave; Pacific service
Samoa News	Newspaper, 5 times a week; American Samoa
SIBC (Solomon Islands Broadcasting Corporation)	Radio
Solomon Star	Newspaper, biweekly
Solomon Islands Voice	Newspaper, biweekly
Sunday News	Newspaper, New Zealand
Sunday Post	Newspaper, part of the *Daily Post;* Fiji
Sunday Star	Newspaper, New Zealand
Te Reo o Tefana	Radio, Maori Service of Radio NZ

Source: PACNEWS bulletins, PACNEWS Archives, January–July 1994.

Put the debate in a different perspective. If you had been a news editor in Hawaii in 1779, would you have reported the event-centered story of how Captain James Cook lost his life at the hands of a group of Hawaiians in terms of the tragic hero? Or would you have reported the process-oriented story of massive loss of Hawaiian lives from measles, syphilis, and other diseases as a result of European contact? Or would one story have included the other?

This issue of news characterization has been as much obscured as clarified by the greater NWICO debate. The answer of the moment is that "events" are culturally determined and thus the media are essentially slanted. "Facts-in-the-news" are essentially subjective and oftentimes "false." This is the popular view, but it is not unchangeable—nor necessarily right.

In the context of this debate, then, the concept of the news net presents itself as a metaphor with some dangers. The first occurs when we slip from using the term as metaphor and start using it as an analogy. As an analogy, the news fish swim along in the Pacific Ocean; if they are of sufficient size or if the net is of a fine mesh, the news is hauled in. The analogy fails straightaway because in the case of PACNEWS, the ocean of news does not have fish of every Pacific stripe and not all the fish in the net have news in their belly. Additional Pacific issues, such as government control over many broadcasting units in the region, also influence the catch of the day.

Indulge the analogy a little further. With major international news agencies the analogy also fails. They don't cover all countries, and anyway, so the argument goes, their nets are flawed because they're made by major powers, and they don't go fishing with the same kind of fish in mind. As a result, some of the "facts-in-the-news" escape, in part because of the methods used to gather them, in part because of who does the gathering and with what means. Should we adopt this analogy, *all* media fail. Of course, one would do well to remember that media, as in the everyday practice of communication, constitute neither social science nor philosophy—something academics tend to disregard.

The media environment in the Pacific is more complex than meets the eye. To put the net metaphor into perspective, consider radio news from the standpoint of sources of the news. Well over 50 percent of PACNEWS dispatches has as their source local radio station newsrooms, an overwhelming majority of which are newsrooms in Pacific states. If we look at the total number of news stories, the importance of the radio connection is even greater. Who decides what's news, to borrow from the title of Herbert J. Gans' book, *Deciding What's News,* depends in part on the professional judgments of a wide variety of individuals and institutions, well before PACNEWS editors have their chance to cull, refine, or augment the day's offerings.

A good many of the stories PACNEWS distributes come from radio stations that are government-related, if not government-owned. A close examination of that relationship will give one a feel for what some of that Pacific media environment is like—a view that may not easily fit into preconceived notions. The general debate about uneven news flows in South countries is sometimes far too abstract to capture the texture of radio journalism in the Pacific, or elsewhere. It behooves one to look in the newsrooms of a few Pacific island stations to understand the picture more fully.

Thank you for not yet striking down anyone of those in this House who fabricate stories over the radio knowing quite well of their potential gain.
—Fata Sano Malifa, *A Kava Bowl Called Paranoia*

Around the Radio's central station, this iron castle, where clouds of wires stream out like strands of hair, there will surely be posted a skull and cross-bones with the familiar inscription: Danger! For the slightest halt in the working of the Radio would produce a spiritual swoon of the entire country, a temporary loss of its consciousness.
—Velimir Khlebnikov, *Radio of the Future*

5

In the Newsroom

Radio Newsrooms

At one end of the room is a Yaesu shortwave receiver with a Deutsche Welle program schedule tossed on top. The radio is on. Reception even during the day is fair to good, but during the hours of darkness it gets better. The set is usually tuned to Radio New Zealand International and sometimes to Radio Australia. When the reception is good, the world news from RNZI is recorded and edited for rebroadcast. By world news, people mean non-Pacific news. There is a reel-to-reel tape recorder and a sound mixer. Some edits are done in this open newsroom, but with the overlay sound—shortwave broadcasts and the normal patter of work conversations—it is a difficult task. Regional or Pacific news comes by fax from PACNEWS, the news exchange of the Pacific Islands Broadcasting Association, three times a day.

This newsroom at Radio Tonga isn't so grand. A large table nearly fills the room. On any one morning a Mason jar of flowers will sit in the center of the table. To one side, unscreened, louvered windows look out on an empty field of weeds.

Various and sundry items adorn the walls. There is a calendar from National Panasonic—the Radio Tonga Store is agent for this as well as a few other equipment manufacturers—and a Royal Tongan Air schedule. Posters and QSLs (listener acknowledgment cards) from other stations are pinned or pasted up: Jazz 88.5, WGVU-FM, West Michigan Public Broadcasting; Radio Japan; Deutsche Welle; WDTC 1450 Detroit; WDR Publik; Hundert 6 Neues Radio für Berlin.

The Macintosh Classic stacked in a corner doesn't work; it is the wrong voltage.

On the common table, an edition of *Interradio* lies in a pile with the most recent PACNEWS fax transmissions. News staff will incorporate the PACNEWS copy into the noon news spot. *Pacific Newsline,* a monthly newsletter sent out by the U.S. Information Agency office in Suva, Fiji, is also tossed onto the stack. One article reads "US to Enforce Driftnet Moratorium with Boardings," but the lead article warns "US House Backs Ban on AIDS-Infected Immigrants." These materials are rewritten and occasionally used, "if there is something appropriate." There are cassette tapes of weekly programs from Voice of America that the Worldwide English Division of VOA airmails to the station.[1] The one-hour program is called "VOA Pacific." Radio Tonga receives five hours' worth a week and selects what it will use.

One of the more whimsical features of this newsroom is two maps on Mercator's projection, placed side by side. One is a map of the world, the other of the United States. Someone has drawn in the Bermuda triangle with a black felt-tip pen.

Media Freedom Day decals are stuck here and there.

Down the hall is the broadcast booth. When the engineer is on air and when the air conditioning is not working, the door will be propped open. Tonga's climate is pleasant, but in the Tongan summer—December to April—temperatures range from 25° C to 33° C (77° F to 91° F) and the humidity can be oppressive, particularly during the rainy season. Because of the open-door policy, street sounds may occasionally reach the radio audience, and a few words from passing conversations too. Around the station you have to step lightly and be careful what you say.

Mele Laumanu Petelo, the controller of news and current affairs at Radio Tonga, presides over the newsroom. At one time, this was an all-woman newsroom, although sports was read by a man. The sex barrier is now broken as several men have joined the staff. The news staff assembles around the common table. They do everything—collect the news, write in English and Tongan, present the news over the air in both languages. They also translate world news sources from English, primarily, into Tongan, as they do with PACNEWS dispatches.

Petelo does not have a journalism degree, but her professional journalism experience is considerable. Her formal training at university was in English at a time when no journalism courses were available. Since then she has taken advanced radio courses on newswriting and presentation. Petelo has reported Commonwealth meetings and was a Jefferson Fellow at the East-West Center in Hawaii. She has traveled widely.

Petelo's on-air persona has the quality of control. The news is read in a superb voice, power veiled in understatement and not oversold. The controller of news, an unfortunate title, is also a singer and has performed with her own group. For the most part, her singing is a private matter, reserved for the church choir. She doesn't sing or preach the news, but there is clear resonant authority, a pacing for secular radio with a hint of lauds.

When she thinks an unfolding event in Tonga may have Pacific regional interest, Petelo will write the story and submit it to PACNEWS. Perhaps the story will detail a government trade surplus. The trade balance is normally in deficit, but a niche market for squash, exported to Japan and Australia, usually pushes the November figures into the black. If Tonga holds a national election, results will be reported along with some analysis:

> 77 PERCENT OF THOSE WHO VOTED FOR THE PRO-DEMOCRACY GROUP DID SO BECAUSE THEY VALUED ACCOUNTABILITY; 10 PERCENT WANTED POLITICAL CHANGE; 5 PERCENT CAST VOTES BECAUSE PRO-DEMOCRACY CANDIDATES WERE RELATIVES; OTHER REASONS, UNREPORTED.

An announcement at the High Commissioner's Residence of an association between Tongan and New Zealand business concerns might be reported to PACNEWS, and locally as well. Tongan deportees from Australia, New Zealand, the United States, or Samoa, usually for overstaying their visas, might also make the news—locally certainly and maybe regionally as well. At the least, the story would be faxed to PACNEWS for editors there to decide its newsworthiness for the day's bulletin. For their submissions to PACNEWS, neither Radio Tonga nor the local reporter receives compensation. A stringer for RNZI or Radio Australia would. The benefit you get from submitting a story to PACNEWS is that you get the news out and you get regional news in return.

Not only in Tonga, but in Vanuatu and other locations across the Pacific, you can watch the same weekday routine: newspeople sending out stories and receiving a news bulletin three times daily from the offices of PACNEWS, now in Port Vila, the capital of Vanuatu. When PACNEWS was headquartered in Honiara, Solomon Islands, Harold Obed, then a reporter for Radio Vanuatu, submitted a story reporting that Father Lini, former prime minister of Vanuatu, had been banned from Pentecost Island by a local chief. The next morning, Obed's story was read on RNZI, picked up from the PACNEWS bulletin.

In the PACNEWS offices themselves, it is not unusual to hear a story over Radio Australia or on the Pacific broadcasts of RNZI that has only moments before been faxed by PACNEWS to its various respondents scattered around the Pacific, which of course include Radio Australia and RNZI. Note that this is not the way pundits have theorized about the flow of news. In fact, the direction of the flow is exactly the reverse.

The commonly held view assumes a media imperialism, pointing to the cultural impact of transnational media organizations on South countries.[2] According to the theory, transnational media giants—Time Warner, Sony, CNN, Reuters, Agence France-Presse, and the like—overwhelm the local voice of South nations, the so-called Third World. Global products from a few North, developed countries—the United States is blamed for a lot—dominate the international market in communications, in music tapes and CDs. Western news agencies dominate the flow of information. Western television production companies dump cheap reruns, the same as regards comics, movies, and animated films. Intuitively we know what this means. Turn on Italian TV. You can't help but see animated programs that are Japanese in origin and that have been dubbed into Italian. But the same is true on Saturday morning in the United States, only the same Japanese animated programs have been dubbed suddenly into English. So the phenomenon is not unique to the Third World.

A metaphor of flow is supposed to explain the paradigm—a flow from North to South, with little reciprocal flow, and scant intraregional exchange.[3] But the news stories that Laumano Petelo files from Nuku'alofa and Harold Obed submits from Port Vila, the dispatches sent by Dykes Angiki from Honiara, and the rest of the reports from across the Pacific which flow across the desk of Jonas Cullwick, PACNEWS senior editor, lead to doubts about the viability of the theory in the Pacific. At least there is reason to question this matter when it comes to news production.

The flow theories and characterizations of media behavior emerged partly as a result of historic and technical conditions during and immediately after the colonial period. The theories may once have had currency, and even now in some countries and in specific areas of media—movies, television, and books—these characterizations prevail. But the point to be made here is that as a simple formulation of the flow of media, and particularly of news from North to South regions, old assumptions require a corrective lens. Based on the development of institutions such as PACNEWS and on actual conditions and content of radio news, the picture that has emerged looks quite different.

Direct Foreign Content

With or without PACNEWS, with or without locally generated stories, Pacific radio stations have always broadcast programs that have come from developed nations, international agencies, and foreign broadcast services. The Voice of America, Deutsche Welle, and the BBC, to name a few, contribute the usual fare of programs on culture, health, and rural agricultural development. Interviews with agricultural specialists and health care officials seem to predominate. These commentators may be earnest, dedicated experts, but their on-air personality hardly cuts it on radio. They are often dreadfully dull, and one wonders who listens.

Among programs sent by the Voice of America, through the U.S. Information Agency, is a professionally produced, hour-long stereo program, mostly of popular music.

FROM THE GULF OF THAILAND TO THE CORAL SEA: THIS IS VOA PACIFIC.

The musical offerings range from "Cold Hearted" Paula Abdul, Bruce Springsteen, the Beatles, Sting, Michael Jackson, Bryan Adams, the Eagles, the Wilson Sisters, the Osmonds, Amy Grant, to the June Blossoms. Spots punctuate the music: the travels of Peace Corps volunteers, the annual egg-dropping contest by engineering and architecture students at the Cooper Union, Sting's efforts to save the rain forest, the perils of smoking and drunken driving.

On rare occasion, foreign programs of this sort will prove to have local appeal. One such program aired by Radio Tonga a few years back proved to be terrifically popular. The audience demanded a repeat broadcast, and the station staff was forced to hold up production of one of their own programs until the foreign program could be rebroadcast. Ordinarily one might not make a connection between the two events, but blank recording tape was in short supply at the time, and the station was preparing to reuse the tape of the foreign program, which is to say, to record over it. Indeed, stations in low-income countries are happy to receive public information tapes from abroad because the high-quality tapes, on which the foreign programs have

Muddy Tapes

The tape recorder is an emblem of the uphill battle facing many Pacific radio stations. In a salty, humid climate, sometimes beyond the reach of electricity, even something as basic as a tape recorder takes on larger dimensions.

First of all, as with other equipment at a radio station, professional quality is essential. Not any cheap, handy cassette recorder off the shelf will do. Tape hiss on a machine used in the home may not be very noticeable, but on air the hiss can sound like a steam radiator. Furthermore, under very humid conditions, recorders are known to "scream" on playback—again not a desirable effect on air. So equipment has to be rugged and reliable. Pacific stations do not have the luxury of ringing Kansas City to get some Sony parts sent out. In the United States, you would have your parts in a week to ten days. Who knows how long you would have to wait in the Pacific? As for the more common repairs, station technicians try to fill the breach.

Professional recordings, if they are going to be rebroadcast, require sound level controls with built-in meters. Ideally, a tape recorder should have a VU-meter (volume unit meter) or a PPM-meter (peak program meter) to ensure good sound fidelity. When recording speech, for example, the rule of thumb is to set the VU-meter so that the peak readings do not exceed 0 dB and, to be safe, to adjust controls so that peaks do not go higher than -3 dB.

As a speaker shifts position and moves closer to or farther from the microphone, the reporter must readjust the setting. The aim is a balance between a recording level too high, which results in sound distortion, or too low, which will cause a hiss loud enough to drown out the interview. Of course, there are automatic recording controls, but they present problems of their own. During silent moments of an interview, or when a speaker responds less volubly, the automatic controls readjust, amplifying unwanted background noise. Sometimes this background noise—the rumbling of cars or other conversations—will render the interview unintelligible.

Then there is the editing. Reporters want their presentations to be lively. An entire story in one voice tends to be dull. Out of an interview or news conference, only a clip of about 20–40 seconds is typically usable. With analogue tape, organizing the story physically can be accomplished in two ways. One is by cutting and splicing together the recorded material, where any *uh-huh,* throat clearing, and *ahh* at the end of a sentence are deleted with a sharp razor blade. This produces a whole, continuous clip. A reporter's questions are similarly eliminated, long pauses disappear, parts of answers are joined. Reporters in the North prefer to edit by this method because the result is, paradoxically, "seamless" and clean. Dub-editing—accomplished by copying an original tape onto another tape, stopping and starting again to create the story tape—is looked down upon because sound quality degrades in this process.[1] In the Pacific, however, dub-editing is preferred because it is *physically* seamless, producing no cuts that have been spliced together on the tape. To cut tape is to cost the station money.

Broadcast workshops outside the Pacific teach young Pacific journalists how to edit by cutting and splicing. (Digital editing is not in the immediate future for most Pacific stations.) But back home, when one reporter got out a splicing block, marked points on the tape with a grease pencil, and was about to make a diagonal cut on the shiny vinyl, his general manager intervened. Recording tape is a precious commodity in the Pacific and is by rule recycled. A tape that has been spliced over a few times has a shortened life span. Moreover, in a hot climate without air conditioning, the adhesive tape used to secure the cut ends of the recording tape gets sticky and gums up the machines. A news director observed wryly, "When the tape begins to screech during an interview, that's when I know it's time to change the tape." At his station, tapes were recycled until no longer shiny.

There are other reasons for dub-editing. The chance

that an inexperienced reporter might destroy a taped interview is lessened. In one country, there is the benefit of providing an exact record of the interview, necessary in the event political dispute arose over what was actually said; it was the general manager's "tape insurance."

But dub-editing is far from optimal. Two machines are required, so where equipment is scarce, reporters have to share resources. Under constraints of news deadlines, the trial-and-error aspect of the process also takes longer. You have to play back the original tape many times to get the precise spot you want to isolate, and the *uh-huh*s and *ahh*s are likely to remain—hence, muddy tapes, a far less "professional" sound, and far fewer clips from interviews.

---

1. Produced in Washington, D.C., National Public Radio (NPR) has a distinctive sound and is rightly famous for its aural presentation surrounding news. Thomas Looker captures the feel and technique of this fine art of tape cutting for news production in *The Sound and the Story: NPR and the Art of Radio* (Boston: Houghton Mifflin, 1995); see also Marcus D. Rosenbaum and John Dinges, eds., *Sound Reporting, The National Public Radio Guide to Radio Journalism and Production* (Dubuque, Iowa: Kendall/Hunt, 1992).

been recorded, are a resource they receive free. In one Pacific newsroom, the current affairs in-box contained tapes from five different external services being (re)used in this way.

But this valuable commodity of reusable tape is drying up. The BBC, for example, now sells its programs through the Tropical Tapes section of the BBC World Service. Radio Fiji, Radio Kiribati, NBC Papua New Guinea, and Radio Tuvalu all subscribe, some at reduced rates because, as Russ Willey, marketing manager of BBC Tropical Tapes, discreetly puts it, some broadcasters "are not well off."[4] Three of the four stations use the BBC educational program "Future Perfect." Other educational, public affairs listings in the BBC Tropical Tapes catalog include "Your World," "International Call," "Health Watch," and "International Money Program."

The foreign origin of this kind of programming is obvious. VOA is explicit about it:

HI, I'M JIM BURTEL AT THE VOICE OF AMERICA IN WASHINGTON AND THIS IS VOA PACIFIC.

The same for the other foreign services.

There is no pretending: news is another arena where direct foreign news content enters the programming day. At various times during their broadcast cycle, stations will air news feeds from Radio Australia, RNZI, and the BBC, among others. The extent of this news programming differs from Pacific station to station. In the North Pacific, one is more likely to hear a relay from VOA. In the South Pacific, RNZI and Radio Australia are more commonly heard.

RNZI, which is funded by the New Zealand Ministry of Foreign Affairs, produces a number of programs specifically for Pacific audiences. From a transmitter site at Rangitaiki, about four hundred kilometers north of Wellington, RNZI broadcasts "Pacific Regional News," "Calling Cook Islands," "Pacific Island News from New Zealand," and "News in Tongan." Listeners throughout the Pacific tune in to these shortwave broadcasts on five different frequencies, which may change from hour to hour due to co-channel interference at various times of the day. "Pacific Regional News" is heard at 0400 UTC and every hour from 0700 to 1000 UTC. RNZI also broadcasts sports.

Upon closer examination, however, when it comes to Pacific regional news, the nature of flow changes radically. RNZI relies to a large degree on PACNEWS as its source. Or to state the fact in other terms, a significant portion of RNZI Pacific news originates from the very newsrooms of the countries RNZI is targeting with their broadcasts. The same is true, though to a lesser degree, in regards to Pacific news stories on Radio Australia. As shown earlier, these news stories have been prepared by local Pacific radio stations and faxed to the offices of PACNEWS, where they are edited by Pacific news professionals. The resulting PACNEWS bulletins are then faxed to all subscribers and members of the Pacific Islands Broadcasting Association for use as they see fit. RNZI uses these island news dispatches for its own news programs, which may then be picked up by individual Pacific radio stations, and the circle closes.

So you can imagine how the flow metaphor—described as one-way, top-to-bottom, rich-to-poor—may not be inviolate. Where is the information flow from "'high'-ranking nations" to "'low'-order" South countries and territories?[5] The hypotheses and assumptions about pecking orders no longer hold; if anything, the direction of flow has been reversed. These RNZI news programs are foreign in origin, with the above qualifications, even if they are rebroadcast directly over the frequencies of local stations. And what Pacific audiences are hearing is an echo of their own voices.

At Radio Tonga, for example, on the AM service the news of the day in a typical weekly program schedule begins at seven in the morning, Monday through Saturday, with a fifteen-minute segment of the BBC World News. The station does not broadcast on Sunday until the evening program, which starts at five o'clock with a classical concert hour. Sunday's broadcasts end with world news and weather in Tongan. At eight in the morning, Monday through Saturday, Australian Broadcasting Corporation's World News is on for fifteen minutes. Weekdays at 4:30 P.M. there is an RNZI feed, "News Headlines."

Radio Tonga also provides its own news throughout the broadcast day, except for Sunday. At 7:45 A.M. world news is in Tongan; the 11:00 A.M. slot is for news headlines; the 1:00 P.M. broadcast is "Today's News"; at 3:00 P.M. listeners hear news headlines; slotted for 7:00 in the evening is local news; and at 8:00, Radio Tonga provides local news interspersed with ABC feeds. Just before sign-off at 10:45 at night, the last programs of the day are world news and weather. This sample of the weekly program schedule for Radio Tonga is not necessarily typical; relative to other stations in the region, Radio Tonga uses more foreign news feeds. Nonetheless, only the news from the BBC is clearly out of region, as even ABC uses PACNEWS dispatches and local stringers.

The situation was not always like this. When Tavake Fusimalohi, the general manager at Radio Tonga, first arrived at the station in the 1970s, there was only a "primitive form of the news"—more on the order of announcements mixed with Tongan translations of news stories monitored from the BBC and Radio Australia. Pacific news sources were primarily Radio Australia, RNZI, and the *Pacific Islands Monthly,* a news magazine published in Fiji. Regional news was scarce.

The newsroom at Radio Tonga today is the creation of Fusimalohi. He has trained staff members. By design, most employees at the station can perform a variety of tasks, which makes for flexibility in staffing. If for some reason a staff member is absent, another is able to fill in. Thus, reporters can announce. If necessary, technical staff can also fulfill different tasks.

In the 1970s, "you rarely heard Pacific news in the daily bulletin on Radio Australia." Today, Fusimalohi receives, in Nuku'alofa, his PACNEWS bulletin by 3:00 or 3:30 in the afternoon. At 5 o'clock he can tune in to the RNZI Pacific regional news and hear stories from the day's PACNEWS bulletin read almost word-for-word. The echo effect can sometimes be heard on Radio Australia. "Maybe they don't pay enough [to receive PACNEWS]," Fusimalohi laughs, thinking about how times have changed.

The inclusion of fifteen-minute foreign news feeds over the course of the broadcast day has several sides.[6] For the Kingdom of Tonga, the broadcasts provide an alternative view to the news produced locally in a station closely tied to the government. The prime minister, after all, sits on the board that oversees the station. If the foreign news presence is representative of what some impute to be cultural imperialism, in this instance, at least, there is a different balance struck—as well as a balance effected—between two regional powers, Australia and New Zealand, and Britain. This balance lends some diversity of opinion to the news dispatches that are, in any event, much more mixed in their news sources than the label Radio Australia or RNZI indicates. (Note that this discussion is absent any mention of international wire services such as Reuters or Associated Press. The reason is straightforward: the wire services are not cheap, and most Pacific broadcasters "are not well off." Even if they could afford these news services, they would find very little Pacific news.)

Rhetoric divides the world into neat categories of North versus South, developed versus developing. But the division is in fact not so easily drawn. In the case of the Pacific, first of all, there are significant differences in view and policy between the two regional developed powers, Australia and New Zealand. And second, a good deal of the Pacific news that they broadcast originates from PACNEWS, a service that derives its material from regional stations. Listeners of Radio Tonga hear these broadcasts. They do so daily, along with a more frequent local view in Tongan. That this diversity exists in radio, a media of such importance to the country, is remarkable, a tribute to the news staff as well as to the general manager. And in this regard, Radio Tonga is not unique.

From Self-censorship to Outright Pressure

Radio Tonga is not, however, without controversy. During the early 1980s, the pro-democracy movement (recall that Tonga is an absolute monarchy) sponsored a monthly radio program. The talk show invited panelists to discuss elements of government policy. One topic was what constitutes a fair distribution of wealth. "This program was, from the point of view of Cabinet, so outrageously critical of the government that it ordered the Tonga Broadcasting Commission to have the [program] axed. [Activist and newspaper publisher, 'Akalisi] Pohiva was dismissed from the civil service soon after and others were reprimanded."[7] To place this situation in context, high government ministers are members of the Tonga Broadcasting Commission. The distinction between government and broadcast commission is not always clear.

Just after the election in February 1993, the *Tonga Chronicle,* a government-controlled paper, cautioned in an editorial: "The continual sly hints of corruption and dishonesty against His Majesty's Government without proof is going to rebound with multiple traumatic consequences on those concerned."[8] Remarkably, this was "news" before the event in fact occurred, but the editor had it right. A series of legal actions against *Ko e Kele'a* publisher Pohiva soon followed. Charges of libel and threats of legal actions, needless to say, are one of a variety of means that are used against journalists the world over to harass and to create a chilling climate that discourages the further reporting of potential scandals and malfeasance.[9] Even where journalists have large organizations to back them up with time and money, a caution sets in where courts and lawyers enter the newsroom. In Pohiva's circumstance, he has represented himself in a number of actions brought against him.

Pohiva, who is a parliamentarian, also faces an attempt to cut off another avenue available to him to make and publish statements critical of the gov-

'Akalisi Pohiva and *Ko e Kele'a*

'Akilisi Pohiva is a newspaper publisher, pro-democracy activist, and elected member of the Parliament of the Kingdom of Tonga, one of the few remaining absolute monarchies in the world. Nine members of parliament are appointed by his royal highness, King Taufa'ahau Tupou IV, nine members elected by the nobility of the land, and nine representatives popularly elected by the people.

According to the *Fiji Times,* the government has sought to restrain the *Ko e Kele'a,* Pohiva's eight-page monthly newspaper, after publication of confidential documents that have embarrassed the government.[1] Despite government demands, Pohiva has refused to reveal his sources. Indeed, even if Pohiva were predisposed to do so, he might not be able to. It appears, according to news reports in the *Tonga Chronicle,* that Pohiva's informants may have been civil servants acting "in breach of their obligation of secrecy under the Official Secrets Act."[2] Individuals from Nuku'alofa indicate that pro-democracy supporters sometimes toss a packet of information on Pohiva's lawn in a late night drive-by. While the means of obtaining information is unconventional, it has provided some telling revelations.

An example of Pohiva's reportage:

> Government Duty Free Operation was started in the late 60s as part of the Dateline Hotel operation. . . . Chronicle of events: 1. Late May, rumors of Princess Pilolevu taking over Duty Free Operation started to spread. 2. Mr. 'Etoni Tonga returned from New Zealand to work for the Princess in early June. 3. Earlier on, the Minister went to America on invitation of friends/partners of the Princess in San Francisco to inspect their duty free facilities. . . . 4. Between July and August, the Princess also registered a new company, called Sovereign Distributors. The two main shareholders are Princess and 'Ana Tupou. . . . The Princess was appointed a member of the Duty Free Committee

> on 21/07/92 by Cabinet. . . . On 14 August 1992, the Committee appointed Mr. 'Etoni Tonga as Manager despite the fact that there were other qualified applicants. . . . Comments: Mr. 'Etoni Tonga on the other hand has no appropriate qualifications, no management experience at all. He worked only in bar and restaurant services in New Zealand. . . . He wears two hats and conflict of interest is obvious. His responsibilities do not warrant such a salary (of T$15,000 per annum). . . . The strange arrangement with Sovereign Distributors means diverting government duty free orders to be handled by inexperienced people whom the Princess has engaged. . . . The Princess and the Minister do not know what they're up to.[3]

Under Tonga's constitution and the Official Secrets Act, Pohiva argued, it is not illegal to receive documents and then to publish them. But it is illegal to provide them. The government contended that Tonga's laws protect state secrets from exposure to public scrutiny, in the press and elsewhere. Secrets are interpreted to mean anything not officially released. In part, the courts sustained Pohiva's position. But in 1993 the Tonga Constitution was amended to read: "It shall be lawful for all people to speak, write, and print their opinions, and no law shall ever be enacted to restrict this liberty. There shall be freedom of speech and of the press forever, but nothing in this clause shall be held to outweigh the law of defamation, official secrets, or the laws for the protection of the King and the Royal Family."

Legal action against Pohiva continues. Public officials have sought large damages specified under the amended Section 7. His Royal Highness Crown Prince Tupouto'a sued for libel over an article that implied his appropriating T$1,090,000 in aid from the Republic of China to establish the Royal Beer Company.[4] The Crown Prince claimed defamation of character, that he had been made the subject of public ridicule, odium, and contempt, suffering damage to his reputation and public standing. He was awarded T$50,000.

Other cases have come in a series that seem designed to silence the *Ko e Kele'a* and to destroy Pohiva financially. He has lost a number of actions, requiring payment of substantial sums.

Pohiva is not a journalist by training. He was a school teacher and a civil servant. The nature of his reporting, as evidenced above, is somewhat free-form, relying on rumor and insinuation, which have not helped his cause in court. Even so, the actions against Pohiva-the-journalist are part of a larger shadow play involving Pohiva-the-pro-democracy-movement-leader.

Pohiva's plight also demonstrates the cultural sensitivity which journalists face. In Tonga citizens take royalty seriously. Even pro-democracy advocates accord great honor to the monarch. Linking royal names with corruption and impropriety offends traditionalists who might otherwise be sympathetic to some form of change. When a sense of respect and order is offended, one of the press's vital roles as the conscience of society is easily forgotten.

Elsewhere in the Pacific as well, chiefs and politicians use tradition, custom, and honor of authority as immunity from criticism and charges of malfeasance. Speaking to this problem, University of the South Pacific professor Epeli Hau'ofa notes, "The danger is not from traditional culture, it is from our leaders who use traditional culture as an excuse to muzzle freedom of expression."[5]

In the case of Tonga, the crown prince is on record as saying that there is a need for democracy to develop. He adds that it is necessary that the change be one of evolution with the development of an organizational structure. A political party system is an example of what he has in mind. Others are not so sanguine. One noble minister indicated that change would not come without a battle, and no one should expect nobles to hand over power without it.[6] The minister of police, also chief executioner, reminded radio audiences prior to elections in 1993 that sedition was a capital offense.

Despite the intense conflict, candidate Pohiva has appeared on Radio Tonga, along with other candidates for public office. In what must have been a difficult interview to conduct, the conversation with Pohiva degenerated into an on-air argument. Nonetheless, the candidate had his time on the radio.

---

1. "Tongan Leaders on Gay Issue," *Fiji Times*, July 15, 1993. In a odd juxtaposition, the article contained two stories, one about increasing numbers of *fakafefine* (cross dressers), the other about the Tongan government's action against Pohiva. See as well Martin Tiffany, "Political Party for Kingdom," *Pacific Islands Monthly* 64:9 (September 1994): 17.

2. "Court Refuses to Restrain Publication of Gov't Secrets Pending Trial on Constitutional Issues," *Tonga Chronicle*, February 18, 1993.

3. "Government Duty Free Operation," *Ko e Kele'a* 7:6 (February 1993).

4. "Crown Prince Sues Legislator for Libel," *Tonga Chronicle*, March 4, 1993.

5. Sireli Korovulavula, "Culture and the Journalist," *Fiji Times*, March 20, 1993.

6. "Tonga," *Washington Pacific Report* 1:14 (April 15, 1993): 4.

ernment—the reporting of parliamentary proceedings. The Speaker of Parliament, Noble Fusitu'a, argues that Tonga media have too much freedom.[10] He has attempted to remove the privilege of nonprosecution from the ability to publish statements made in parliament, which the Tonga constitution guarantees. Others, including the kingdom's minister of justice, the Hon. Tevita Tupou, have opposed this infringement on press freedom, however. In a sense, Pohiva was attempting to have his cake and eat it too: he could say what he liked as a parliamentarian and then publish it as a journalist in his newspaper.

Tonga is not the only Pacific country with challenges to press freedoms. In Apia, Samoa, at 2AP, the government-owned station, the government presence is clear and explicit. There are strict guidelines about what can and cannot be reported over the air. Incidents of rape, for example, are not reported, nor are most crimes.

Before the news is broadcast, Prime Minister Tofilau Eti Alesana reviews all material that may be considered "sensitive." ("'Sensitive' means anything that might possibly reflect poorly on majority politicians," one visiting journalist states. "They are not worried about Samoa's reputation with regard to crime.") Samoa's foreign relations would be an example of material that is "sensitive," so much so that the PM may actually choose to edit and rewrite the news text before it is read over the air.

The net effect of this interference is that what is broadcast is relevant to the position the government has taken and to its interests and political goals. Radio does not help set the public agenda in Samoa unless the government decides that it will. For all intents and purposes, this constitutes censorship of the news. But it is a charge that the prime minister is, ironically, insensitive to. In response to widespread antitax demonstrations in 1993, he quoted from the Book of Romans: "Whosoever therefore resisteth the power, resisteth the ordinance of God: and they that resist shall receive to themselves damnation." Religion and politics mix freely in Samoa.

There is no live news on 2AP. Instead, news, once it is cleared, is recorded before the broadcast, then rebroadcast several times during the day. On weekends, the news is almost twenty-four hours' stale. A staff of three covers all news—as well as a host of other responsibilities at the station—for a nation of more than 170,700 people; by contrast, at Radio Tonga, eight staff members are directly involved in news production for a population of about 97,800.

Nor is the news staff free to cover the Fono, the Samoan parliament, because discussion of political issues may prove to be too "sensitive." On the other hand, the station does carry the Fono live, which would seem risky for the government but is probably safe enough. Samoa has a distinguished tradition of oratory, and as you walk along the streets in downtown Apia, you can wander in and out of the sound of the debates of the forty-nine honorable Fono members because practically every store has the radio on. As *Pacific Islands Business* columnist Ulafala Aivao puts it, radios are tuned to 2AP's live coverage of the Fono's "prayers and insults. . . . As long as they shout their piece inside the meeting chamber, they are safe from court action, but not necessarily from each other. Like any game, there is a score-card. Parliament-watchers glued to their radio sets award points in [various] categories."[11]

Emotions often heat up in the Fono, and the excitement can captivate the radio audience. In one incident, a member of the opposition party was so outraged by actions summarily taken by the Public Accounts Committee, without consultation, that with all due flourish and drama over the radio he resigned his committee position; 2AP's live coverage afforded him that indulgence.

Debate has been known to spill outside the Fono as well. While the government station may be enjoined from covering politically sensitive issues, the policy apparently does not extend to Magik 98 FM, a small commercial station in Apia. When an opposition member, furious at proceedings in the Fono and attempts to silence him, stormed out of parliament, he vowed to carry on the debate over radio. Probably the government smiled. But rather than heading for 2AP's studios across the street, he appeared at Magik 98's studios downtown, which promptly put him on the air.

In July 1994, some visitors looked in on the 2AP newsroom. A 2AP editor was working late into the evening, faced with a troubling news question: how to handle a breaking story concerning three Samoan students who had assaulted a Fijian student at the University of the South Pacific in Suva. There were compound issues: the alleged crime, rising racial tensions at the university campus, the Samoan minister of education flying to Suva to deal with the matter, and, of course, the sensitivity of the story because it touched upon foreign affairs. The prime minister would have to clear the story, the editor indicated.

As reported later in the *Fiji Times,* the details of the event were as follows: three Samoan students, who had been drinking, went to the room of

Saimoni Tuiqali, a Fijian student at the university, and attacked him with a Coke bottle, rupturing his eye.[12] Knowledge of the incident had spread quickly, and passions were running high. Fiji and Samoa were scheduled to play a rugby match; there was the potential for wider violence.

Fiji won the match, but not before Samoa team members were reported, in the Samoan newspapers, to have feared for their safety. Punches were thrown by some Fiji supporters following a late tackle. But there was no further reported violence.

After the Coke-bottle attack, a delegation of twenty Samoan elders, led by the Reverend Faitala Talapusi, principal at Pacific Theological College, journeyed to Fiji to attempt a traditional reconciliation. A peace offering of whales' teeth and an *ie tonga,* a distinctive, finely woven Samoan mat, was made to a chiefly group in Fiji. There was also the offer of the prime minister of Samoa to pay for the student's medical costs and to compensate him for injuries.[13] But the efforts at peacemaking were rebuffed by the injured student's family. As reported in the *Fiji Times,* the family was offended that the delegation paid tribute first to a *vanua,* the chiefs of Nadroga, rather than directly to the family—an act complicated by the fact that although the student's family did currently live in Nadroga, they were originally from Nacula in Yasawa.

Rev. Talapusi stood on the integrity of his mission: "If the *lotu* (church) and *vanua* (traditional set-up) are taken seriously, then the matter has been cleared at the *vanua* level through this ceremony." Responsible Fijian leaders subsequently sought to ease tensions. Memories are long, however, and whether or not the family has accepted this attempt at reconciliation through traditional channels is not known.

But all this took place sometime after the fact. In the 2AP newsroom that evening, as the initial events were unfolding, the news editor was sweating a deadline. The cabinet was in session, the prime minister unavailable to review her text. Clearly the story was of sufficient magnitude that the prohibition of crime stories or any story reflecting poorly on the country could not be honored. The rugby match was pending. A minister was en route to Suva. Fiji media were reporting the incident, and local papers in Samoa would report it too; 2AP could not pretend the event had never occurred. If there was nothing on the newscast, 2AP's credibility would be severely questioned. Further, there were Pacific journalists and broadcasters in Apia for the annual meetings of the Pacific Islands News Association and the Pacific Islands Broadcasting Association. They would be listening to what the station reported. The pressure was on.

A pack of cigarettes and a lighter lay on the desk in the dim room. Stacked on shelves in one corner were records, their covers frayed from repeated handling. The reporter's story, on coarse paper, was half stuck in a manual typewriter. The text was light from an old ribbon, but *e*s and *o*s were black dots from the dirty keys. The delay complicated matters: if she did not report the story, there would be a news hole and nothing to fill it with. The reporter had been at the station all day from an early hour. When the visitors left, the reporter sat in the gloom with many facts to expect and few to report.

The next day, encountering her visitors at the broadcasters' meeting, the reporter disclosed that she had ultimately filed the story without getting approval from the prime minister. She got the story right, she felt certain; there was nothing in it that would cause the government concern.

While an observer may be reassured to know that, for all the concerns at play, the news did get reported, the issues of censorship and self-censorship emerge large. Journalists in the Pacific indicate that pressure to shape a story in a certain fashion often originates from government, rarely from business, in part because the pattern of public ownership provides the opportunity and because of politicians' sensitivity to any criticism about their behavior and activities. The effect of this sensitivity as perceived by the media is a more subtle, more effective *self*-censorship, which is probably more typical than the outright editing or proscription of news. Rather than receiving direct governmental interference, journalists in the region describe themselves to be under societal constraints which indirectly control their autonomy and shape their judgments.

"What should cub reporters in Pacific countries know about ethics and professional standards in journalism?" Frederick Yu asks rhetorically in a publication distributed by the Pacific Islands News Association. "This is not a question that can be answered adequately in a brief manual," he concludes. "The answers should come from the journalists and media in the region."[14]

As a practical matter, however, the answers come from government, from politicians and other public officials, and the answers rarely resemble journalistic ethics or professional standards. Broadcasters, particularly those from government-run stations, are caught in the middle. While they must depend on government sources for information, they cannot so easily keep a professional distance. In this respect, they are like beat reporters from North nations who at times feel pressure from sources to shape a story and do, on occasion, give in.

Because the politically powerful are often the economically powerful in the Pacific, even in the best of times politicians have ready access to the media. Radio journalists' freedom from political pressure is easily compromised; they do not take their professional autonomy for granted. After all, in Samoa, news staff have the same civil service status as plumbers. In such context, a mix of news sources, even when the origins are from abroad, provides an important contrast to what gets broadcast locally and, equally important, what does not.

Certainly the presence of extraterritorial news broadcasts, then, is not a neutral event, as postcolonial critique bears witness. Should it not be obvious, the foreignness of language, most commonly French or English, articulates the difference. That media power is uneven goes without saying. More interesting to colonials and postcolonials, minorities, migrants, and exiles is not the transnational role of programs and language in themselves, but the discourse that is induced by their presence. That is, we are made increasingly aware of our own stories and of how those stories are constructed and invented.

In addition, the social context—regional radio—tends to localize the utterance of what comes from afar. The process engages as the listener differentiates among the range of stories to discover the *who, what, where* of journalism on the listener's own terms. That sometimes means accepting what one hears, at times reforming news into one's own story, and at other times rejecting and turning a deaf ear to what is broadcast. In this enterprise, Pacific radio listeners are no less adept than the rest of us.

A local reporter may not tell the same story about nation, economy, race, gender, class, and the like that his or her metropolitan counterpart does. It is the point made in the next chapter—that the story of the storm from afar is not the story of the storm nearby. Journalists are not, however, without intelligence or resources. Sometimes they deploy an asymmetry in stories—their own and those from outside—to their own purposes, finessing ethnic, national, political, and other categories in service of a news story they want to report.

For example, many journalists labor under circumstances in which they are able to report a story only after it has been carried elsewhere. If that story comes from PACNEWS, which has wide Pacific regional distribution, they are at greater liberty to pick it up. News on Radio Australia and Radio New Zealand also grants such license, because these broadcasts are readily received on shortwave radio by local listeners, whether or not the stories are rebroadcast directly over autochthonous stations. When the story in their own culture is out, so to speak, through such circuitousness, journalists feel freer and safer to cover it in their own voice. The foreign report removes a taboo and becomes a peg on which the story the local reporter really wants to broadcast can hang. In this case, the novelty of a local story being reported from afar outweighs the customary demand for freshness.[15] That is, the news has been given a renewed shelf life. Although the story may be stale or unstated locally, the fact that it is of interest beyond national borders gives the event a different currency. Thus the journalist has license to raise the matter anew.

That cross-cultural transmissions from foreign broadcast services occur is less surprising than that they occur with such frequency on Pacific stations that are publicly supported. Given the chilling political climate and recent press curbs in areas across the Pacific, one would imagine that political figures might prefer to silence, or at least limit, outside media voices. On occasion they do.

On May 14, 1993, in "Solomons-Jamming," PACNEWS Morning Edition carried such a case. Relays of news from overseas radio stations were jammed in the Solomon Islands as part of a ministerial ban on broadcasting any item concerning the Bougainville crisis. It is believed locally that the national police used an emergency transmitter to broadcast on the SIBC frequencies at the very moment the overseas relays were aired, producing interference to shut out the foreign news. This case of jamming is exceptional. More often, Pacific governments have moved in the direction of press regulation and not infrequently on the caprice of particular politicians.[16]

The Cost of News

Far more often, the constraints on news reporting are economic. Running a radio station is a costly proposition to begin with, and the news division can take up a large chunk of the station's yearly budget. One of the continuing laments of general managers is lack of funding. At a PIBA meeting, James Kilua, Solomon Islands Broadcasting Corporation general manager, recalled that to increase revenue, SIBC at one time resorted to repairing small electronic equipment and selling electronic parts. In the Norfolk Islands, part of the external territory of Australia, broadcast manager Margaret Meadows complained that Radio VL2NI, a medium-wave station run by the Norfolk Island Broadcasting Service, suffers from revenues "hardly adequate to cover the costs of running the service."[17] Indeed, the station relies heavily on volunteers.

Alligator Creek

In 1993 the Pacific Islands News Association awarded special recognition to Dykes Angiki, news director at the Solomon Islands Broadcasting Association, for his defense of the media in the Solomon Islands. Angiki had taken a stand against a ban on news broadcasts concerning the Bougainville conflict imposed by the prime minister of the Solomon Islands, Solomon Mamaloni. In his acceptance speech, Angiki began by saying how this experience could be likened to walking a tightrope over Alligator Creek, the World War II battle site in the Solomons famous for its alligator infestation. An excerpt from his speech:

> The notion of media freedom conjures a double meaning in the minds of Solomon Islanders who either through involvement in the work of radio and newspapers or simply as listeners and readers come to form some opinion of what media is to them.
>
> To a majority of the nearly 300,000 population who live in rural areas and remote islands, the media—more radio than any other media—basically exists to provide news of happenings in and around the country and beyond, reports about the weather and shipping, and of course some entertainment.
>
> But this simple analysis of the expectation that this largely rural-based audience has come to have of radio broadcasting, a service designated by law as "essential," gets somewhat complicated when we come to consider and indeed deal with a mere handful of people—the country's elite, leaders, and politicians.
>
> They too want news of current events, up-to-date weather information, shipping news, and entertainment. But when we come to talk about the media as having a "watch dog" role, that it represents the voiceless, that the government

as well as the opposition be given equal air time, the argument normally degenerates to irrelevancies, including who pays for the service.

So while the debate on media interest in developed countries has shifted emphasis to focus more and more on the changing role of the media and indeed its future in a technologically fast-changing environment, the situation in the island nations of the South Pacific, Solomon Islands in particular, remains that of a struggle to maintain the basic right and freedom to publish or broadcast.

The situation is further complicated by a fact of history, that in the small island states, radio stations, and in some cases newspapers, originally evolved as part of the former colonial information service, that even today independent island governments continue to exercise and maintain varying degrees of control.[1]

1. Dykes Angiki, Acceptance Speech, PINA Annual Meeting, Apia, Samoa, 1993, typescript.

Throughout the history of the Pacific Islands Broadcasting Association, as evidenced by assembly reports, stations have faced funding difficulties—low revenues, cost cutting, and funding cutbacks. Stations are, by and large, dependent on their governments and vulnerable to a continued squeeze for funds. When they get squeezed, their on-air presence shows it.

News is expensive. The costs include staff—editors, announcers, and engineers; subscriptions to wire services and other sources; news vehicles; tape recorders; sound mixers; shortwave radios; typewriters, personal computers, and more. Travel to cover news outside the capital city can be significant, particularly if an outlying island is concerned. In Fiji, going from Suva on Viti Levu to pursue a story on Rotuma Island, the northernmost island in the country, north-northwest of the capital, is a distance of about 386 kilometers. There are two weekly flights at about F$200 each way. Even a few such trips can easily eat into the slim budget.

Ideally, a reporter would prefer to be on the scene because it makes for a better story. There is no substitute for seeing a situation with one's own eyes and having personal contact with a source, from whom information may have context. News conferences, briefings, and public meetings can be valuable as well. But circumstances in the Pacific do not always lend themselves to active coverage, and the result is that, in many cases, telephone contact is the rule more than the exception.

Even then, it may not be so simple. On the island of Lau, Fiji, for example, water shortages can be severe. At times of the year, villages may simply run out of water.[18] Water must be secured from some distance, on occasion even by ship. Rationing is required, and supplies are turned on for but a few hours during the day. Laundry is done in streams along the coast. In one such drought, after a village had been without water for three months, visiting government officials, before the day's meetings, had to join locals in bathing in the sea. To cover this story, Radio Fiji chose not to send a reporter to Lau, and instead, an attempt was made at telephone contact. Lau has a radio telephone—kept open only during certain hours—but no direct lines. When the news reporter tried to get through, however, the radio telephone operator was off duty. To reach the operator, a service announcement was read over the air from Radio Fiji broadcast studios in Suva. Someone on Lau, having heard the appeal, got in touch with the operator, who then opened up the connection, and the news reporter was able to find an appropriate person to interview for the story.

Such complications notwithstanding, the telephone offers alternative means of access, but the ramifications of its use for news gathering may be unfortunate. In a part of the world where the overwhelming majority of the population is not hooked up to telephone, those who do have telephones obviously represent a certain social and economic stratum, and reliance on telephone builds a bias into reportage.

The cost of news can be apparent in what some newsrooms in the Pacific do *not* have: equipment and basic training. As the public affairs director in another Pacific newsroom put it, "If I could spare someone I would, but some of the staff are high school graduates. If we could spare a tape recorder and find the tape, the guy who goes down [to cover a speech by a politician] may not know the right end of the tape. Assuming he brings something back, it may be unusable."

In the face of such handicaps, even the most conscientious news director will sometimes settle for making do. He may accept as fact the written text of a speech without taping, and comparing against, the actual speech made. Often enough the two are the same, but not always; yet given the newsroom's limitations, there is little choice but expediency. In one case, the news director expected a minister's speech opening a conference to contain little news, to be a repeat of a speech given the week before. So he took the risk of not having a reporter on the scene. The follow-up would be by telephone. "I have to be careful," the news director laughed. "Maybe his car broke down and he didn't make the speech after all." Stories are always a compromise forced by time and resources.

Perforce, then, reporters find themselves searching through handouts, news releases, and statements for something that has news value. They will rewrite at length, not only to get the material into radio broadcast style, but to make fresh something said earlier. They read between the lines and follow up over the telephone for clarifications, cross-checking, and background information. As a matter of necessity, they may fax an official's statement to the opposition, or vice versa, then call for comment.

Why don't reporters get out more if that is what they prefer? Simple unavailability of vehicles is often the reason. At Radio Fiji, where a pool of two automobiles exists for the entire station, the news department must stand in line like everyone else. There is no vehicle at its disposal, and reporters must resort to taxis, which can be expensive, or use the telephone. At the Solomon Islands Broadcasting Corporation, the general manager has a car but the newsroom does not. It is a similar situation throughout in the Pacific, falling under the category of inadequate resources to cover small populations and scattered settlement. To some extent, a Pacific reporter's inability to physically get from one place to another gives an advantage to "official" news and news about officials, news about the capital, from the capital.

The general manager, who oversees the operations of the station, plays a critical role in the allocation of funds that a newsroom sees. To be sure, the GM must balance competing interests of the various divisions—engineering, programming, public affairs, news—to keep the station functioning and economically viable. But in the Pacific no less than anywhere else, the budget is a powerful tool, something that the general manager may use as a lever of control. The same with personnel appointments. Both have serious implications for the news. Several news directors complain, for example, that personnel policies set by the general manager mean they can only afford to hire high school graduates. Indeed, personnel policy—as regards, say, the very number of people in the newsroom—can determine news policy, whether or not the radio station can sustain "specialty" coverage. Too few reporters means only general assignment reporters, with no one assigned to specific beats like parliamentary affairs, business, and so on. This is understandable in a microstate, but beat reporters are to be found in only one or two of the larger Pacific island countries.

In countries where even the general managership of a radio station is a political appointment, nepotism and political favors handed out in the form of a radio job can be rife. News directors have had to accept people in the newsroom with few qualifications for the job. This situation increases the burden of news directors, who must start these appointees with basic training and get them into workshops offered by PIBA and other organizations.

General managers are not one of a kind, however. One news director remarked that his "GM reports to the prime minister's office, so he keeps us on a tight leash with his tight-fisted ways. He knows his political interest." But another felt his general manager defended the newsroom from political pressure and rarely intervened in the newsroom—either in hiring or in news stories. This GM's main concern was that he not be blindsided with a sensitive story that the government might complain about. The greater problem was that, although he was evenhanded in his allocation of funds among the various divisions, there simply wasn't enough money to go around.

A general manager can exert power and influence but he must at the same time be more sensitive to politics and political pressure than are salaried employees at a station who may be protected by labor laws. Even where his station has been privatized, a GM usually holds his position on sufferance. He has to worry about contract renewal, about pleasing a commission or board of overseers whose members are politically appointed. At times the concern is with "public journalism," a sort of reporting that respects the complexity of Pacific issues, providing information and leaving the audience the job of assessing it. And all too often the concern is with maintaining a public front, ensuring that the bad is not magnified, and sometimes not reported at all.

A general manager's concerns with the newsroom are not, however, always unwarranted. The GM from Kosrae was called out of a meeting with a complaint from a government official. The station had just run a program on the importance of education, after which the deejay on duty segued to the Pink Floyd lyric "don't need no education." He says he had to "talk to the deejay." As a practical matter, it is not simply through hands-on management that general managers influence things. The financial choices and overall policy set by them influences who and what gets into the news broadcasts from their stations, even where they do not approve story-by-story what is aired.

In the News

Who gets into the news on a Pacific radio station? Table 3 lists subjects reported on in the evening news broadcasts of the Solomon Islands Broadcasting Corporation. The information comes from a three-week review, during which certain individuals and institutions, such as the prime minister, appeared multiple times. The typical format for the evening news during weekdays is five to six national stories, three to four regional stories, and one or two international stories. Local news staff conduct interviews and otherwise gather news for the national stories on SIBC. Pacific regional stories come primarily from PACNEWS. The occasional international story is likely to be pulled off Radio Australia, BBC, or RNZI, as the station does not have the funds to subscribe to a wire service. Of the 116 national stories broadcast during the first three weeks of July 1994, more than half (54 percent) concerned public officials and government institutions. The remaining 46 percent concerned nongovernmental officials and nongovernmental institutions.

There were few stories about social disorder such as crime. Some nonpublic individuals who had violated, or were alleged to have violated, the law—burglary, for example—were named. This follows a typical pattern in

Table 3
Local People and Institutions On Air (Evening News Broadcasts, SIBC)

Academic	Minister of Posts and Telecommunications
Brownies, school clubs	Ministry of Provincial Government
Churches of Western Province	National Provident Fund
Commission of Inquiry	Nurse
Director of Public Prosecutions	Parliament spokesman
Finance Minister	People of Kwara'ae
First settler, fishing village	Police Association Officers
Foreign Minister	Premier Ratu
Four prison inmates—released	Prime Minister
Government spokesman	Provincial Ministers
Governor General	Public sector unions
Home Affairs Minister	Residents of Honiara
Honiara Town Council Vice President	Sailors (take over vessel)
Hospital Superintendent	Science Society
Industry spokesman	SIBC (on occasion of receiving PIBA awards)
Island resort spokesman	Speaker of the Parliament
Leader of the opposition	Sports figures, soccer stars
Malaita man (accused of theft)	Sports figures, other sports
Man from Dai Island off North Malaita	Teachers Association
Marovo people	Technicians, telecommunications
Member of Parliament	Town Council Vice President
Minister of Health, Medical Services	Water Authority spokesperson

Source: Solomon Islands Broadcasting Corporation, News Archives, month of July 1994.

news reporting the world over, but what marks a major difference from some North media patterns is that there were relatively infrequent mentions of crime—only two or three in a week's time. While most of the individuals in the evening news were public or semipublic figures, such as union officials, teachers, and sports figures, there were also a few "unknowns," such as the "first settler" of a fishing village, who were not violators of the law. A number of nonpublic institutions did get into the news, such as public sector unions, but they received coverage because of protest and disagreement over government decisions or policies.

That news of known government officials predominates is expected, but the mix that the SIBC news staff manages is creditable. In a number of South nations, news is "whenever a minister is present," resulting in something of a cabinet diary. That is, news is what happens to public officials, whether or not it is new or relevant.

News Values

To the journalist, news values may be similar North to South—timeliness, nearness, audience significance, government action, human interest, and so on. There are differences too. Development journalism may be an ill-chosen term, but it is intended to convey the idea that a central function of media in developing states is not entertainment and distraction alone—although certain cultural transmission, local music, for example, is part of the positive reporting activity required of development journalism. While present, there seems to be less news about exotic paradises and uncanny events in Pacific journalism than there is in news about the Pacific filed from industrialized nations. In the North, on the face of it, development journalism might be considered quaint, discredited with its focus on creating a "public sphere," which is a sense of universality in cultures that are diverse and have only recently achieved nation status.

Development journalism is a special category of "new journalism," which looks beyond the professional values of detachment and journalistic objectivity that North reporters pride themselves on. Media critics argue that developing countries should adopt development journalism in the same way that North countries ought to strive for more "public journalism." As applied here, development journalism translates into less cynicism and less negative coverage of complex public events and specifically into positive reporting of economic and social development. The idea is that stories about economic growth, per capita income achievements, and other significant developments of society require purposive news attention and should be reported in a positive light.

Western media, critics charge, seems to focus on conflict, coups, the negative, and the bizarre.[19] But Pacific media has been known to wallow in that mud too. "Man Bites Off Ear" read the headline in one Pacific newspaper, the article reporting the nightclub activities of a Tongan man in a Brisbane, Australia.[20] Obviously, sensationalism sells everywhere.

Development journalism, on the other hand, emphasizes events that reflect attempts "to find solutions to enormous development problems."[21] Various formulas have been proposed for this journalistic mode: Focus on positive social changes, welfare in the largest sense. Focus not only on what has been achieved; focus on people. Focus on the demands and strains of development. In a sense development journalism is the Third World's public journalism.

Then, is there such a thing as "development journalism" on Pacific stations? Dykes Angiki, the director of news at SIBC, answers, "Yes."

Can you provide an example?

"No."

Well, are Pacific radio news values different from news values elsewhere?

"No," he says, "news values are the same North to South. Of course we use our professional news judgment, and we are event-centered because we can't always get out of the station. That is a difference. But no."

Because most of the Pacific—so-called South nations—falls in the economic category of developing nation, one could reasonably expect development journalism on the radio. There are examples. Population, a controversial topic regardless of geography, might be appropriately reported using a development journalism formula. Here is an illustration, as broadcast by SIBC:

SOLOMONS—POPULATION

SPEECH

11.7.94

THE CHIEF MEDICAL OFFICER, MATERNAL CARE, JUNILYN PIKACHA, HAS REVEALED THAT THE NUMBER OF BABIES BORN IN SOLOMON ISLANDS PER DAY IS QUITE HIGH.

INSERT TAPE CUE IN: "TODAY, LONG COUNTRY . . .
CUE OUT: . . . I UMI LONG SOLOMONS."
TAPE DURATION: 22 SECONDS.

DOCTOR PIKACHA WAS SPEAKING IN HONIARA THIS MORNING AT A GATHERING TO MARK WORLD POPULATION DAY.
SHE SAID THE BIRTHRATE IS A RESULT OF IMPROVED LIVING STANDARDS RESULTING IN THE REDUCTION OF INFANT MORTALITY.
DOCTOR PIKACHA SAID SUCH A HIGH BIRTHRATE IS A BURDEN TO THE GOVERNMENT, WHICH HAS TO PROVIDE SERVICES SUCH AS HEALTH AND EDUCATION FOR THEM IN THE FUTURE. SHE THEN URGED INDIVIDUAL PARENTS TO CONSIDER THE SIZE OF THEIR FAMILY.
ENDS ///[22]

This story included a relatively lengthy, 22-second tape clip of the Solomons' chief medical officer's speech, in Pidgin.

Another SIBC story, carried a day later, concerned Lake Tengano in East Rennell, Solomon Islands, the largest freshwater lake in the Pacific. Lake Tengano was being considered by UNESCO for a World Heritage listing, and an EC-funded road, under construction, would connect the lake to human habitation. The story explained straightforwardly how the road was anticipated to improve the local economy and to open up possibilities for ecotourism.

In a North political climate, where debate about the role of media often centers on how to emancipate it from the state on behalf of the market, such a blanket appropriation under the guise of a notion of development journalism is often met with skepticism. On the other hand, North media are also subject to demands for balance and empowerment of a variety of competing voices—women's advocates, environmentalists, indigenous people, gay men and lesbians, the religious right, and, one must add, commercial interests, among others. These demands in the North are honored by media laws enforced by the state and by professional codes of media practice. These are different terms and different demands from those in the public service-oriented South, but even in a swell of deregulation, they are respected and enforced, sometimes in the breach, by the state no less. Similarly, to divorce Pacific radio, public service or commercial, from its role in political society is shortsighted, as much as it would be to divorce the market in those countries from the same influence.

For Pacific broadcasters there is little shelter. If development journalism's doctrines do not undermine independence, the imperatives of profitability and commercialization will. As Darryl Ware, a PIBA media trainer, describes the situation, "When you're a government station, there are always pressures, sometimes helpful and sometimes mistaken, that land on the person behind the microphone. Steering a way through these conflicting demands takes a solid background of understanding about radio philosophies and ethics, particularly when some of the critics neither know nor care about these qualities."[23]

This is but one difference that indicated a Pacific broadcast environment somewhat in contrast to that of North broadcasters. Radio is central to the domestic culture of these Pacific states, a role that is no longer assured in the North. In the Pacific, what gets broadcast is of interest to everyone who listens—and local audiences do listen, if for no other reason than that there are, literally, so few communication channels. As a result, it seems inevitable that journalists will on some occasion run afoul of government interest in reporting the news.

Given the mix of racial, class, religious, linguistic, economic, and other categories that exist within and between Pacific nations, it is understandable that the state would be concerned with messages heard over the air. Many of the political units that comprise the Pacific have only recently known independence, and geography, ethnicity, and development divide as well as unite. While the nature of the state is not at issue here, it is impossible to escape the practical problem of uniting those categories into some governable form. Perhaps for this reason Papua New Guinea's National Policy on Information and Communication, adopted by parliament, is unabashed in stating that "the power of the media to influence is based largely on its contents. Because of this, priority must be given to encouraging Papua New Guinea cultures, Christian values, and promoting national aspirations and development objectives."[24] This distinct appropriation of media for social purposes has been the source of much controversy and has not gone unopposed. To some extent, government involvement in Papua New Guinea as elsewhere is a reflection of the social perspective of the Pacific societies involved. Social restraints on reporters, as mentioned elsewhere, also influence what gets reported.

State ownership and control, direct and indirect, will continue even where there is a mixed system of privately owned media alongside public interest stations that have commercialized. Stations are commercializing in the hope that they may generate much-needed revenue. Where this proves successful, commercialization may bring on market pressures that will offset certain relationships between media and the state. But as a commercial venture, radio is unlikely to be sustained by market forces in the smallest of Pacific countries, for the simple reason that the markets are simply too small and expectations for revenue too great. There is, furthermore, the practical issue of what gets squeezed off the air if six to ten minutes of each half hour of air time is devoted to commercials. In a national environment with few broadcasting stations, those few minutes of commercial air time add up to a sizable proportion of total broadcast time. Where public service radio survives, it must be supported.

Commercials and jingle production will be a part of that support, and inventive economic solutions, such as the Radio Tonga Store, no less. The information heard on Pacific radio, however, will be a public service, or it may not be heard at all, which is to say that without some sort of government support there may be no radio and in some locales no newspaper either.

Commercialization or not, meager resources impose limitations on daily programming, regardless of its nature. Because news is by far the most expensive kind of program broadcast, the capacity of journalists to perform their jobs is practicably constrained, and the trend seems likely to continue. As radio shifts from analogue to digital technology, the terms of radio grow increasingly intricate. One of the saving graces of radio, however, is that as a medium of sound and writing—as opposed to television, which incorporates visuals as well as sound—production can remain of smaller scale. A staff of six to ten can run a radio station, a feat that would be impossible for even a modest TV station.[25]

Radio, Palimpsest to the Region

The circumstances facing Pacific broadcasters are not at all the same from station to station, nor are they similar, North developed to South less-developed region. Not that the North is consistent in this respect either. The presence of authority may or may not mean a lack of press freedoms; nevertheless, radio is often seen as a tool for the advancement of the country and as an extension of nationalist culture—as exemplified by development journalism—even as politicians see it as a means to maintain their position, status, and career.

For all of that, there are unique local media—heard by most on radio—despite the presence of outside broadcasts and news. But even outside broadcasts are subject to interpretation because, at times, those very nonlocal voices open up domestic broadcasts to material and interpretation that might not have been aired in their absence. Asked what would happen if SIBC cut out the foreign broadcasts, Dykes Angiki answered with a shrug: "Nothing." But then he added, "The ex-pat community would miss them, but most probably have shortwave. Our audience would lose balance and a view of the outside, larger world."

In addition, it is not at all clear that outside media—transnational media—have been incorporated into Pacific national media environments as they have in the North. To the extent that national systems of communication have not yet been challenged by internationalization, a clearer distinction remains between what is local and what is not. Foreign broadcasts are, notwithstanding, a North-to-South distribution. Be that as it may, Pacific radio audiences have recourse to intraregional and at times international information that is not dominated by the North: PACNEWS, a news source of their own creation and control. Indeed, this local dimension acts as a more than effective counterweight. Radio is that aural space, a fleeting palimpsest, where the region's voice is broadcast, erased and rerecorded, broadcast again.

Radio retains its intimate dimension—primarily a local sound that one yet hears throughout the Pacific.

THIS IS THE CALL OF THE FRIENDLY ISLANDS . . .

THIS IS RADIO SUNSHINE . . .

THIS IS RADIO HAPPY ISLES . . .

OUTSIDE

The air seemed filled with the rush of something. The house quivered and vibrated, and they heard the thrumming of a mighty note of sound. The windows rattled. Two panes crashed; a draught of wind tore in, striking them and making them stagger. The door opposite banged shut, shattering the latch. The white doorknob crumbled in fragments to the floor. The room's walls bulged like a gas balloon in the process of sudden inflation. Then came a new sound like the rattle of musketry, as the spray from a sea struck the wall of the house.

—Jack London, *"The House of Mapuhi"*

6

The Storm

Bad News

On a small Pacific atoll during the height of the pearling season, a storm rages. Trees are vibrating like tuning-forks, and rain hits like lead pellets. The wind makes it hard to breathe. Our narrator ties himself to a tree, lest he be blown away. His clothes are ripped from his body, but he holds on and he survives. Others are not so fortunate; many wash out to sea and drown. On the island all habitation is destroyed, the tops of coconut trees snapped off and strewn about the landscape.

The account of this storm comes from a writer one usually associates with tales of colder climes, but in this short story, "House of Mapuhi," London's setting is the Tuamotu Archipelago, a group of islands east of Tahiti, in a remote part of Polynesia where the French fifty years later would detonate a series of nuclear devices. The area is noted by some eighty atolls, pinpoints on a map, which stretch in two roughly parallel chains over a distance of 1,400 kilometers (870 miles). In "House of Mapuhi," London documents how, as the barometer drops precipitately, a tropical storm in this little-known part of the South Pacific gathers and dispenses its enormous, terrifying force. Whether from London's prose or from the sheer force of detail, we sit up and take notice.[1]

A symbol in literature as often as background, weather discriminates against none and exists outside social context. The weather spares no one; the weather is not cultural. Because of this apparent neutrality, weather, particularly when bad, becomes a means by which we experience locales that may be faraway and remote and that we may otherwise have no reason to care about. We share in the weather experience, the force of the meteorological event, and in doing so, we share in a cultural event, the objective fact experienced subjectively by a people, by specific individuals.

In news, weather performs a related function. Weather draws our attention by its sheer power and by its indifference. Bad weather is bad news, which is big news, no matter where it hits. But as in literature, while the givens of the story may be basic and similar, the drama is all in the telling, and context to a large extent determines content.

The Storm from Afar

"POWERFUL QUAKE REPORTED, NO ONE HURT ON REMOTE ISLAND"; "DESTRUCTIVE TYPHOON IN THE MARSHALL ISLANDS . . . "—headlines and lead sentences of this sort typify much of the news reporting about the Pacific, an area of the world that comprises about 35 percent of the earth's surface. The topic: the storm from afar. The date: irrelevant. The theme: man as victim of unknown and unshaped forces of nature. The details: probably unnecessary. Indeed, reporting of the storm—any storm, as long as we are not ourselves in its path—tends to be so similar as to be generic, and because of this, details—who, when, where—become extraneous.

Consider, for example, the following account from the *Japan Times* (January 20, 1992):

> TYPHOON RAVAGES MARSHALL ISLANDS
>
> Majuro, Marshall Islands (Reuter-Kyodo)—The Marshall Islands' government has appealed to the United States for food after a typhoon destroyed crops and damaged fresh water supplies in the central Pacific nation, an official said on Saturday.
>
> Neal Palafox, senior US public health officer in the Marshalls, said in an interview that huge waves that flooded the country had contaminated food supplies and may cause a shortage in vitamin A among children. "The disaster is yet to come," Palafox said, warning of food shortages if no help arrived soon from the United States. "The nutrition situation on the outer atolls is so fragile," he said.

In the storytelling rules of the news, an inverted-pyramid convention is characteristic of contemporary reporting; a drama—quick, dirty, familiar—is fashioned from the disaster.[2] The hard facts are part of the lead—the toll taken, crops destroyed, water supply contaminated—and together they constitute a conventional narrative form that we understand as "the storm," a destructive force beyond our control.

The storm subsumes a variety of natural phenomena—typhoons, tsunami, earthquakes, floods. It meets several news values, but specifically it represents the news value of negativity common to disasters, war scandals, conflict, and crime. These negative news narratives contain a central complication. They play on the reader's emotions—fear, pity, awe, sorrow, idle curiosity, the urge to gawk—and carry within them an interpretive code or filter by which we decipher the information. Our response to these stories is anticipated, even as we know what to expect when we encounter these stories. It is not unlike the detachment of the voyeur.

As with most news forms, we expect the storm to have a beginning, a middle, and an end. Where there is disaster or conflict from afar—in distance if not in mind—if the beginning is the hard, unpleasant reality of the event, the middle can be surprisingly wanting. In these accounts, seldom does one find much elaboration on the facts. The range of personalities is minimal. People are not individualized by name or by concern for them. Instead, people are victims, vehicles for the force of nature; they have no voice and are not quoted. In the Reuters-Kyodo dispatch on the Marshall Islands typhoon above, the one individual who is quoted is not local to the region. Usually this is sufficient for our purposes.

Finally, with didactic precision, we look for the storm to draw somehow to a satisfying end: a hero emerging to solve problems left in the storm's wake. Particularly if rescue comes from abroad, that fact is given featured attention. In the case of the dispatch here, we observe that the expected hero is the U.S. government. This is the uplift awaited. With variation and sometimes inventiveness, this narrative form can be observed in stories about the Pacific over and over.

Obviously the actual event of the storm is not so clean or self-contained. But given the state of our interest—literally as well as figuratively—in the storm from afar, reporters maintain an aesthetic distance between the reader and the scene of destruction. The news conventions of objectivity, lucidity, and clarity require this distance. The reader-audience should be witness to an event, not participant at the happening. Under these dispassionate terms, the storm is presented as a dramatic occurrence, the news report centering on a crucial portion of what is an ongoing episode, usually that period immediately after the destructive force has spent itself, when the damage is assessed.

But make no mistake, the destructive force of typhoons on the lives and economies of Pacific island nations can be devastating and wide ranging. Typhoon Namu, which struck the Solomon Islands in 1986, left the country in a shambles that was far more than topographical. Prices shot up 24 percent in a year. Harvests of copra and palm oil, major exports, declined drastically, at the time when prices for these commodities in the world marketplace were falling. Gross domestic product, US$145 million, dropped by 90 percent, remained unchanged in 1987, and did not regain prestorm levels until two years later.

Typhoon Ofa, which struck Samoa in 1990, had a similar devastating effect. Local food supplies were destroyed. Agricultural capacity, primarily in taro and banana, was not restored for six months and then at only 80 percent capacity. Breadfruit crops were demolished, the trees leveled.

A few years later, a tropical cyclone struck Samoa with such magnitude that people knocked holes in the concrete tanks used to collect rainwater, drained the contents, and crawled inside for shelter. In addition to such "usual" devastation, the storm blew the roof off the studios of the government-run radio station, 2AP, and water flooded into the transmitters. Amazingly, the station's transmitting antenna on Mulinu'u Peninsula withstood the storm, and 2AP was able to stay on the air throughout the ordeal. Yet, several years later the station still relied on a portable studio, a trailer, provided by the Australian government.

In the disaster narrative from afar, long-term effects of this kind are rarely found in the news. The action is confined, the narrative complete, complications that follow unnoted. Perhaps the fuller story is too familiar, too unrelieved, lacking really in a hero. The news consumer may weary of the sudden steep inflation, the food shortages, decline in exports, reduction in GDP, increase in government deficit and external debt, the foreign disaster relief, the small direct or declining foreign investment, the widening balance of trade deficits often amid falling commodity prices. The loss of life and suffering inflicted by these acts of nature so far away, while terrible, may be un*newsworthy*.

This distancing of the storm from afar has its correlation in the way environmental issues are currently viewed. While disaster and storm reports in the news have long preceded interest in the environment, the greater sophistication about the causes of natural disasters and awareness of how certain environmental acts—global warming, deforestation, coastal zone habitation, and so on—contribute to these phenomena may influence attitudes. In environmental matters, the difference between a "condition" and an environmental "problem" seems, in some respects, to be related to increased media coverage in conjunction with environmental activism. The mere presence of pollution, for example, does not necessarily promote a condition to a problem worthy of news attention.

Unlike environmental issues, natural disasters are not typically seen as a "problem." Natural disasters—storms—are unlike disorders in the social, moral, environmental, or technological realm. Natural disasters are viewed as a "condition." From afar, natural forces are the agency of action, an act of God, and therefore beyond our ability to ascribe cause, which is part of the drama. An example is "Problems in Paradise," a story from the *Australian Financial Review:* "Six weeks ago, the tiny South Pacific island nation of Tuvalu (population 9,043) lost about 7 percent of its 26 square kilometer land mass during a cyclone. It just washed into the ocean with devastating economic consequences for the island."[3] Closer to hand, where the effects can be felt, the view of the storm is different, and so is the reporting.

The narrative often takes on a personal cast. In the following story about a hurricane on the neighbor island of Kaua'i in the *Honolulu Star-Bulletin and Advertiser* (September 13, 1992), one notices immediately how reporters David Waite and Jan TenBruggencate have narrowed the social distance between the event and the audience-reader. There is an introduction of personalities and appreciably more detail, layered and full, than in the wire-service story about the Marshall Islands typhoon.

> Hurricane Iniki's rampage across Kaua'i on Friday was far more destructive than Iwa's was 10 years ago. As news finally filtered out of the Garden Island yesterday, it was all grim. . . .
>
> "I saw total destruction—it broke my heart," Kaua'i Mayor JoAnn Yukimura said after a 90-minute helicopter flight with Gov. John Waihee across the island's battered landscape. "There is incredible human suffering in terms of loss of homes and dislocation of their lives."
>
> President Bush declared most of Hawaii a federal disaster area.
>
> The storm, which slammed into Kaua'i on Friday afternoon packing winds up to 165 miles per hour, left at least three people dead,

according to Bob Blair, spokesman for the Federal Emergency Management Agency. Another hurricane-related death was reported on Oahu.

A 91-year-old Kaua'i woman was killed when her house collapsed and a 76-year-old man died after being hit by flying debris. A third person was reported to have died of a heart attack during the storm, Blair said. . . .

Two others may have been lost at sea after the storm smashed their boat off Waimea, the Coast Guard said. One of three aboard the boat was rescued, and a search continued for the others throughout the day yesterday.

At least 98 people were injured on Kaua'i, said Phil Palmer, president of Wilcox Hospital, the island's largest. Seven people were hospitalized, said Palmer, who added that lacerations were the most serious injuries.

Yukimura had set preliminary damage estimates at $350 million to $500 million. But after her tour, she said the cost of repairing the destruction could reach $1 billion.

The storm left at least 8,000 people on Kaua'i homeless and inflicted perhaps three times the damage of Hurricane Iwa, which smashed Kaua'i a decade ago, FEMA spokesman Blair said.

"Our initial survey is far from complete, but we expect to be sheltering 8,000 people whose homes were destroyed," he said. Many more homes are partially damaged and may be habitable with minor repairs or plastic covering, he said.

"You might see some tents, but I don't think you'll see tent cities (which cropped up in hurricane-devastated south Florida). People may prefer to stay in their homes while repairs are being made." . . .

Sudden destruction was everywhere.

"I thought it was World War II," said Moro Kaneko of Kekaha. "Boom! And half the guy's house was gone."

Note how background in this article provides a context to a more emotional, personal recounting of events. "I saw total destruction—it broke my heart," the mayor is quoted. Victims become individualized as people—an elderly woman, an elderly man, lives lost at sea, the injured, the homeless, local residents with names. Clearly the reporting is of a real presence, a human event as well as a natural one.

From this close, local perspective, the details of the storm narrative do not simply act to convince us of the likelihood of the action. Wind speed, barometric pressure, temperature, the hard facts of people killed or property damaged would be sufficient for that purpose. The details move beyond mere reportage to spotlight human conflict and suffering. The event is not arrested in time—the period of destruction—but becomes a continuing drama where the quotes demonstrate to us the pathos of the situation, the emotions and difficulties people must endure over some interval. Circumstances unfold. There is immediacy—local people, local color, local facts.

The topic of the story is easily recognizable. It is really no different from the storm from afar, but the theme of the narrative has been altered significantly. A manifestation of nature provides the backdrop, a sort of frame against which human drama is played out. In this sense, the storm is secondary. Human beings are primary and have been thrust into the foreground —something quite contrary to the narrative of the storm from afar, where people, if they do appear, are aggregates and abstractions.

The point here is that there is an inside view of an event and an outside view. Depending on whether the event is near or afar, we tell and read our stories very differently, especially if the afar is foreign, nonwhite, or nonmetropolitan. That is, in the news of the world, most often it is the metropolitan powers—generically, the industrialized North—that most often tell, and consume, the story, and in the telling there is a reshaping and a reordering of the raw data. In this regard, the account of the Kaua'i hurricane occurs as an interesting case in point, as the Hawaiian Islands are not only part of a metropolitan power but also in the North Pacific. Thus, in a sense, we speak to ourselves. If the story is our own, heavy seas, high winds, torrential rain, and storm surge are sometimes only props in the news narrative. When these facts are not the full storm, then who tells the story—and for whom—may make the difference.

In a variation on the storm from afar, the following article, Batiri Batua's "Lost on the Way to Wedding," from the *Marshall Islands Journal* (April 13, 1992), offers yet a different take on the inside/outside view of news. First of all, the reporter has written the story from the perspective of a Pacific islander, for a primarily Pacific island audience. They are *inside.* The metropolitan North is outside.

Tarawa March 27—Six Maiana men who were heading to Tarawa for a wedding function on the 26th of February but went off course and were lost at sea for a period of more than two weeks have landed safely at Nauru.

The men, Utimawa Taken, Konene Biribo, Takarebu Teweti, Roten Kamoriki, Bsiribo Itara and Aboro Tatang, met a sea storm when they were half-way between Maiana and Tarawa.

The sea began to rise, and the wind got stronger, accompanied by heavy rainfall. The aluminum boat could not speed fast enough because of its heavy loads, and have in order to reach Tarawa before it got worse.

When they surrendered, strong currents took them away from land and Tarawa was not in sight. They searched for land the following days but all they saw was the darker blue of the ocean color.

The men were carrying enough food and drinks on board, and have little difficulties while adrift. The only thing they missed was their wives and kids back on Maiana.

The men must have been pretty lucky, because in less than two weeks, they were taken fast by strong currents and wind to the mouth of the Nauru Harbor.

They reached Nauru on a Sunday, and their boat was seen by the i-Kiribati community working for the Nauru Phosphate Corporation. A boat out in the sea on a Sunday at Nauru is a rare sight for the i-Kiribati, unless you are a Seventh Day Adventist.

Only the Nauruans cruise on Sunday for fun. But this boat here is a rare sight and their curiosity actually brought them to the harbor and by Christ, they saw less weakened i-Kiribati on board, they do not see them much on the island.

Straight away someone yelled, they must be drifters, and the crowds drew nearer until the Maiana people on Nauru recognized their fellow countrymen.

According to the drifters, they were taken straight to Maiana mare where they were changed, washed and fed. Later the beginning of the long story was rewound.

The Maiana men have returned home via Tarawa, with new fatty handbags full of new clothes and other Nauru products.

And what about the wedding function? "Forget it," says Utimawa.

> "We have attended a better function, which gave us life experience when you are out in the sea, the opportunity to meet Maiana people on Nauru and stuffs we brought back from Nauru."

In the drama that unfolds, the storm is transformed to something well beyond its physical facts. The reader-audience witnesses less the ravages of nature than the Maiana men cast in a struggle against nature: Caught by a rising sea, strong currents, and heavy rainfall, they flounder helplessly in an open aluminum boat for two weeks. In the recounting, there is little distancing, which makes the story, for those of us who are now outside, difficult to appreciate fully. Yet, unfamiliar though we may be with some details of the story—"new fatty handbags," geographical locations (Tarawa in the Gilbert group in Kiribati), unexplained references to groups of people (Maiana and i-Kiribati), even the use of nonstandard English—the immediacy and the emotional force of the narrative are clear. The storm has receded into a backdrop against which an almost unrelated human drama has been played out—"Later the beginning of the long story was rewound." The subject of Batiri Batua's article is obviously not the high seas and heavy rain.

"Lost on the Way to Wedding" is a moral tale. At a critical time, the men sight land as their boat drifts toward a harbor on the island nation of Nauru, an ocean-distance away from their starting point. Their potential tragedy is transformed into a much larger moment: "We have attended a better function, which gave us life experience when you are out in the sea." In broader terms, the story invites us, its readers, to consider, to participate in, a human experience—a real plight, a problem, a sensibility—not merely an act of nature.

In each of these three news narratives—the Marshall Islands typhoon as reported by a wire service for a worldwide audience, the Kaua'i hurricane as reported locally for a Hawaiian audience, and the storm at sea as written locally for a Marshall Islands audience—the storm serves as a vehicle. But the subject represented, and the mode of expression, changes the closer the reader-audience is to the event. The storm from afar has no cause: weather is an act of nature. But the closer it is to hand, the more aware we grow of frailty and vulnerability. Acts of nature become knowable through human suffering and response.

It goes without saying that news, for an audience outside the culture of the story, can sometimes be hard to grasp. Even if the reporter wants to achieve a wider appeal, so much of the news must be telescoped and condensed that a fuller, global view may be impossible to convey. A cultural compression, for want of a better term, is what is often effected by a reporter or editor, leaving much that is understood and unstated.

For example, the subtext of "Lost on the Way to Wedding" reverberates with the Micronesian tradition of navigation and voyaging canoes. Yes, these men lost their way in an aluminum boat. But the unheard echo is of a common cultural knowledge, of sennit made from coconut fiber lashed to a gunwale, the stain of kukui nut oil, the sap of breadfruit trees bled for caulk, a koa log chipped out and carved for a hull. Yes, these men lost their way, but the unwritten saga is of master navigators like the Micronesian Mau Piailug and the Tahitian Rodo Williams and of canoe builders such as Tava Taupu of the Marquesas, who can still lash a vessel's twin hulls together and know the sequence of turns, through the gunwale strake holes, around the boom and around the spreader. "Lost on the Way to Wedding" does not report news, in the sense of disseminating information or sending a message, as much as it invites the reader to share in an ancient identity, a way of life. From an imagined Pacific cultural space, canoes still regularly cross the ocean, and compressed into news, this storm story reminds us of a ritual aspect of communication.

News is embedded in culture, and the culture provides the interpretive code for news when it is produced and when it is consumed. That is to say, the various news narrative forms—the storm, say, the invitation to travel, or the sports battle—are in fact so culture-embedded to us that they almost automatically yield themselves to a set of expectations invoked by their codes. Our interaction with the narrative form—for which we have a certain anticipation—and the handling of details, the context, provide the answer to the question: What is this story really about? What really is the content? The answer is always more than wind speed or other objective details. *Who writes about where for whom* thus determines what the code will be.

We all want to tell, want to hear, our own story. Myths and interpretive codes shift. Whereas a sports story may be uplifting, may have lessons for overcoming difficulty and adversity, the storm story, which is one of but a few stories, is a reenactment of a ritual of sense-of-community disaster stories—community coming together to overcome shared adversity, hopeless against outside forces but reminded of sense of community in the face of that adversity.

Survivors—Four Months at Sea

PACNEWS carried a "people story" about three men from the island nation Kiribati who were adrift on the high seas for more than four months. The story originated with Radio Kiribati but was edited in the PACNEWS offices in Port Vila, Vanuatu, for distribution throughout the Pacific. The story is written in a rip-and-read format. Novelty is one of the appeals. It was also a "balance" story, a positive note among stories concerning dengue fever, a civil war ultimatum, and a drug shortage. The story, written and edited by Pacific journalists for a larger, nonlocal non-Kiribati, Pacific audience, also contains a social distancing. As radio format demands a compact style, there are no names of survivors and little personal detail.

> KIRIBATI—SURVIVORS: RADIO KIRIBATI, PACNEWS[1]
>
> THREE KIRIBATI FISHERMEN WHO'D BEEN ADRIFT ON THE HIGH SEAS FOR MORE THAN FOUR MONTHS HAVE BEEN FOUND AND ARE IN GOOD HEALTH.
>
> THE THREE, WHO WERE REPORTED MISSING EARLY FEBRUARY, WERE FOUND ON JUNE 5 BY THE POLYNESIAN SHIPPING SERVICE VESSEL *THE SAKARIA*, ON HIGH SEAS 400 MILES EAST OF TARAWA. THEY WERE ADRIFT IN THEIR 18-FOOT WOODEN BOAT.
>
> THE KIRIBATI FOREIGN AFFAIRS DEPARTMENT SAYS THE THREE MEN HAVE BEEN DROPPED OFF AT PAGO PAGO, AMERICAN SAMOA, AND ARRANGEMENTS ARE BEING MADE FOR THEIR RETURN TO TARAWA.

1. "Kiribati—Survivors," PACNEWS bulletin, 2d ed., June 6, 1991 (Port Vila, PACNEWS Archives, 1991).

Someone Else's Other: Pacific News Narratives

We are long accustomed to receiving reports about events far from wherever we happen to be. William Randolph Hearst was an early innovator in communication at a distance by creating the concept of a news syndicate.[4] The Hearst International News Service provided newspapers in various parts of the world with common material, such as reviews, editorials, and reports on science, that could be purchased and published. Hearst's syndicate was followed in 1915 by the King Features Syndicate, of which one "product" was comics. How this development in production of news communications and entertainment material came about is not clear, although it does seem certain that, in this process of the commodification of communication, we all became someone else's *other* in a cosmopolitan/local division of the world. News changed in this process, a change analogous to what happened in comics.

For one, cartoon material became more standardized and homogenized.[5] Clothing, political and religious differences, as well as regional characteristics were blurred, or eliminated, in the process of the internationalization and interregionalization of mass communications. And yet the very nature of mass communications across time and space involves us in a larger paradox. To some extent, we all become cartoon characters in someone else's comic strip. So too with news, a commodity structured for the market or a specific intended audience, most often a metropolitan audience. Where that market is not local, the nature of material alters as the viewer shifts perspective. As this process continues to evolve, with the introduction of CNN and Star Satellite networks, the perspective will shift again. This somewhat platitudinous point applies to our view of what constitutes a storm no less than to other events.

Thus, most news stories, about the Pacific or elsewhere, are cast in a narrative form that is simple, has immediate appeal and understanding, and does not require "education" to understand. At the same time, the audience-reader is both receiver and source of the news content cast within the narrative. That is to say, readers have certain expectations about what media messages should constitute, and are active, if unaware, in appropriating their own meaning from them.[6] Accordingly, the form or the way a story is framed is, to some extent, as important as the content, the purported facts, of the story. This rule applies not only to the weather but also to most news we read.

Types of News about the Pacific

The news that most of us, who reside outside the Pacific, read about those who live within its confines may have minor differences from paper to paper and place to place, but the similarities and specific patterns are striking. These print news categories include such topics as travel as fantasy, the Pacific as a shadow play in East-West conflict, environmental matters, ethnicity and nationalism viewed as civil rights, and development assistance as humanitarian aid. Herewith, a brief review of these narrative news forms about the Pacific from English-language newspapers.

Travel in "Paradise"

A category of Pacific narrative forms in the news media might be termed "Travel in Paradise," as exemplified by the headline "Reporter's Notebook: And Now, Time for a Dip," AP, October 29, 1990. Azure seas surround peaceful, unspoiled islands, littered with white sandy beaches and palm trees. Or as the *Cleveland Plain Dealer* noted, "gambol on the beaches with their bluest of waters, revel in the lush beauty of a rain forest and sip a mai tai as the sun sets over the ocean in a blaze of coral, pink and gold" (in "An Education in Paradise Oahu Wants You to Enjoy, But Also Learn the Islands," October 8, 1995). Bananas are for the picking in these stories. Of course the natives are real friendly. The frame of these travel stories is a pastoral ideal—the South Pacific garden of all-sufficing beauty and abundance, a sexy, spontaneous Eden.[7]

Travel reporting in general, and specifically here, tends to emulate an Enlightenment view of the state of nature and then to veer off in the direction of the cult of the Noble Savage. At its best, the narrative teaches us about a world where life is lived differently. At its worst, the narrative is part of a larger discourse that one might be tempted to call racist.

Regarding the Pacific, travel stories perform a function not unlike "Claude glasses," the tinted, framed spectacles produced in the 1680s with the traveler in mind. When gazed at through the lens of Claude glasses, which were mounted on a handle, landscapes could be transformed into pastoral illusions that evoked the romantic paintings of Claude Lorrain.

In much the same way, we willingly put on our Claude glasses as we scan the travel section of the Sunday paper to indulge our yearnings for the primitive and our dreams of tropical paradise. Reconstructing our own versions of reality, we pursue redemption from civilization. Travelers usually aren't eager to have reminders of daily life or unpleasant social forces intrude upon their mythic island worlds. Travel is not meant to be a field trip.

The form that travel stories take is not the result of sinister intent or pressure from advertisers. While there is no denying that transportation firms, hotels, eating establishments, and travel agencies supply important revenue to newspapers, national travel ministries are known to get into the act themselves. Surely all parties, the reader no less, participate in the conceit of travel narratives.

Except for an occasional travel advisory, the substance of travel sections rarely reflects the news in the rest of a newspaper. Rising suicide rates in Micronesia, undernourishment and hypertension in the Marshall Islands, or proposals to tattoo criminals in Papua New Guinea, to give three examples, do not fit a pastoral fantasy of the Pacific. Nor does the reader expect, or care, to hear about such things. News is not the issue here. In a complicated process where commercial considerations actually play only a small part, the ritual in travel stories is regularly reenacted where readers create their own meaning. Demographic studies have shown audiences to be quite active in decoding information that may be quite apart from content.[8] What we read goes beyond the catalogue of factual material. With the storm narrative, the story is not just the details of weather, and in a travel section, the story is not just the cost of airfare and a hotel room.

East-West Conflict in the Pacific

Until 1990 and the end of the Cold War, political stories about Pacific island nations tended to portray a shadow play of international alliances, of the broader conflict of East versus West, the Soviet Union versus the United States. Fishing agreements, in particular, were subject to such analysis in the news. When, for example, Kiribati and Vanuatu signed a fishing treaty with the Soviet Union in early 1985, they were portrayed in wire-service stories as having "played the Soviet card." This was followed by "French Polynesia Leader Warns of Russian Pacific Threat," AP, August 3, 1985; "US Admiral Raps Pacific Nation's Plans for Ties with Libya," AP, May 17, 1986; and "Vanuatu Signs Fishing Pact with Soviets, Allows Port Visits," AP, February 10, 1987.

Polemic was strong on all sides during this period. News stories in the United States by and large chose not to mention that the U.S. government had refused to recognize new maritime laws or that American tuna trawlers were fishing within the 200-nautical-mile zone of Pacific states without paying compensation. Instead, the economic issue was transformed into part of the East-West conflict as China, Libya, Vietnam, the Soviet Union, and North Korea "gained influence" in the region that had been primarily under Western sway and former colonial control.[9] Stories about the granting of fishing rights were framed in terms of the East-West conflict.

With the end of the Cold War, the tune changed, and many of these conflicts shifted news category. The international political and ideological friction of the 1980s became the economic and environmental stories of the 1990s: John J. Fialka, "From Dots in the Pacific, Envoys Bring Fear, Fury to Global-Warming Talks," *Wall Street Journal,* October 31, 1997. This shift, while not inappropriate, has brought on other obstacles for getting into the news.

Newspapers divide into topical pages and sections. Classification of articles, sometimes called the coding of a story, determines whether that article is deemed an international story or, say, an environmental story, which could then go on back pages. So-called general topics—local, regional, international, occasionally financial, and other specialized topics—are placed in the first pages of "factual" or "hard-news" material. Specialized topics such as business, financial, and sports appear in separate back sections.

Independence came to the vast majority of the Pacific islands in the 1970s and 1980s, but newspaper databases in the West will sometimes list Pacific news under the category of general rather than international news. Even with a country as regionally important as Fiji, this is often the case. An editor of a major daily in the United States, however, is not likely to scan general news when canvassing for international material to include in the day's edition, and the result is that as stories about the Pacific shift category from political or international to business and environment, placement of the articles moves to back pages. This is a somewhat mixed blessing. While the frame is no longer the East-West conflict, perhaps a positive change, articles about the Pacific may now receive less play in the news.

But the larger problem of reporting on the Pacific is substantive. The nations within the region are small and not well known to many readers of metropolitan powers, in addition to the fact that their political status is extraordinarily complicated. Tonga, for example, is an independent kingdom that was never colonized. Wallis and Futuna is an overseas territory of France, existing as part of French Polynesia. Constitutionally it is an integral part of France but with a degree of self-government. Kiribati is an independent republic. The Northern Mariana Islands, formerly part of the U.S. Trust Territory of the Pacific Islands, were proclaimed a U.S. Commonwealth by President Ronald Reagan in 1986; residents are now U.S. citizens.[10] Hawaii is the fiftieth state in the union of the United States. Guam, one of the principal U.S. defense fortifications in the Western Pacific, is an "organized unincorporated territory" that seeks to become a commonwealth of the United States in the way that Puerto Rico and the Northern Marianas are. Niue is a self-governing state in free association with New Zealand, but Tokelau is a territory of New Zealand.

The Cook Islands have truly ambiguous status. While self-governing, the Cooks do not enjoy the status of an independent state under terms acceptable to the United Nations because of links to its former colonial power, New Zealand, which looks after their defense. Yet the Cooks are to some degree responsible for their own foreign affairs. American Samoa is an unincorporated territory of the United States. Nauru, a single oval coral island with rich deposits of phosphate, is a republic. Easter Island, which is part of Chile, is administered as a unit of Valparaiso Province. The Galapagos has a similar status with Ecuador.

Norfolk Island is a dependency of Australia in the southwestern Pacific Ocean, about 1,496 kilometers (930 miles) east of mainland Australia. The Republic of the Marshall Islands and the Federated States of Micronesia have a Compact of Free Association with the United States with separate security pacts, yet are considered sovereign and self-governing. The listing is far from complete, particularly if we add in various reefs, atolls, and the yet smaller islands: Jarvis Island, Palmyra Atoll, and Kingman Reef, which are unincorporated outlying territories of the United States; and the uninhabited atoll, Clipperton Island, south of the coast of Mexico, which is a component of French Polynesia.

Sovereignty is clear only in the case of Fiji, Kiribati, Papua New Guinea, Solomon Islands, Tonga, Tuvalu, Vanuatu, and Samoa. The Pacific is a difficult place to classify—so much ocean, so many islands. In a practical way, given the complicated nature of sovereignty and colonial status, how does a news editor decide where to place stories about the region? As perceived political independence is unclear, the answer is far from consistent or certain. If these political units were truly sovereign, stories about Pacific island states would correctly be classified as international. Because that is not always the case, for the most part, it's the storm, if not the Edenic isle, we read about.

Environment

As changes in geopolitical relations have removed the East-West conflict in the Pacific as a news category ("Vanuatu Will Not Approve Nuclear-Free Treaty," AP, August 10, 1985), articles addressing some of the same issues from an environmental angle have become more common. Nuclear testing by France on Mururoa Atoll, southeast of Tahiti, is reported as environmental protest and outside activism ("France Seizes 2 Ships Owned by Greenpeace," *New York Times,* September 2, 1995); and at other times as a matter of anticolonialism in the guise of antinuclear demonstrations ("Detonation in the French Pacific: Colonialism's Last Gasp," *New York Times,* September 10, 1995). Press reports from outside the region focused on denunciations of the French nuclear tests by Australia and New Zealand, as well as Chile, Peru, and the Nordic countries. If Pacific states were mentioned at all, they were typically referred to collectively as "nations of the South Pacific."

Other environment stories include driftnet fishing ("Japan to Reduce South Pacific Driftnet Fleet," AP, September 19, 1989) and global warming ("Bush Discusses Environmental Concerns with Small Pacific Nations," AP, October 27, 1990).

Many articles detail the vulnerability of the ecosystem, citing most often the "greenhouse effect." On islands where land mass rises only a few meters above sea level, should rising temperatures melt polar icecaps, the danger of inundation by the sea is real. Also real is the concern of residents who depend on fishing for subsistence. As regards nuclear testing, articles will also make passing reference to reports of radiation-related illnesses in French Polynesia ("France, Despite Wide Protest, Explodes a Nuclear Device," *New York Times,* September 6, 1995).

France isn't the only country with a nuclear legacy in the Pacific. This regionally important, sensitive issue was given tongue-in-cheek treatment in "Godzilla's Home Opens Its Arms to Scuba Divers," by Nicholas D. Kristof, in the *New York Times,* June 22, 1997. The article had as its focus Bikini Atoll where the United States dropped twenty-three atomic and hydrogen bombs in the 1940s and 1950s. In a feat worthy of a "reporting paparazzo," Kristof managed to combine a travel story with one on the environment. In another reporting coup worthy of this reporter, Kristof interviewed Imata Kabua, the president of the Marshall Islands, in a hotel bar that he was known to frequent. Showing surprising disrespect and even arrogance, the reporter wrote that the president's "tongue was loosened and he appeared to be drunk" ("Bikini Journal: An Atomic Age Eden (But Don't Eat the Coconuts)," *New York Times,* March 5, 1997).[11]

Within the region, issues surrounding development and the environment dominate the agendas of various multinational institutions. Major concerns include the dumping and storage of radioactive wastes and incineration of chemical weapons. Other issues include control of marine pollution, management of natural resources, management of coastal resources, climatic change, sea-level rise, conservation of biological diversity, environmental education, and management strategies.

As reported by the press of the developed North, however, Pacific environmental issues are viewed with sometimes shocking myopia. Kristof, above, provides one such example of this. Another is the frequent depiction of strip-mining disruptions on the island of Bougainville as economic loss to mining companies and hardships to Australian miners and the copper industry. Rarely is there consideration of the Bougainvilleans themselves, who have borne the environmental burden of the industry.

Ethnicity and Nationalism: Through the Prism of "Civil Rights"

"In a South Seas Eden, A First Taste of Race Strife" read the headline in the *New York Times,* May 1, 1987. The finger was pointed at the snake in the garden—ethnic chauvinism, that is to say, racial conflict with an overlay of nationalism, so the reporter believed. This was the fashion in which the two coups d'état in Fiji were characterized by the metropolitan press.

For the outsider it was not an unreasonable analysis, though perhaps misguided. By now an international fact of modern political life, where few but the most homogeneous nations in the world are exempt, ethnic strife is a prominent daily feature in the news: Eritrea, incorporated into Ethiopia in 1962 after a protracted civil war, independent in 1993; Estonia, Latvia, and Lithuania, former Soviet republics, now independent states; in Germany, reunified in October 1990, Nazi skinheads attack immigrants; Inuits granted sovereignty over 20 percent of Canadian territory; Aboriginal people in Australia awarded rights to large tracts of land in the 1992 Mabo ruling by the High Court, which recognized prior ownership; Slovakia splits from Czechoslovakia; native Hawaiians start an independence movement; Hokkaido Ainu claim the Northern Territories of Japan; the former Yugoslavia splinters; insurgents on Bougainville plead their case against the government of Papua New Guinea before the UN Commission on Human Rights in Geneva. The list is long and varied.

But viewing the cascade of news reports as an extensive inventory of the same essential phenomenon can be deceiving—particularly when events are portrayed as an extension of the American civil rights movement, which they are not. To do so fails to comprehend a wide range of phenomena and confines them within a single category. Ethnicity, it is true, may be a common contingency in these developments, but beyond that a full set of theoretical assumptions is required to link the situations we observe. The point is, Pacific islanders do not constitute unified empirical data—members of an ethnic or a social class whose collective reality exists as a thing and gets reified as an event. Looking at an incident and categorizing it under "Papua New Guinea" and "payback killing" does not close the matter by transforming it into incontestable reality needing no deeper analysis. Ethnicity is the starting point, a concern to be explained. Where there is collective action, ethnicity is the result of the action, not the cause. As we have seen, however, the techniques of reporting do not lend themselves to such understanding or investigation.

In general, a reporter locates the facts in the news by pointing to specific events. The truth claims of facts cannot always be checked, but events can be verified. Sakeasi Butadroka, a nationalist in the Fijian parliamentary opposition, did in fact propose that all people of Indian origin in Fiji be deported to India at the expense of the former colonial ruler, Britain. There is proof of these comments being made. The events point to the facts of racial conflict but do not go very far in explaining them.[12]

This brings us to another feature of much of the reporting on ethnicity. As in the *Seattle Times* story, "Once A Coup Leader, Rabuka Faces Wrath Of Ethnic Fijians," May 15, 1997, the *who* is often cast as either hero or villain. The background to the ethnic story is the narrative of tragedy—a "two-plane writing"—which maintains a parallel structure between the contemporaneous ethnic event and a known ending—most often an unhappy one that culminates in conflict. The parallel image is nurtured in our minds, a hidden narrative that animates our understanding of an otherwise unknowable event about an unknown place. As in the storm, juxtaposed to the present event is a saga whose story line is familiar. The characters in the story are in role too: "We are on course for another explosion in the near future." The ethnic conflict is viewed as a deterioration into barbarism, unless the story turns unexpectedly happy, in which case civilization is seen to be maintained.

As the media view from afar tends toward generalities and formulaic drama, so the actors in these events are described in stock terms: Fijian nationalists, Bougainville separatists, Aboriginal spokesmen. Names and faces are few, aggregates many. The Bougainville secessionist crisis in Papua New Guinea is reported as ethnic nationalism combined with rascalism, implying criminal activity, random violence, and industrial terrorism.[13] The Bougainville Revolutionary Army, whose actions have centered on independence from Papua New Guinea, is identified in Australian and PNG newspapers as rebels, terrorists, brigands, gangsters, saboteurs, criminals. Yet, as many are wont to point out, one side's saboteur is another's freedom fighter.

In reporting on New Caledonia, the French Overseas Territory in the South Pacific, here too the news frame is often race relations—a conflict between indigenous Kanak and metropolitan French.[14] Political independence, the right to self-determination, and the issue of French colonialism are background issues to the usual framing of the news narrative. The facts one finds central to a story—examples of ethnic conflict, in this case—structure understanding. The characterization becomes self-validating as specific details of violence between Kanaks and French colonials are recounted.

A story form may demand particular sources and particular facts. When the story relates to racial issues, a common reporting practice is to go to the police and the authorities for official details and quotes regarding, say, violence. When the story relates to self-determination, however, if the authorities are colonial representatives or government officials, then one can assume that details and quotes will reflect a decidedly metropolitan point of view—usually in terms of destruction of personal property or violence to non-Melanesians. Even choosing to refer to a country by a certain name can affirm a point of view, as in the case of New Caledonia, a large island with outliers in the Loyalty group, rather than Kanaky, which the local Kanak leaders prefer.

Development Assistance as Humanitarianism

"The ODA story," overseas development assistance, is another category of coverage of the Pacific region. Stories such as "Shultz Promises Assistance to Western Samoa," AP, July 4, 1987, are told primarily from the point of view of the donor state. This perspective is maintained whether the aid will increase or decrease. Where news articles are more explicit, the rationale tends as well to be couched in terms of the donor nation—protecting investments in commerce, banking, tourism, shipping, retailing, and strategic interests.

It would be naïve to think that aid was unrelated to strategic interests, of course, but it is a link that often goes unstated. Instead, as reported by metropolitan press, aid would seem to be a purely humanitarian gesture, a theme that might also be woven into a disaster story. Australia, not unlike other developed countries, provides substantial aid to nations and institutions in the Pacific, but seldom are news stories as unsubtle as this Australian Department of Defense report: "Australian development assistance policies support strategic and defense policy objectives in [Oceania]. . . . Such considerations are of particular relevance in the South Pacific where strategic considerations are heavily influenced by the economic security of the island countries."[15]

The aid patterns of the United States, likewise, show clear strategic interest in the Pacific. At least five defense agreements, including the bilateral treaty with Japan, are in the Asia-Pacific region. U.S. defense forces are deployed throughout the Pacific. In the Marshall Islands, elements of the Strategic Defense Initiative program and missiles have been tested. In Palau, the United States has an agreement to use two airports, at Airai and Angaur, and one harbor, Malakal, for military purposes. The agreement also allows use of parts of the island of Babeldaob to train forces in tropical conditions. In the Northern Mariana Islands, air facilities have been upgraded because of its strategic location. The Federated States of Micronesia and Guam similarly lie close to major sea and air routes across the North Pacific. Where aid is given, the strategic link is rarely expressed, but it would not be a stretch to conclude that a country's strategic and military value to the United States has been rewarded by aid under humanitarian guise.

France is also very much in evidence in the Pacific. The French Pacific Forces are based in Papeete, Tahiti. While the United States has not completely decolonized the Pacific, in the case of France, sovereignty for their colonies is elusive. But the French are clear about their strategic interests—the importance of nuclear modernization, for example, exploitation of seabed minerals, and use of exclusive economic zones that surround French Pacific possessions. Subsidies from the metropolitan government to New Caledonia and French Polynesia are significant.

Wallis and Futuna, as well, depends heavily on France for modern infrastructure, services, and aid. Most of the islanders live elsewhere—France, New Caledonia, Fiji. In a typical pattern, most of the workforce of about nine hundred in Wallis and Futuna earns salaries primarily from government-sponsored jobs.[16]

In general, aid in the Pacific remains a vexing issue. The economic outlook is grim: a declining standard of living in the majority of states; high standards of expectation based on emigration experience in New Zealand, Australia, Hawaii, and the U.S. mainland; greatest per capita aid-dependence in the world; and little evidence of moving into self-sufficiency.

Famous and Not-So-Famous People

News the world over is largely about people, famous and known.[17] If the person is not famous, or infamous, then the person has probably engaged in some negative activity—robbery, rape, vandalism, protest, riot: "More than 100 Inmates Break out of Prison, Flee into [Fiji] Jungle," AP, September 23, 1987. But sports aside, many of the stories about the Pacific are not about famous figures from the Pacific at all. They come from elsewhere: "John Paul Beatifies a Papuan Martyr," Alan Cowell, *New York Times,* November 17, 1986; "Japanese Ambassador to Fiji Killed in Car Crash," AP, June 8, 1990.

If an accident involves more than one unknown, and these unknowns happen to be from a dominant national power, the incident may be considered newsworthy: "Six Americans among 11 Killed in Fiji Plane Crash," AP, December 27, 1987. Victims from a metropolitan nation will be named; local islanders, unless they are known, are normally not identified. Few articles that appear outside the region will name an "ordinary person," and unknowns, if they are named, are primarily reported as statistics and aggregates. This remains true the world over.

Studies from the seventies and eighties show that, before a disaster becomes news, a substantial number of people who are not the same nationality as the audience are required to die. Metropolitan victims of a plane crash, for example, require a minimum of five deaths to get in the news.[18] But nonmetropolitans, particularly when a great distance from a metropolitan state, must perish in more sizable numbers before receiving press attention. Given the physical distance, as well as the social and cultural differences, a significant number of people have to die in Honiara, Nuku'alofa, Port Vila, or some other Pacific capital before it makes the news in London, Tokyo, or New York. This is a pattern of reporting that really has not changed in the last two decades.

The usual test of newsworthiness is this: To reach print, disasters and accidents outside the target audience's frame of reference must be considerably more serious than an equivalent disaster within the target audience's frame of reference. The story, in other words, must possess sufficiently great impact to hold audience attention, thereby underscoring the need for content skewed to metropolitan interests. Where these criteria hold, it is more likely a story will appear. In the world of a commercial press, this rule of newsworthiness will assign an importance rank to stories and thus to what gets into the news and what does not. As regards the Pacific, generally well outside the metropolitan scope of interest, it would be naïve to expect otherwise. These priorities at work may help to explain why the storm is one of the most common news narratives of the Pacific we know.

Without Relevance, Silence

Most typical of all is silence. That is, compared to other parts of the world, the Pacific and the island nations that compose the region receive little attention in the world's press. The reason is simple enough. One of the constraints that define news values is "proximity." Proximity can be viewed spatially, ideologically, economically, or culturally. Many Pacific island nations stand as some of the more physically remote spots on the globe. Transportation is difficult or infrequent. For many audiences, the Pacific as a news event is remote culturally as well. The population of the area, let alone of the countries themselves, is small, the demographics particular unto themselves. Gathering information about them is difficult. To take two cases at random, Tokelau has a population of about 1,500, and the Republic of Palau a population of about 18,100. News of these countries would seem then to hold little relevance for many outside the region if for no reason other than the lack of interaction, knowledge, or social or economic interest.

Again, the net result is that many news articles follow ready-made narratives, such as "the storm," which tend to be scripts, or even stereotypes, within the boundaries of metropolitan familiarity. This is not unusual to this area of the world or even to understanding in general. That is, events close to us yield richer material for news narratives for a variety of reasons but in part because messages from the media can be based on more complete and available understanding by the audience. As a rule, we reduce information overload by resort to ready-made stories. They are easily updated, and they are commonly understood and responded to.[19]

Of news values, relevance for the reader is essential for a story to enter the news stream. News that contains pertinent information about events and actions—pertinent to a large grouping—receives greater media attention and a larger audience. If we select economics as one indicator, the Pacific cannot capture a large audience for the press of the industrial world based on relevance: many of the economies, typhoon or not, are stagnating. Primary exports are noncompetitive agricultural products such as sugar or copra. There are extensive social and political problems that preclude development—attitudes regarding land ownership, for example. A number of these small and remote places rely on aid and remittances from nationals residing abroad, often in metropolitan countries. These inflows keep the per capita income reasonably high by world standards, but the figures are misleading. To cite one example, in 1988 the GNP of Tokelau was US$1 million and the total aid flow was US$3 million. Throughout the Pacific, growth is stalled, and per capita income has begun to fall. The birth rate is high. The Solomon Islands, for example, had a 3.8 percent increase in population, per year, through the 1980s. Vanuatu had a similarly high birth rate at 3.4 percent. Employment opportunities are scarce. The public sector is often the largest and in some cases the only employer. The regional characteristics are gloomy for these, the smallest economies in the world. Gloom is not news.

One notable exception was the initial coverage of the coups d'état in Fiji in 1987, which prevailed by the sheer sensationalism of the event. Here was a story sufficiently out of the ordinary to warrant broad outside attention. So too with the 1997 crisis in Papua New Guinea over contracts for mercenaries. Economic news, especially if a metropolitan country has Pacific ties, also commands attention, so it is not uncommon to encounter news of a specific Pacific nation on the business pages.

In metropolitan communities where there are sizable numbers of expatriates from one or a number of Pacific islands, coverage of the Pacific may be given on back pages to meet the demands for "news from home." On the other hand, with only eight hundred residents of Wallis and Futuna (population 14,200) living in the French metropolis, it is unlikely that press coverage in French dailies will be systematic unless a negative issue suddenly emerges.[20] Look instead to the specialty publications, such as *Pacific Islands Monthly* and *Pacific Islands Business,* if at all.

Probably the most up-to-date source of news about the Pacific is the overseas shortwave services of ABC and RNZI (and now the East-West Center's PIR, the Web-based Pacific Islands Report). In its programming RNZI seems to have made a concerted effort to cover news developments specific to Oceania. One of the benefits of both ABC and RNZI news broadcasts is that some stories originate on the scene, as it were. Although there have been cutbacks, ABC has a few reporters stationed in the Pacific. It broadcasts directly from Port Moresby and sometimes from Suva. Often political and other figures are interviewed by telephone and then a recording is retransmitted over the Pacific service. Both of these shortwave services routinely make extensive use of news bulletins from PACNEWS.

There is much talk of global or world culture. These days, one can find cosmopolitans—people who live their lives in a global framework rather than in a national or local context—almost everywhere, even in the Pacific. These people attune to one or more global flows of information; they are in touch across frontiers. But most of these flows of information are extensions of the cultures of major economic powers. Indeed, one might even say that at the present time global news is disseminated from Western Europe and North America. In terms of information flow, which includes news of the world, cosmopolitan dominance could not be more evident. Excluding Australia and New Zealand, the population in the states of Oceania—something on the order of 6.3 million people—totals somewhat less than that of greater Tokyo—which hovers around 30 million. There is no city in the Pacific of any significant size.

In 1992, at a regional meeting in Rarotonga, the five smallest nations of the South Pacific banded together to form the Small Island States. Yet in 1997 the group, composed of Kiribati, Niue, Nauru, Tuvalu, and the Cook Islands, approaches a combined total population of no more than 126,600. While their association unites them on such issues as fishing rights, the environment, and economic concerns, it would be fanciful to expect to see much news of the Small Island States in the developed North.

Spread over a vast ocean, Pacific populations compose rich and varied cultures in no way homogeneous. The cultural diversity and heterogeneity are something of an appeal. This very diversity, however, creates a minority relevance in global news flows. The vast geographical area of the Pacific, with its scattering of population, is constituted primarily of local cultures. It is, if we accept the cosmopolitan-versus-local argument of globalization. But the result is, in the domain of information, local concerns go under-covered, and reportage, on a basic level, suffers, at least from the perspective of locals. And in the world flow of information, if these local concerns are going to be covered at all, they will likely be covered from a perspective outside the region. One unintentionally comic news wire story described the Kingdom of Tonga as "three islands a few kilometers north of New Zealand." This does not bode well for the state of knowledge of metropolitan readers.

Within and without the region, however, developments in New Zealand

and Australia have always been reported quite differently. True, these nations are not always considered part of the Pacific, or even Asia.[21] On the other hand, both have extensive trade relations in the Pacific, and both have sizable numbers of Pacific island populations in residence. Australia, the larger country and larger economy, receives more press coverage than New Zealand.

Even among more developed economies, news flows are discriminating. Japan and New Zealand are a case in point. In terms of trade, Japan received about 17.3 percent of New Zealand's exports in 1989, up from about 14 percent in 1976. Yet no Japanese correspondent is stationed full-time in New Zealand.[22] Indeed, according to the New Zealand embassy in Tokyo, there is no full-time correspondent from New Zealand stationed in Japan either, although there are occasional visiting journalists who stay for short periods.[23] The fact remains, readers of news in both Japan and New Zealand, two not entirely minor nations, likely rely on wire-service stories for news of each other. Given that, what can one expect for some of the more remote spots in the region?

The Case of Niue

There are no nearby islands. Its nearest neighbor, Tonga, is 386 kilometers west. The Cook Islands are to the east, American Samoa to the north. New Zealand, its "patron," is 2,500 kilometers southwest. Niue, situated just inside the tropics, in the central Pacific, stands alone. At 260 square kilometers, about 58 kilometers in circumference, it is one of the largest coral islands in the world. Its highest point is a mere 60 meters above sea level.

Niue has endured a long, sad history of exploitation.[24] In the 1860s Peruvian slavers and British blackbirders virtually depleted the island of its population. Today the main town is Alofi, and the island population hovers around 2,100; it is a decline of 3,000 since 1970.

Niue became self-governing, in free association with New Zealand, in 1974. It has an elected assembly, Fono Ekepule, which chooses the premier. When they travel, Niue islanders carry New Zealand passports.

Employment on Niue is primarily governmental—almost 90 percent is on the payroll of the government development board. A few residents do wage work and engage in subsistence farming. Taro is commonly grown, as well as yams, manioc, passion fruit, and bananas. There are some agricultural exports, probably to New Zealand, but reports indicate their having been curtailed because of inadequate transportation and high shipping costs. The economy is solvent only on the basis of grants, aid, and remittances from relatives who live abroad. Hurricanes, drought, a dengue fever epidemic, and a severe emigration of population have added to the island's woes. Twelve thousand Niue islanders are estimated to live in New Zealand.

If you read a developed, North metropolitan newspaper, you are unlikely to know the name of any "known" figure from Niue except, possibly, that of Constable Alan Makani. Constable Makani was quoted in a telephone interview on the occasion of typhoon Ofa, which isolated and devastated much of Niue in 1990. Or it's possible you might have read his comments on the closing of the nation's only jail due to a cut in aid. But it is improbable that Constable Makani ever caught your attention.

The other "known" figure might have been the late Sir Robert R. Rex, who was Niue's long-time premier.

In any event, public figures quoted or referenced in the news concerning Niue are generally not from Niue but from New Zealand—associate minister of foreign affairs, minister of external relations and trade, and the like. Also, outside business figures are sometimes cited. It would be rare indeed to read the words of a Niue resident in the foreign press.

But contrary to what one might expect, news coverage of Niue does exist. For this tiny, isolated Polynesian nation with a diminishing population, there has been a surprising amount of press coverage. Niue crops up regularly in wire-service coverage. Of course, wire-service mention does not necessarily mean that the articles will appear in newspapers that subscribe to the service. The choice of a story for inclusion in a daily news edition is based on a number of criteria. Often very mundane matters such as functional or technical constraints—deadlines, space, time, money—will determine whether a wire-service item is used. Hundreds of stories come over the wire in any one-day period. Editors exercise choice, and, as discussed, there is a pattern to that choice that we observe over time: in a ten-year period there have been but one to two dozen wire stories, except for the Asian/Australian News wire service, where there have been more than a hundred—primarily because New Zealand papers are included in the database. What did all of this net? Two or three mentions in major U.S. papers over that same ten-year time span. And in Japan? Mostly nothing unless Niue was mentioned in passing.

In many of the references to Niue, disasters, as expected, crop up. In 1990, for example, tropical cyclone Ofa struck, leaving Niue inhabitants stranded. Coverage of this event focused on islanders' isolation and dependency on New Zealand and on the former colonial power's humanitarian efforts on behalf of islanders. What is striking about most categories of

Radio News Broadcast, "Niue People"—SIBC, Evening News

Below is a transcript of a news story read in English and Pidgin on the evening broadcast of Radio Happy Isles, Solomon Islands Broadcasting Corporation.[1] The source of the news is the Pacific regional service, PACNEWS, Port Vila, Vanuatu. PACNEWS is primarily distributed within the Pacific region and carries stories on Niue several times a week.

> NIUE—PEOPLE [ENGLISH VERSION]
> PACNEWS / ABI
> OCTOBER 7, 1994
> THERE'S A MOVE TO GET NIUEANS BACK TO NIUE, BUT TOO MANY AT ONCE COULD CAUSE PROBLEMS.
>
> UNITED NATIONS POPULATION AND DEVELOPMENT AGENCY OFFICERS WANT TO CARRY OUT A RESEARCH PROJECT IN NEW ZEALAND TO FIND OUT HOW MANY NIUEANS WOULD BE INTERESTED IN RE-SETTLING ON NIUE. THIS WILL BE A SECOND STAGE OF A DEVELOPMENT PLAN FOR THE ISLAND WHICH HAS A RESIDENT POPULATION OF 2 THOUSAND, WHILE ABOUT 13 THOUSAND NIUEANS LIVE IN NEW ZEALAND.
>
> NIUE PREMIER FRANK LUI SAYS HE WANTS AROUND 500 NIUEANS A YEAR TO RETURN AND HELP DEVELOP THE ISLAND, BUT ECONOMISTS SAY THIS TARGET COULD BE TOO HIGH AND WOULD PUT A STRAIN ON ESSENTIAL SERVICES. THE UN POPULATION AND DEVELOPMENT OFFICERS HAVE TOLD THE NIUE GOVERNMENT THAT LIVING STANDARDS SHOULD BE EQUAL OR BETTER THAN THOSE IN NEW ZEALAND BEFORE PEOPLE WOULD WANT TO MOVE HOME.
>
> ENDS/////

NIUE—PEOPLE [PIDGIN VERSION]
PACNEWS/ABI
OCTOBER 7, 1994
WAN FALA TING TING HEM STAP FO TEKEM BACK PIPOL BLONG NIUE KAM LONG COUNTRY IA, BUT PLANDE TUMAS LONG WAN TAEM SAVVE KOSIM PROBLEM.

POPULATION WEITEM DEVELOPMENT AGENCY OFFICERS BLONG UNITED NATIONS I LIKE FO KAREM OUT WAN FALA RESEARCH PROJECT LONG NEW ZEALAND FO FINDEM OUT HOW MANY PIPOL BLONG NIUE NAO I LIKE FO SETTLE BACK MAO NAO LONG NIUE. . . .

POPULATION WEITEM DEVELOPMENT OFFICERS BLONG UN IA TALLEM LONG GAVMAN BLONG NIUE DAT LIVING STANDARDS HEM MUST SEM SEM OR GUD GO MOA WINNIM NEW ZEALAND, BIFOA PIPOL BAE LIKE FO GO BACK LONG NIUE.

ENDS/////

1. "Niue—People" (English and Pidgin transcripts) (Honiara, SIBC Archives, October 7, 1994).

reporting on this small island is the point of view, which is predominantly that of the New Zealand government. For example, in stories about New Zealand's aid to Niue, the only known person to appear is typically the New Zealand minister of external relations and trade. No political figure from the Niue government is quoted, despite the obvious interest of Niue in the issue. This pattern of reporting is much complained of by Pacific islanders.

In most wire-service stories, Niue is a fleeting reference, usually in association with political issues that face a grouping of southwestern Pacific island nations, with no specific details supplied about Niue.

The surprising aspect of wire-service news coverage of Niue is not that it simply follows the typical pattern of reporting in developed-developing or center-periphery flow of news—it does so with all too depressing regularity. Most foreign news the world over is about England, France, Germany, Italy, Japan, Israel, Egypt, Russia, China, and the United States. The surprising aspect of the coverage of Niue is that for such a small and isolated place on the face of the earth there is so *much* news. That 2,100 people in what is an economically insignificant political unit that cannot sustain itself without aid and remittances should receive as much wire-service coverage as it does is truly remarkable. Indeed, the findings are contrary to many expectations about the incidence of international news coverage. Perhaps novelty is the news allure of Niue?

Coverage but One-Way View of News

For the most part, the perspective reported of political relations within Oceania are those of major regional or global powers—Australia, New Zealand, France, Japan, the United Kingdom, the United States. Environmental news appears with such viewpoint, as does business news. And there will always be disaster reporting. As is true in many domains of news, the Pacific states will most likely enter the news flow where there is novelty, deviance, and negativity—as long as there is perceived consonance and relevance. Here too, each of these criteria is conditioned by a certain presupposition. That is, the news is dependent upon preexisting knowledge and beliefs about the region.

But this presupposition also indicates the scripts and frames that an audience can be expected to understand and that the press is trapped by. In 1992, Robert Tickner, Australian minister for Aboriginal affairs, complained that mass media did not represent the views of Aboriginal people or their interests fairly.[25] He noted, moreover, the presence of "false stereotypes and prejudice" in the media. The minister's concern about prejudice in reporting on Aboriginal people, however, is likely a minor problem. As the minister conceded, the press is, for the most part, highly professional, and journalists who publicly express their biases rare. The real issue is more fundamental.

On the other hand, information that steps outside the frame of presuppositions is uncommon and conveyed only with difficulty. There are no news frames for a "paradise" in which life consists mainly of subsistence agriculture, primitive fishing, and poverty, or where, as in a number of Pacific island nations, cultures are dying from large-scale immigration.[26] Typhoons, lack of adequate harbors, declining commodity prices, and increased freight costs keep cash economies in a depressed state.[27] Nor is there a frame for the devout, unsexy, Sunday-is-for-religion practice that is much in evidence.

News follows certain scripts or models that contain "known information"—defined at an audience-by-audience level and understood as conventional stories about weather and other familiar forms. Because newswriting demands compression, partial expression in news stories is a delicate art. Where we know the story, the compression of details goes unnoticed. Anyone who has tried to read a newspaper from a country out of his or her cultural understanding, however, has some awareness of the vast assumptions and conventions that embody something we so lightly designate by the generic term, *news*. "Lost on the Way to Wedding," the *Marshall Islands Journal* article cited earlier, is a case in point. The difficulties involved in understanding the content of the story are immense when you do not know the story form, the context. Without comprehension of the news conventions, the text is unfathomable. This is not to say that change cannot come in understanding but that the prejudice of journalists—which can be serious—is an easier problem to solve than the stories preconceived by a audience.

So in this view there are no villains—unless all are villains who live in metropolitan locales and participate in the global flow of news and entertainment. Journalists do not contrive to distort our view of the Pacific. Journalists do report stories from our perspective as outsiders. We simply have to understand that this is not the view from inside, the view that Pacific people have of themselves.

But there are other media differences too. For the most part, Pacific islanders do not read about themselves in the news, nor do they watch themselves in the news—even in their own media. The Pacific is a sea of sound where people are tuned to radio.

KHBC

Aia i ka la'i *ula lae ho*	There in the calm *ula lae ho*
O Keaukaha la *ula lae ho*	Of Keaukaha *ula lae ho*
KHBC *ula lae ho*	KHBC *ula lae ho*
Ka home a'o Pele *ula lae ho*	The home of Pele *ula lae ho*
Ke'anapa nei *ula lae ho*	Sparks *ula lae ho*
Ka uwila makeneki *ula lae ho*	The electric magnet *ula lae ho*
Mea 'ole ia loa *ula lae ho*	Distance is nothing *ula lae ho*
I ka hana ka uwila *ula lae ho*	For the electricity's work *ula lae ho*
Na ka uwila *ula lae ho*	Electricity *ula lae ho*
E hali nei *ula lae ho*	Carries *ula lae ho*
Ka leo mele *ula lae ho*	The singing voice *ula lae ho*
A lohe 'oukou *ula lae ho*	So you all hear *ula lae ho*
Ke hea nei *ula lae ho*	It calls out *ula lae ho*
Ke mele nei *ula lae ho*	It sings out *ula lae ho*
'Auhea 'oukou *ula lae ho*	Pay attention, all of you *ula lae ho*
E ho'olohe mai *ula lae ho*	Listen in *ula lae ho*
Ha'ina ka puana *ula lae ho*	The story is told *ula lae ho*
Ua mele 'ia *ula lae ho*	It is sung for *ula lae ho*
KHBC *ula lae ho*	KHBC *ula lae ho*
Ka home a'o Pele *ula lae ho*	The home of Pele *ula lae ho*

Vickie I'i Rodrigues[28]

APPENDIX A

Glossary, Abbreviations, and Acronyms

A3Z	Call letters for Radio Tonga, Nuku'alofa, Tonga.
ABC	Radio Australia, Australian Broadcasting Corporation.
ABCs	Accuracy, balance, and clarity: the so-called ABCs of professional journalism.
ABU	Asia-Pacific Broadcasting Union, an association of broadcasting organizations in Asia, Pacific, and the Middle East.
AFP	Agence France-Presse, a French international wire service.
AM	Amplitude modulation.
AMIC	Asian Media Information and Communication Centre, Singapore.
AP	Associated Press, a U.S. international wire service.
arbeitervolkslieder	German workers' folksongs.
backtime	The time in a newscast at which each story must start in order to remain on schedule and end the newscast at the proper time.
band	A large group of frequencies of the radio frequency spectrum as defined by the ITU for a particular use; e.g., MF (medium frequency).

BBC British Broadcasting Corporation. Broadcasting service, including radio and television services as well as external service for broadcasts abroad.

BCN Broadcasting Corporation of Niue.

Black Liberation Radio A low-wattage station in Springfield, Illinois, established by Mbanna Kantako to address inner-city housing issues and other needs of local residents. The station is on air 24 hours a day, 7 days a week, with community-oriented programming.

BIG Bougainville Interim Government.

BRA Bougainville Revolutionary Army. *See also* BIG.

bulletin An incoming wire story; a story that has been marked as high priority by a wire service.

CBA Commonwealth Broadcasting Association, an organization of public broadcasting authorities in Commonwealth countries.

clandestine radio Term applied to "unauthorized" stations, usually with some political motive, and contrasted to authorized public or private stations. Pirate stations, on the other hand, usually have some commercial motive. So-called freedom radio broadcasts for a social or political motive. There is no accepted definition of clandestine radio. *See* Radio Free Bougainville.

commercialization Trend in public service broadcasting to accept advertising for some portion of the broadcast day while the station remains in government or public hands.

contact noise A rumbling sound caused by touching or handling a microphone.

dB Decibel.

Deutsche Welle German external radio service.

development journalism News that concentrates on development-related items and efforts, with a focus on positive and cohesive efforts in a society.

external service A government broadcasting service aimed at foreign countries. Such services are often part of international diplomacy and typically make use of shortwave radio. NHK, for example, manages the overseas broadcasting service of Radio Japan. Programming concerns Japanese life and culture, politics and economics, etc. The general service is broadcast in English and Japanese. Regional services in twenty-two different languages broadcast for a total of sixty hours a day from seven broadcasting locations around the world.

FBC Fiji Broadcasting Corporation.

FCC Federal Communications Commission, a U.S. government agency that regulates broadcasting.

FES Friedrich-Ebert-Stiftung, a German foundation whose media department provides media and broadcast funding in developing nations. FES supplies funding to PIBA.

FM 96 Communications Fiji, Ltd., private broadcaster, Suva; FM 96 broadcasts in English and Fijian.

FM 98 Nambawan Call letters for the FM station in Vanuatu.

free flow doctrine A policy of encouraging unimpeded exchange of information across national boundaries without government interference. Contrast to NWICO.

FSM Federated States of Micronesia, including four states—Kosrae, Pohnpei, Chuuk, and Yap.

GM General manager, the top administrator of a radio service; sometimes termed director-general.

GTZ Deutsche Gesellschaft für Technische Zusammenarbeit, Agency for Technical Cooperation, Germany. GTZ has supplied technical equipment and consulting to PIBA members and other projects.

IPDC International Program for the Development of Communications, a UNESCO-based source of information about communications development needs and resources. Established at the 21st UNESCO General Conference in Belgrade in 1980.

ITU International Telecommunications Union, a UN agency formed to regulate wire and wireless communications and to manage the electromagnetic spectrum in the common interest. The basic statute for ITU is the International Telecommunications Convention and is supplemented by the Radio Regulations established by the World Administrative Radio Conference (WARC).

jamming — Electronic interruption of radio broadcasts.

kHz — Kilohertz.

KISS-FM — Rock station in New York City, 98.7 MHz.

kW — Kilowatts.

MacBride Report — Report by MacBride Commission on findings of New World Information and Communication Order, published in 1980 by UNESCO.

media imperialism — Alleged cultural and economic domination of South nations by the industrialized North through a flow of media, primarily from international news agencies and syndicated programming.

MHz — Megahertz.

micro-radio — Term inspired by Black Liberation Radio. Sometimes called pirate radio or people's radio, micro-radio serves a local community through nontraditional and often illegal transmissions from low-wattage transmitters.

mixed system — A national broadcasting system in which two or more types of programming goals exist together. E.g., public service broadcasting and commercial broadcasting.

Navtarang — A Hindi-language station run by Communications Fiji, Ltd., Suva.

NBC — National Broadcasting Commission of Papua New Guinea.

needle time — The amount of time a station can play a portion of copyright recorded music without paying.

NFP — National Federation Party, Fiji, composed primarily of Indian Fijians.

noncommercial station — Term used to designate stations held or run by not-for-profit organizations. These stations fall outside the typical commercial pattern of ownership in Pacific countries, which generally follow the U.S. regulatory model.

North Term used to indicate industrialized nations or high-income nations.

NPR National Public Radio. Created in 1971 with offices in Washington, D.C., NPR produces not-for-profit radio programs such as *All Things Considered* and *Morning Edition.*

NWICO New World Information and Communication Order, a set of goals proposed for reforming communications to make them fairer to South countries. NWICO opposed some market-oriented policies practiced by some North nations. *See also* MacBride Report.

NZ On Air Funding agency of the Broadcasting Commission of New Zealand, established by the Broadcasting Act of 1989. The agency is responsible for the collection of the public broadcasting fee and the allocation of funds to television program production, radio broadcasting, television and radio noncommercial coverage, and television and radio archives.

ODA Official Development Assistance.

Pa'anga Currency of the Kingdom of Tonga.

PACBROAD Technical assistance arm of the Pacific Islands Broadcasting Association.

PACNEWS Pacific News Service, news exchange of the Pacific Islands Broadcasting Association; offices in Port Vila, Vanuatu.

PIBA Pacific Islands Broadcasting Association, association of public service and commercial broadcasters in the Pacific; office in Port Vila, Vanuatu.

PINA Pacific Islands News Association, an association of news people, principally print media but also of other media.

PIR Pacific Islands Report, Web-based news source of the Pacific Islands Development Program at the East-West Center.

PNG Papua New Guinea.

PNGDF Papua New Guinea Defense Forces.

popping Sound resulting from a microphone held too close to the sound source. With voice, *b*'s and *p*'s tend to sound plosive and *s*'s become sibilant.

PPM-meter	Peak program meter on a tape recorder; gives peak readings of recording level.
prime time (U.S.) / golden hours (Japan)	Segment of a TV broadcast day—evening hours—when viewers are at a maximum. These hours vary from country to country.
privatization	Trend toward the transfer of the control over communications media from government domination to the private sector.
program guide	Listing of the program schedule and times of broadcast.
proximity effect	"Colored sound," which gives a voice a warm, close feel resulting from talking closely into a microphone (5–20 cm). Directional microphones can eliminate this effect by using the voice or "S"(peech) switch.
public service broadcasting	Broadcasting in which the "public interest" is given priority over commercial broadcasting. Some authorities have now "commercialized" so that advertising appears but is usually not sufficient to run the broadcasting service.
QSL	Confirmation of reception. Shortwave hobbyists collect verification-of-reception cards—the more the better. QSL is Morse code shorthand for "I acknowledge receipt."
Radio Free Berkeley	Micro-radio station in Berkeley, California. *See* clandestine radio.
Radio Free Bougainville	Clandestine radio of the Bougainville Interim Government. Its shortwave frequency (3880 kHz) is variable. Station has often been off the air due to the conditions of insurgency warfare. When possible, broadcast times were 0750–1120 UTC.
Rarotonga Declaration	Proposed statement of the roles and responsibilities of news media and governments—South Pacific Forum states, 1990.
rebroadcasting	Broadcast material picked up from another broadcasting station. Many stations in the Pacific rebroadcast Radio Australia and Radio New Zealand.
Reuters	A British international news agency.
RFO	Société Nationale de Radio Télévision Française d'Outre

	Mer, a French agency that serves the broadcasts needs of French overseas territories—in the Pacific, French Polynesia, and New Caledonia.
RNZI	Radio New Zealand International.
service announcement	For a per-word charge, personal messages read over the air on public service and commercial stations.
SI$	Solomon Islands dollar. In the early 1990s, US$1 = ± SI$0.32
SIBC	Solomon Islands Broadcasting Corporation, Radio Happy Isles.
slug	Word or brief description that easily identifies a news story. Synonyms are *catchline* or *title.*
South	Term used to designate less-developed countries, low and medium income; sometimes Third World.
spillover	Communication signals that cross national boundaries.
stylebook	Internal guide in newsrooms that specify preferred word usage.
tok pisin	Regional dialect of Papua New Guinea—pidgin.
TV Blong Vanuatu	Government-owned TV station in Port Vila, Vanuatu.
UNESCO	United Nations Educational, Scientific and Cultural Organization, Paris. Charged with promoting peace through education and the diffusion of information.
UTC	Universal standard time (sometimes called GMT, Greenwich mean time), the mean solar time of the meridian of Greenwich, England, used as the basis of standard time throughout the world. UTC is used to indicate the number of hours ahead or number of hours behind UTC. E.g., Tokyo is +9 UTC while Hawaii is -10 UTC.
V99.9 FM	Station in Marshall Islands.
VAT	Value-added tax.
Vatu	Currency of Vanuatu.
VBTC	Vanuatu Broadcasting TV Corporation.

VOA Voice of America, an official U.S. external service operated by the U.S. federal government by the USIA (United States Information Agency).

VU-meter Volume unit meter on a tape recorder, usually marked on a scale from -30 dB to +3 dB. Used to adjust for sound levels.

WARC World Administrative Radio Conference. Convened by the International Telecommunication Union (ITU) every twenty years.

WNYE A Brooklyn, New York, community radio station.

Demographics of the Pacific Islands: Mid-year 1997 Estimates

Country/ Territory	Year of last census	Mid-1997 population estimate	Median age	Urban population (%)	Population density (POP/km²)
Melanesia		5,870,300			
Papua New Guinea[a]	1990	4,311,500	18.2	15	9
Fiji	1996	779,200	20.1	46	43
Solomon Islands	1986	401,100	15.8	13	14
New Caledonia	1996	201,300	22.9	71	11
Vanuatu	1989	177,200	17.6	18	15
Micronesia		495,000			
Guam	1990	145,400	24.6	38	269
FSM[b]	1994	111,800	16.0	27	159
Kiribati	1995	83,400	19.9	37	103
Marshall Islands	1988	60,000	14.1	65	331
CNMI[c]	1995	65,100	26.9	90	138
Palau	1995	18,100	25.2	71	37
Nauru	1992	11,200	N/A	100	533
Polynesia		599,600			
French Polynesia	1996	222,300	21.1	54	63
Samoa	1991	170,700	17.8	21	58
Tonga	1996	97,800	18.1	36	131
American Samoa	1990	61,100	20.4	48	306
Cook Islands	1996	19,000	19.5	59	80

(Continued on next page)

Demographics of the Pacific Islands: Mid-year 1997 Estimates (continued)

Country/ Territory	Year of last census	Mid-1997 population estimate	Median age	Urban population (%)	Population density (POP/km²)
Wallis and Futuna	1996	14,200	17.8	0	56
Tuvalu	1991	10,900	24.8	42	419
Niue	1997	2,100	21.5	32	8
Tokelau	1996	1,500	19.3	0	125
Pitcairn	1996	47	32.3	0	1
All Pacific Islands		6,964,900			

Source: Adapted from South Pacific Commission, *Pacific Population Bulletin* (Noumea, New Caledonia: Statistics Section, South Pacific Commission, 1997).

[a] The figures for Papua New Guinea do not include the North Solomon Province, Bougainville. Because of insurgency, accurate census figures are unavailable.

[b] Federated States of Micronesia: Yap, Chuuk, Pohnpei, Kosrae.

[c] Commonwealth of the Northern Mariana Islands (U.S.).

NOTES

Introduction

1. Graham Balfour, *The Life of Robert Louis Stevenson,* vol. 2 (New York: Charles Scribner's Sons, 1901), 129–130.

2. William A. Hachten, *The World News Prism: Changing Media of International Communication,* 4th ed. (Ames: Iowa Sate University Press, 1996), 157ff.

3. "Mass Media Declaration," Article VI (Paris: General Conference Resolution 4/9.3/2, 1978), and Mark D. Alleyne, *News Revolution: Political and Economic Decisions about Global Information* (New York: St. Martin's Press, 1997).

Chapter 1 Radio Happy Isles

1. Before the 1986 coup d'état in Fiji, roughly half the population of Fiji was ethnic Indians brought to Fiji by the British, originally to work in the sugarcane fields. About 45 percent of the population was indigenous Fijians and 5 percent was "other" —Chinese, Europeans, other Pacific islanders, etc. These percentages have shifted slightly since the political turmoil. Large numbers of Indians and educated Fijians are reported to have left the country. For the first time since 1946, Fijians now comprise a majority. See A. R. Crosby, *Urban Trends,* Working Paper 3.2, Urbanization and Monitoring Project, Asian Development Bank Technical Assistance for Institutional Strengthening (Suva: Asian Development Bank, 1992).

2. Kalinga Seneviratne, "Giving a Voice to the Voiceless: Community Radio in Australia," *Media Asia* 20:2 (1993): 67.

3. Jan Corbett, "Air Heads," *Metro* 141 (March 1993): 62–71. See as well *NZ On Air—Iriangi Te Motu, Annual Report, 1992–93* (Wellington: Government of New Zealand, 1993). Radio Australia also suffered budget cuts; see http://www.abc.net.au/ra/default.htm Internet pages for a variety of information about ABC, including the full ABC charter.

4. William Drozdiak, "As Crises Mount, French Blame U.S., the Usual Culprit," *International Herald Tribune,* September 22, 1993.

5. Daniel Newman, "The Gospel According to Disciple," *DJ,* August 12–25, 1993, 24.

6. Corbett, "Air Heads," 66.

7. *Jurassic Park,* directed by Steven Spielberg, screenplay by Michael Crichton and David Koepp, Universal City Studios, 1993. Stephen Jay Gould, "Dinomania," *New York Review of Books* 40:14 (August 12, 1993): 51–56.

8. UNELCO, the Vanuatu electrical utility, reminds users that it costs 1.6 vatu to listen to the radio for 32 hours and the same amount to listen to 90 minutes of a cassette. A football match on TV might cost 6–8 vatu in electrical charges.

9. One need not require the extreme arguments of Cees Hamelink, for example, to appreciate that a lack of advertising codes poses problems in terms of manipulative advertising and economic exploitation. Baby foods, tobacco products, fast foods, and pharmaceuticals are usually cited as areas where Western multinational corporations exploit Third World markets. Cautions about misinformation are reasonable. The view that citizens of low-income countries are illogical consumers is not, however, well founded except in anecdotal material that might be termed the literature of "false class consumer consciousness." The commercial market potential of many Pacific island nations is insignificant in world terms, and there is a general lack of advertising codes. See Hamelink, *Cultural Autonomy in Global Communications* (London: Longman, 1983).

10. Elihu Katz and George Wedell, *Broadcasting in the Third World: Promise and Performance* (Cambridge: Harvard University Press, 1977), Table A-2.

11. Christopher Mellor and Donna Snell, "New Music Seminar," *DJ,* August 12–25, 1993, 20.

12. Yothu Yindi includes indigenous instruments, including *bilma* (percussion sticks), in its repertoire, and the music combines contemporary rock with Aboriginal music. The heavy doses of political issues in the lyrics do not seem to have hurt the group's popularity: "Well I heard it on the radio / And I saw it on the television / Back in 1988 / All those talking politicians." The reference in this song, "Treaty," is to former Australian prime minister Bob Hawke's unsuccessful attempt to seek reconciliation with Aboriginal people in the bicentenary year of white colonization. "Treaty" broke through the Australian charts, and the band has toured Japan.

13. Michael Webb, *Lokal Music: Lingua Franca—Song and Identity in Papua New Guinea* (Port Moresby: National Research Institute, Music Department, 1993). This monograph is part of the series called Apwithire: Studies in PNG Music.

14. Author's interview with David Palapu, program manager, SIBC, Honiara, March and November 1993.

15. Webb, *Lokal Music,* 53.

16. Don Niles, "Editor's Preface," ibid., xiv.

17. Ruth Finnegan, *Hidden Musicians* (Cambridge: Cambridge University Press, 1989). A number of studies are beginning to emerge showing the relation of "new" media technologies to a thriving local popular culture. An early study is Roger Wallis and Krister Malm, *Big Sounds from Small Peoples: The Music Industry in Small*

Countries (New York: Pandragon, 1984); and more recently, Peter Manuel, *Cassette Culture, Popular Music, and Technology in North India* (Chicago: University of Chicago Press, 1993).

18. Manuel, *Cassette Culture,* 63, argues that the music industry in India was effectively restructured in the mid-1980s as tapes and inexpensive tape recorders became available. Cassettes in India account for 95 percent of the recorded music market. Records and now CDs can only be afforded by the wealthy.

19. Per capita GNP was US$820; Rodney V. Cole and Somsak Tambunlertchai, eds., *The Future of Asia-Pacific Economies: Pacific Islands and the Crossroads?* (Canberra: Asian and Pacific Development Centre and the National Centre for Development Studies, 1993), 46.

20. Mary Ann Cordova, "Music Man Goes Digital," *Marshall Islands Journal* 24:42 (October 15, 1993). Hitkicker Studios produces albums as well as jingles for radio as far away as Palau. Although the population in the Marshall Islands is only a little over fifty thousand, between a half dozen and a dozen local tapes have been produced.

21. John Connell and John P. Lea, *Planning the Future: Melanesian Cities in 2010* (Canberra: National Centre for Development Studies, Australian National University, 1993), 25ff. South Pacific Commission data show, nevertheless, that Papua New Guinea, Solomon Islands, Tokelau, Vanuatu, and Wallis and Futuna have some of the lowest levels of urban concentrations among Pacific countries—0–18 percent.

22. Mel Gordon, "Songs from the Museum of the Future: Russian Sound Creation (1910–1930)," in *Wireless Imagination: Sound, Radio, and the Avant-Garde,* ed. Douglas Kahn and Gregory Whitehead (Cambridge: MIT Press, 1992), 209. On the technological relationship of music, see Douglas Kahn, "Track Organology," *October* 55 (Winter 1991).

23. This phenomenon is pervasive and not solely the experience of low-income countries. See the case of Austria in Kurt Luger, "The Sound of Music Country: Austria's Cultural Identity," *Media, Culture and Society* 14:2 (April 1992): 185–192.

24. Benedict Anderson, *Imagined Communities: Reflections on the Origins and Spread of Nationalism* (London: Verso, 1991). Although Anderson is interested in the historical origins of nationalism, his arguments could equally apply to the Pacific, where many "nations" are of recent origin. The point here is that many communities and cultural entities are "imagined" through media. Quite a different but related view is that of Eric Hobsbawm, who argues that traditions are invented and that the imagined "deep roots" in culture are questionable. Eric Hobsbawm and Terence Ranger, eds., *The Invention of Tradition* (Cambridge: Cambridge University Press, 1984); and Eric J. Hobsbawm, "Nationalism and Ethnicity," *Intermedia* 20:4–5 (August–September 1992): 13–15.

25. See, for example, Judith A. Bennett, *Wealth of the Solomons: History of a Pacific Archipelago, 1800–1978* (Honolulu: University of Hawai'i Press, 1987).

26. Roland Barthes, *Mythologies* (London: Paladin, 1973), 100.

27. The process also runs in the opposite direction as when groups reject modern means of expression and take up "traditional" ones. For example, in Hawaii there has been a resurgence of ancient hula. See as well Jocelyn Linnekin, "The Politics of Culture in the Pacific," in *Cultural Identity and Ethnicity in the Pacific,* ed. Jocelyn Linnekin and Lin Poyer (Honolulu: University of Hawai'i Press, 1990), 149–174. Fred Fejes, "Media Imperialism: An Assessment," *Media, Culture and Society* 3:3 (1981): 281–289, argues that there are a number of assumptions about media impact on Third World culture but little specific understanding and too much attention on institutional aspects from a First World view.

28. South Pacific Commission, *Pacific Population Bulletin* (Noumea: SPC, 1998). Connell and Lea, *Planning the Future,* 38–39, estimate the 1990 population of Port Moresby at 194,295 and the 1986 population of Suva at 141,273.

29. One way to look at media is to look at where media are used. In the United States about 71 percent of all bedrooms and 56 percent of all kitchens are equipped with radio. In any event, radio is used very differently in developed nations, where it is often seen as radio-as-companion, diverting and alleviating isolation and loneliness, with a predominantly youthful audience. See Peter Fornatale and Joshua E. Mills, *Radio in the Television Age* (Woodstock, N.Y.: Overlook Press, 1984).

Chapter 2 Distantly from the BBC

1. Wolfgang Hoffmann-Riem, *Regulating Media: The Licensing and Supervision of Broadcasting in Six Countries* (New York: Guilford Press, 1996), 40.

2. For an interesting history of U.S. commercial radio, and resistance to it, see Susan Smulyan, *Selling Radio: The Commercialization of American Broadcasting, 1920–1934* (Washington, D.C.: Smithsonian Institution Press, 1994); and Michele Hilmes, *Radio Voices: American Broadcasting, 1922–1952* (Minneapolis: University of Minnesota Press, 1997).

3. The Canadian Broadcasting System is charged to "promote national unity, to develop a national consciousness, and to interpret Canada for Canadians." William H. Melody, "Communication Policy in the Global Information Economy: Whither the Public Interest?" in *Public Communication,* ed. Marjorie Ferguson (London: Sage, 1990), 22. See as well George Wedell and Philip Crookes, *Radio 2000: The Opportunities for Public and Private Radio Services in Europe* (Manchester: European Institute for the Media, 1990).

4. Asa Briggs, *The History of Broadcasting in the United Kingdom* (Oxford: Oxford University Press, 1961–1979), vols. 1–4.

5. Mel Gussow, "V. S. Naipaul in Search of Himself: A Conversation," *New York Times Book Review,* April 24, 1994, 30.

6. "National Radio, Concert FM, and Access Radio," *NZ On Air 1992–93 Annual Report* (Wellington: NZ On Air, 1993), 8.

7. For a discussion of public service broadcasting, see Colin McCabe and Olivia Stewart, eds., *The Future of Public Service Broadcasting* (Manchester: University of Manchester Press, 1986); and Peter M. Lewis and Jerry Both, *The Invisible Medium: Public, Commercial, and Community Radio* (London: Macmillan, 1989).

8. Pacific Islands Broadcasting Association, *Final Report of the Sixth General Assembly, Suva, Fiji* (Port Vila, Vanuatu: PIBA, 1993), 7.

9. Percentages compiled from Pacific Islands Broadcasting Association information and Andrew Sennitt, *World Radio TV Handbook* (Amsterdam: Billboard Books, 1997).

10. Marshall Sahlins, *Islands of History* (Chicago: University of Chicago Press, 1985), xi, 26–31.

11. Also in the region, the University of Hawai'i runs KTUH, 90.3 FM, in Honolulu. "College stations" vary in quality and programming. Professional broadcasters find them a nuisance, but sometimes these stations are the only free-form radio around.

12. Commonwealth of Australia, *Bougainville—A Pacific Solution: Report of the Visit of the Australian Parliamentary Delegation to Bougainville, 18–22 April 1994* (Canberra: Australian Government Publishing Service, 1994), appendix 6, 11.

13. Tetsuo Kogawa, "Free Radio in Japan: The Mini FM Boom," in *Radiotext(e),* ed. Neil Strauss (New York: Semiotext(e), Columbia University, 1993), 90–96.

14. The reference here is to Wilbur Schramm, *Big Media, Little Media* (Beverly Hills, Calif.: Sage, 1977).

15. Lois Baird, "Commercialism," *Pacific Islands Broadcasting Association Final Report of the Fifth General Assembly, Alofi, Niue* (Port Vila, Vanuatu: PIBA, 1992), 52.

16. Malcolm Philpott, "Recognizing the Right to Inform and Be Informed Objectively and Correctly . . . But Who Will Be the Judge?" in PIBA, *Sixth General Assembly,* 93.

17. William Tagupa, "Issues and Directions in Pacific Island History," in *Class and Culture in the South Pacific,* ed. Antony Hooper et al. (Suva, Fiji: Centre for Pacific Studies, University of Auckland, and Institute of Pacific Studies, University of the South Pacific, 1987), 98.

18. Sireli Korovulavula, "Culture and the Journalist," *Fiji Times,* March 20, 1993.

19. Michael Robinson, "Fifty Years in the Doghouse," *Washington Journalism Review,* March 1986, 44–45.

Chapter 3 Fax in Exile

1. Associated Press reported, May 14, 1987, that Fiji's population was 49 percent Indian Fijians, 47 percent ethnic Fijians. The remaining population includes other Pacific islanders and people of European and Chinese descent. As a result of emigration after the coups, these percentages shifted, and Fijians are now the majority.

2. The Fijian military is reported to be composed of approximately 3,700 regulars and about 1,000 reservists. Ethnic Fijians comprise an overwhelming majority. Keith B. Richburg, "Fiji's Leaders Negotiate As Coup Appears to Unravel," *Washington Post,* May 19, 1987. After the first coup, the army was rapidly expanded to about 5,200 regulars. At any one time, about half the army serves with UN peacekeeping forces.

3. Charles J. Hanley, "Fijians Said to Plan Strike to Protest Coup," Associated Press, May 15, 1987.

4. Associated Press (story tag: Fiji), December 5, 1987.

5. Imports to Fiji from Japan are about 14 percent—up from 12 percent in 1987. Asia-Pacific Economics Group, *Asia Pacific Profiles, 1991* (Canberra: Research School of Pacific Studies, Australian National University, 1991), 150.

6. "A significant proportion of educated Indian Fijians and ethnic Fijians have emigrated, a chronic shortage of skilled and professional people has emerged." Asia-Pacific Economics Group, *Asia Pacific Profiles,* 147.

7. Keith B. Richburg, "Fijian Claims Coup Restored Pro-West Stance," *Washington Post,* May 17, 1987.

8. Keith B. Richburg, "Fiji's Leaders Negotiate as Coup Appears to Unravel," *Washington Post,* May 19, 1987.

9. Hendrik Bussiek, "Report on PACBROAD Activities 1986–87," in PACBROAD, *Third General Meeting of Leading Representatives of National Radio Networks in the Region of the Pacific, Final Report,* Nuku'alofa, Tonga, November 30–December 2, 1987.

10. Hendrik Bussiek, Southern African Media Project, Friedrich-Ebert-Stiftung, Harare, Zimbabwe, February 28, 1995, personal communication.

11. Ron Crocombe, *The South Pacific: An Introduction,* 5th rev. ed. (Suva: University of South Pacific, 1989), 202.

12. Peter Higginson, Chief, UNESCO Office for the Pacific States, Welcome Address (letter), in PACBROAD, *Second General Meeting of Leading Representatives of National Radio Networks in the Region of the Pacific, Final Report,* Rarotonga, Cook Islands, July 15–16, 1986, appendix 3(C), 28. Higginson continued: "We are aware of many emerging ideas for future action within PACBROAD, but it is most important that phase one is completed properly before burdening the project's structure with phase two, or for that matter any activity other than training at this stage." No doubt Higginson's caution related to the mandate of a UNESCO thirty-member board of state representatives, which determined the International Project for Communication Development (IPCD) initiatives under which PACBROAD was funded. While UNESCO participation lasted three years, it had to be reviewed by these state representatives for each year of funding.

13. There is great irony in the UNESCO go-slow advice, which was delivered by Dik Henderson, the UNESCO expert involved in 1982–1985 with creating the Carib-

bean News Agency (CANA), a news exchange similar to that being proposed for the Pacific. Henderson was in a difficult administrative situation. On the one hand, Bussiek coordinated training projects overall from Suva. But the arrangement between FES and UNESCO was an "understanding" that had been entered into by Reinhard Keune from the FES Bonn office and by UNESCO representative Frank Goodship in Paris without benefit of formal agreement—see reasons below. The local UNESCO officials in Apia were "pulling Henderson's strings," as one observer put it, because they reported to the education office of UNESCO. Henderson's contract, however, and the office to which he reported at UNESCO headquarters, was quite different. One imagines him in an untenable, uncomfortable position, caught in bureaucratic cross fire and conflicting organizational jurisdictions. UNESCO was not the only go-slow advice. John Nettleton of the Asia-Pacific Institute for Broadcasting Development (AIBD) in Kuala Lumpur, Malaysia, also warned delegates against a news exchange, noting that "some kind of political blessing" would be necessary for it to work. PACBROAD, *Second General Meeting, Final Report,* Rarotonga, Cook Islands, July 15–16 1986, 11–12.

14. The focus of the GTZ–PIBA aid project is primarily on the engineering aspects of radio. The technical coordinator, Kettner, based in the PIBA offices in Port Vila, provides training on equipment maintenance and develops materials for engineers and technicians. He also maintains a database to assist in equipment and spare parts supply. Kettner set up a small sound studio at PIBA Haus, Port Vila; it is used for training and for producing radio programs. He performs a number of other services too, including helping PACNEWS set up a computerized newsroom. The German government also provides direct aid in the Pacific, and through the European Union (EU), indirect aid. Figures indicate that the German government provided AU$15,350,000 to the following South Pacific Forum members: Cook Islands, Papua New Guinea, Solomon Islands, Tonga, Tuvalu, and Samoa. *South Pacific Economies, Statistical Summary: SPESS,* no. 13 (Noumea: South Pacific Commission, 1993).

15. PACBROAD, *Second General Meeting, Final Report,* 11.

16. In a sense, Bussiek's position was akin to that of Henderson, the UNESCO trainer stationed in Samoa, with the following important exception. Bussiek was responsible for the overall coordination of training activity, indicating that he had responsibilities over the UNESCO trainer. The trainer, Henderson, also had wider responsibilities than those simply of a trainer. That is, both individuals represented their respective organizations. According to UNESCO's Jim Bentley, Henderson reported "UNESCO professional inputs to the project in the field, and reports to Headquarters." But the Apia UNESCO office also kept close watch on Henderson. Reading between the lines, one perceives competition as well as cooperation between the two organizations. PACBROAD, *Third General Meeting, Final Report,* 10.

17. There are other regional periodicals as well: *Islands Business,* published in

Fiji since 1984, *Guam Business News,* published since 1983, and *Pacific Magazine,* published in Honolulu since 1975 and which now uses PACNEWS as a source of some of its stories.

18. Radio New Zealand International started broadcasting in 1990. Archive broadcast tapes of "Pacific Link" and background information provided by Rudi Hill, RNZI, March 23, 1995, personal communication.

19. Ibid.

20. Telex is a system of communication consisting of teletypewriters connected to a telephonic network to send and receive signals. The word *telex* is a combination of *tel(etypewriter)* and *ex(change).*

21. PACNEWS, "Samoa TV Debate," July 25, 1994.

22. Hendrik Bussiek, Southern African Media Project, Friedrich-Ebert-Stiftung, Harare, Zimbabwe, February 28, 1995, personal communication. Bussiek indicates that he informed Reinhard Keune of what he intended—a training and trial phase at the end of September 1987 and immediately before that to invite news editors to a workshop. "Keune informed UNESCO in Paris that FES would go ahead, 'with or without UNESCO.' UNESCO agreed to be part of the venture." But lines of communication at UNESCO were tangled; see Keune interview, below.

23. Fusimalohi indicates that Hugh Leonard, Radio Australia, also attended the Nuku'alofa meeting in which PIBA was formally launched and the constitution adopted. Leonard was actively involved in the deliberations. Tavake Fusimalohi, June 21, 1995, personal communication.

24. Tavake Fusimalohi retired as chair of PIBA in 1994 under terms of the association's constitution after guiding the association through the initial years. Hima Douglas, general manager of Broadcasting Corporation of Niue, was elected to replace him. Fusimalohi is also active in associated media institutions. The Pacific Islands News Association (PINA) is primarily an association of print journalists. The regional esteem in which Tavake Fusimalohi is held is demonstrated by the fact that print journalists chose to elect a broadcaster to the position of executive director.

25. Correspondence, Hendrik Kettner, acting project coordinator, PIBA, Takapuna, New Zealand, November 7, 1990.

26. Participants had anticipated some of the difficulties the broadcasting association was to face and made contingency plans: Tavake Fusimalohi made overtures to Radio New Zealand to see if the projects might be accommodated in case of expulsion from Fiji. "This contingency plan was approved by RNZ early in 1990 and was put into practice in May 1990." Correspondence, Hendrik Bussiek, Southern African Media Project, Friedrich-Ebert-Stiftung, Harare, Zimbabwe, February 28, 1995.

27. Gerard Sullivan and Victor T. Valbuena, "PACNEWS: A Study of News Exchange in the Pacific," *Media Asia* 16:2 (1989): 99. *Media Asia* is a quarterly published by the Asian Media Information and Communication Centre, Singapore. AMIC also receives funding from the German nongovernmental organization FES; see below. This AMIC "performance appraisal" of PACNEWS provided a valuable ser-

vice beyond its factual review of activities and news content. In effect, the research was a "shield" for local broadcasters in their attempt to gain independence from government interference to report on regional affairs.

28. Hendrik Bussiek, coordinator, PACBROAD and PACNEWS; interview with Victor Valbuena, Nuku'alofa, October 15, 1988; cited in Sullivan and Valbuena, "PACNEWS." Bussiek, however, has no remembrance of giving a 15 percent figure for stories rewritten from releases. Bussiek and Singh indicate that there were no such figures available at the time. Correspondence, Hendrik Bussiek, Southern African Media Project, Friedrich-Ebert-Stiftung, Harare, Zimbabwe, February 28, 1995.

29. "Media Organizations Want Journalism Training Institute," *Daily Post* (Fiji), July 25, 1994.

30. Some months earlier, in Suva, Fiji, Foreign Minister Tadashi Kuranari proclaimed the "Kuranari Doctrine," which increased aid packages to the Pacific. The response was made in part to "counter Soviet moves in the region." (The USSR had recently signed a fishing agreement and negotiated landing rights with Vanuatu and had previously extended its fishing agreement with Kiribati.) Whatever the intent, the policy reversed forty years of Japanese policy in the Pacific and boosted Japan's presence as former colonial powers gradually withdrew. "Kuranari's Oceania Trip Aimed at Boosting Japan's Presence in Pacific," *Japan Times,* January 6, 1987. *Mainichi Shinbun,* August 3, 1989 ("ODA Blocking Nuke-Free Pacific"), reported that aid to Fiji "shot up after the 1987 coup." The article also quoted a Tongan nuclear-free Pacific activist, Lopeti Senituli, to the effect that Japanese aid reinforced U.S. nuclear and other military aims in the Pacific. The relationship between aid and the coup is tenuous. That is to say, the "Kuranari Doctrine" was planned the year before and announced at the beginning of 1987. The coup came later, as the policy came into effect. Aid was for hospital construction and assistance "not closely related to politics." In addition, recognition of the military regime was by a method known as "silent recognition," which indicates recognition of the effective control by a new government without a decision to be friendly to that government.

31. Strong arguments for press controls, particularly on foreign journalists, are offered on various bases. One is that foreign journalists provide unrealistic expectations in the populace. Other scholars express alarm at threats to media freedom in the Pacific. Suzanna Layton believes that closer ties between Asian and Pacific island countries pose a threat to media freedom. "Media Worry over Regional Relations," *Fiji Times,* July 21, 1994. See as well Michael Kunczik, *Concepts of Journalism—North and South* (Bonn: Friedrich-Ebert-Stiftung, 1988).

32. All telex transmissions are from PACNEWS archives, Port Vila, Vanuatu.

33. "Rip-and-read" refers to the practice of radio station announcers who must rely on news wires such as AP and UPI. The output is literally ripped off the teletype, quickly scanned, and then read over the air with little editing—usually in a five-to-ten-minute slot of short newscasts with a limited number of stories.

34. According to PACBROAD's Kettner, equipment included not only fax

machines but also studio equipment. Funds for technicians and training have also been supplied. Phase 1 funding was approximately DM1.5 million in equipment grants to the PIBA partners. GTZ has funded an additional two phases over the years for about DM1 million in each phase. Funding is for spare parts and other equipment, technical training, and advice.

35. In 1995, Shiu Singh was replaced by Jonas Cullwick, assistant editor of PACNEWS and before that news editor at Radio Vanuatu.

Chapter 4 News Sources—Mostly Radio

1. Just to put things in perspective, it should be noted that U.S. National Public Radio's popular news programs, *All Things Considered* and *Morning Edition,* also monitor the BBC and pull stories and actualities for use on air. Thomas Looker, *The Sound and the Story: NPR and the Art of Radio* (Boston: Houghton Mifflin, 1995).

2. Gerard Sullivan and Victor T. Valbuena, "PACNEWS: A Study of News Exchange in the Pacific," *Media Asia* 16:2 (1989): 100, report similar findings a few years after PACNEWS began. An examination of the contribution pattern over several years varies, but again the reasons appear idiosyncratic rather than structural—personality, event-centered, change of editorship or general manager at local stations, recent access to training.

3. PACBROAD, *Guidelines for Training on News-Exchange (PACNEWS Training)* (Suva: PACBROAD, September 14–18, 1987).

4. After Spanish, German, Japanese, and U.S. rule, Palau joined the UN as a newly independent state. Ian Williams, "United Nations: Palau—The Newest Recruit," *Pacific Islands Monthly,* February 1995, 40–45. Ron Crocombe in *The South Pacific: An Introduction,* 5th rev. ed. (Suva: University of the South Pacific, 1989), 196, comments: "Being constitutionally independent does not make a country politically independent, let alone economically, culturally or otherwise. . . . But balanced interdependence between small island states and populous, powerful nations is unlikely, even in trade; much less so in relation to military, political media, cultural, and other influences. Nevertheless, most Pacific Islanders have wider options than groups of similar size almost anywhere else in the world."

5. Sean MacBride et al., *Many Voices, One World* (Paris: International Commission for the Study of Communication Problems, UNESCO, 1980).

6. See chapter 6, "The Storm," section "East-West Conflict in the Pacific."

7. Muhammad I. Aysh, "Third World Communication," *International Affairs* 68:3 (July 1992): 487–510.

8. Frantz Fannon noted, in the context of French Africa, that "before 1954, radio, on the normal level [was] already apprehended as an instrument of the occupation, as a type of violent invasion on the part of the oppressor, was, in the psychopathological realm, an evil object, anxiogenic and accursed. After 1954, the radio assumed totally new meanings. Foreign technology, which has been 'digested' in the context

of the national struggle, had become a fighting instrument for the people and a protective organ against anxiety." "This Is the Voice of Algeria," quoted in *Mapping World Communication: War, Progress, Culture,* Armand Mattelart, trans. S. Emanuel and J. A. Cohen (Minneapolis: University of Minnesota Press, 1994), 102. See as well Daniel R. Headrick, "The Imperial Telecommunications Networks," *The Tentacles of Progress: Technology Transfer in the Age of Imperialism, 1850–1940* (New York: Oxford University Press, 1988), 97–144; Stuart James Bullion, "The New World Information Order Debate: How New?" *Gazette* 30 (1982), 155–165; and Johan Galtung and Richard C. Vincent, *Global Glasnost: Toward a New World Information and Communication Order?* (Cresskill, N.J.: Hampton Press, 1992), 112, n. 2.

9. Tony Nnaemeka and Jim Richstad, "Structured Relations and Foreign News Flow in the Pacific Region," *Gazette* 26 (1980): 235–257.

10. Ian Williams, "Gearing Up for Barbados," *Pacific Islands Monthly,* March 1994, 17. The summit was organized under a formidable name: United Nations Global Conference on the Sustainable Development of Small Island Developing States.

11. Member states of the South Pacific Forum are Australia, Cook Islands, Federated States of Micronesia, Fiji, Kiribati, Nauru, Palau, Papua New Guinea, Republic of the Marshall Islands, Solomon Islands, Tonga, Tuvalu, Vanuatu, and Samoa. The forum has observer status at the UN General Assembly.

12. Charles W. Holmes, "UN Population Conference Opens Today," *Atlanta Constitution,* September 5, 1994.

13. John Lancaster, "Muslims Echo Pope's Rejection of UN Population Document," *Washington Post,* August 12, 1994.

14. Shiu Singh, "PACNEWS Report, 1991–92" (Port Vila, PACNEWS Archives, 1992).

15. In reporting on Russian military actions in Chechnya, the *New York Times* routinely reported on "military claims," adding such caveats as, "Previous military statements issued since Russian troops entered Chechnya in December have often proved incorrect." See "Russian Military Claims Control of Rebel Capital, *New York Times,* March 7, 1995.

16. "Arawa to Receive Government Services Soon," *Bougainville Today,* press release, 2:108 (July 20, 1994). Compiled by Peter Kasia, Office of the Prime Minister, Papua New Guinea.

17. Republic of Bougainville, "BRA Kills 5 More PNG Soldiers in Central Bougainville," statement (March 20, 1993). The Interim Government, Republic of Bougainville, issues press releases from Brisbane, Australia. This particular press release of March 20 was faxed from within the Solomon Islands. The origin appears to be the office of Martin Miriori, Bougainville spokesperson and humanitarian aid coordinator. The Solomons government has since forced Miriori to be more circumspect in his activities, and press packets now come from Australia.

18. Republic of Bougainville, "PNG Troops Are Hit Harder by BRA Forces on Latest Developments in Bougainville," statement, March 24, 1993.

19. Frank Kolma, press secretary, Office of the Prime Minister, Papua New Guinea, "Situation Brief on Bougainville," statement, March 4, 1993.

20. Chief of Operations, Papua New Guinea Department of Defense, "Blatant and Intentional Misreporting of Security Force Members Deaths," statement, March 25, 1993.

21. The title of a book discussing the "first television war," Vietnam. Marshal McLuhan and Quentin Fiore, *War and Peace in the Global Village* (New York: Bantam, 1968).

22. See, for example, "The Rhetoric of News Discourse," in *News as Discourse,* ed. Teun A. vanDijk (Hillsdale, N.J.: Lawrence Erlbaum Associates, 1988), 82ff.; and Roger Fowler, *Language in the News: Discourse and Ideology in the Press* (London: Routledge, 1991).

23. Gaye Tuchman, *Making News: A Study in the Construction of Reality* (New York: Free Press, 1978), 85.

24. Another difficulty for foreign journalists is visas. According to Monica Miller, former president of the Pacific Islands News Association, "PNG is the hardest [Pacific] country for overseas journalists to enter." "Reporting Bougainville Makes News," *RadioActive* 6 (May 1993): 15–16.

25. Alma Guillermoprieto, "The Unmasking," *New Yorker* 71:3 (March 13, 1995). The writings of Subcomandante Marcos are also available on the Internet.

26. The ban was imposed by the prime minister of the Solomon Islands in April 1993. "Media Gag," PACNEWS bulletin (Port Vila, PACNEWS Archives, April 21, 1993).

27. Geoffrey Reeves, *Communications and the "Third World"* (London: Routledge, 1993), 168–184.

28. UN Commission on Human Rights, 49th Session, Geneva, 3 October 1992.

29. Letter from the Hon. Solomon S. Mamaloni, Prime Minister, Solomon Islands, to the Rt. Hon. Julius Chan, Deputy Prime Minister of Papua New Guinea, February 22, 1993.

30. Jill Nash and Eugene Ogan, "The Red and the Black: Bougainvillean Perceptions of Other Papua New Guineans," *Pacific Studies* 13:2 (March 1990): 1–17.

31. Interview, Honiara, Solomon Islands, March 1993, July 1994.

32. "News-net" is a term coined by Tuchman, *Making News,* 21–24. The idea has older provenance.

Chapter 5 In the Newsroom

1. The World Wide English Division distributes the tapes to other Pacific stations besides Radio Tonga: Solomon Islands; Samoa; Chuuk, Pohnpei, Yap, and Kosrae states in the Federated States of Micronesia; Marshall Islands; Palau; Fiji; Republic of Kiribati; Niue; and Tuvalu. The same program is distributed to locations in Asia.

2. See Johan Galtung and Mari H. Ruge, "The Structure of Foreign News: The Presentation of the Congo, Cuba, and Cyprus Crises in Four Norwegian Newspapers," *Journal of Peace Research* 2:1 (1967): 64–91; Johan Galtung, "A Structural Theory of Imperialism," *Journal of Peace Research* 8:2 (1971); and Johan Galtung and Richard C. Vincent, *Global Glasnost: Toward a New World Information and Communication Order?* (Cresskill, N.J.: Hampton Press, 1992). International news flow studies began in the 1950s by International Press Institute and expanded to other areas of media. See International Press Institute, *The Flow of News* (Zurich: International Press Institute, 1953).

3. Tony Nnaemeka and Jim Richstad, "Structures, Relations and Foreign News Flow in the Pacific Region," *Gazette* 26 (1980): 235–257. The authors test a model of international communication flow developed by Galtung and confirm the model. Print media, not radio, is the authors' research focus. Lack of regional news, which the authors discovered was not lack of interest or simply "colonial-structured political networks," was in great part lack of resources for gathering either foreign *or* interregional news. Many of the Pacific regional organizations and communications structures were nascent in the late 1970s when this research was conducted. Intervening years see change, but the audience for print media remains limited, even as it was at the time of the study. Print is easier to investigate, too, but it contains its own bias, particularly in South countries such as those of the Pacific. News flow studies have been important indicators of a complicated process of interaction across various social and political boundaries. But the news flow metaphor has potential to obscure a greater amount of important detail.

4. Letter, March 21, 1994.

5. Al Hester, "Theoretical Considerations in Predicting Volume and Direction of International Information Flow," *Gazette* 19 (1973): 239–247. One of Hester's hypotheses is that "more information will flow from 'high'-ranking nations in the hierarchy of national systems than will flow from those nations ranked 'low' in the hierarchy." As the distribution of PACNEWS now shows, the hypothesis is not now confirmed in Pacific radio.

6. Ron Crocombe views foreign broadcasts differently: "While each [Pacific] nation has national radio, the cost of making programmes is so high that they simply rebroadcast a lot of news and other material from larger nations which make it available free in return for the exposure they gain." *The South Pacific: An Introduction,* 5th rev. ed. (Suva: University of the South Pacific, 1989), 201. Crocombe's observation lacks precision, but his point that the balance between interdependence and dependence is weighted against island states is well taken.

7. 'I. Futa Helu, "Democracy Bug Bites Tonga," in *Culture and Democracy in the South Pacific,* ed. Ron Crocombe et al. (Suva: Institute for Pacific Studies, University of the South Pacific, 1992), 146.

8. "A Predictable Pattern," *Tonga Chronicle,* February 11, 1993.

9. Futa Helu, "Are Tonga's MP's under Persecution?" *Pacific Islands Monthly,*

June 1994, 33. Philip Shenon, "Singapore Court Finds a U.S. Scholar and Newspaper Guilty of Contempt," *New York Times,* January 18, 1995.

10. "Tonga—Media," PACNEWS First Edition, November 2, 1993. The Speaker's argument was that privilege from prosecution for publishing statements made during parliamentary proceedings should be removed, because a member could be defamed in the House and the defamation published or transmitted without liability.

11. Ulafala Aiavao, "My View: How to Score Samoa's Political Game," *Pacific Islands Business,* July 1994, 21.

12. Rusiate Mataika, "Family Objects to Samoan Peace Bid," *Fiji Times,* July 8, 1994.

13. Still part of Fijian culture, a *tabua* or whale's tooth is presented as a show of respect and sincerity or at other times as a token of esteem or atonement, as in the present example. *Tabua* were traditionally rare items, received in trade with Tonga or sometimes obtained when a sperm whale washed ashore.

14. Frederick T. C. Yu et al., *Get It Right, Write It Tight: The Beginning Reporter's Handbook* (Honolulu: East-West Center, Institute for Culture and Communication, 1985), 84.

15. In fact, some Pacific journalists are not above sending a story to a colleague who in turn reports it for them. A former AP bureau chief reported a similar practice in South America when he was there during the dictatorship after Allende. Robert Ohman recalls occasionally sending stories that had been written by a Chilean colleague to the New York bureau under his own name. Had the story been published under the Chilean reporter's own byline, he would have found himself in jeopardy. The stories would be translated into English for transmission to New York; in New York, the Latin America desk translated the stories back into Spanish and sent them out as New York wire-service stories, which could then be picked up by papers in South America.

Japanese journalists call this process *gaiatsu* (foreign pressure). For various reasons, a Japanese paper may not want to be first to report a story, but if it is reported elsewhere, particularly in the *New York Times* or the *Washington Post,* then the story can be picked up locally.

16. This has been the case in Papua New Guinea, Niue, Fiji, Tonga, Vanuatu, and Samoa, among others. The survey of measures of broadcast freedom and press ratings, issued annually by the media research organization Freedom House, New York City, lists Tonga, Vanuatu, and Fiji as having "partly free" presses. Other measures for the same states indicate considerably less freedom than in the rest of the Pacific. In an editorial, "The Media Freedom Revisited," *Fiji Times,* July 22, 1997, the paper noted that "in developing countries, freedom of the media sometimes depends on the whims of the governing party of parties."

17. PIBA, *Sixth General Assembly, Final Report,* Suva, Fiji, 1993, 8, 11.

18. Netani Rika, "Water Crisis Hits Islands in Lau," *Fiji Times,* July 29, 1994.

19. "The press nearly always magnifies the bad and underplays the good," so the charge goes. William Glaberson, "The New Press Criticism: News and the Enemy of Hope," *New York Times,* October 9, 1994. One problem with development journalism is that while the "developmental role" of a journalist ideally encompasses criticism, politicians and officials associated with governmental institutions concerned with development do not see the journalist's role in the same way. Criticism often goes by the board where media are government controlled.

20. *The Solomons Voice,* July 15, 1994.

21. Paul A. V. Ansah, "International News: Mutual Responsibilities of Developed and Developing Nations," in *World Communications: A Handbook,* ed. George Gerbner and Marsha Siefert (New York: Longman, 1984), 86.

22. SIBC Evening News (Honiara, SIBC News Archives, July 11, 1994).

23. Comment by Darryl Ware, PIBA announcing and presentation trainer, "It's All in the Timing," *RadioActive* 12 (December 1994): 8.

24. Quoted in "PNG Media Freedom Comes under Threat," *Pacific Islands Monthly,* May 1994, 9.

25. The Cook Islands Broadcasting Corporation provides an illustrative case of the difference between television and radio. TV is in the Cook Islands because it was an election promise of the ruling party led by Sir Geoffrey Henry. But the station is only on the air from 5 P.M. until 10:30 or 11 P.M. daily. There is a news staff of six and a production staff of thirteen, not including management. Weekdays there is a half hour of local news and a half hour of local cultural programming. Staff time has to be devoted to commercial production. In cooperation with TV New Zealand Pacific Service, imported programs, including sports, are used to fill most of the day's programming slots. Radio production is far less labor and technology intensive than television. "Station Profile: Cook Islands Broadcasting Corp.," *RadioActive* 5 (January 1993): 10–11. (CIBC has since become privatized.)

Chapter 6 The Storm

1. "The House of Mapuhi," in A. Grove Day, ed., *Jack London: South Sea Tales* (Honolulu: Mutual Publishing Paperbacks, 1990), 25. Technically, London is writing about a tropical cyclone, the correct term for a storm in the South Pacific, which should be substituted for the word *typhoon* or *hurricane.* The term *typhoon* is used to designate tropical cyclones occurring in the region from the Philippines to the north. *Hurricanes*—a similar weather phenomenon—are Atlantic and Caribbean storms with winds greater than 74 miles per hour. The Tuamotu Archipelago came under French protection in 1844 and was later annexed as part of French Polynesia in 1880.

2. The inverted-pyramid style is a reporting narrative convention in which facts or documentation in a news story are provided in decreasing order of importance. In general, there is considered to be a descending order of importance in a news story,

starting with the lead sentence and paragraph. In this manner, stories are fit into the available space with paragraphs at the bottom of a story omitted as editors see fit.

3. Geoffrey Barker, "Problems in Paradise," *Australian Financial Review,* May 12, 1997.

4. Early communication at a distance was primarily about financial and commercial information. Some of the beginning services were those of the Frenchman Havas (1835), the German Wolff (1849), and the Englishman Reuters (1851). In September 1866 a reporter from the *New York Herald* used the trans-Atlantic marine telegraphic cable to send a message about the Austrian defeat at Sadowa. This scoop, reportedly the first use of cable communications in this fashion, cost the reporter's paper 36,000 francs—an unbelievable sum at the time. Armand Mattelart, *La Communication-monde: Histoire des idées et des strategies* (Paris: Éditions la Dévouverte, 1992), 23.

5. R. Gubern, *El Lenguage de los Comics* (Barcelona: Ediciones Peninsula, 1974), quoted in Mattelart, *La Communication-monde,* 26.

6. J. Lull, *World Families Watch Television* (Beverly Hills, Calif.: Sage, 1988); and Stuart Hall et al., eds., *Culture, Media, Language* (London: Hutchinson, 1980).

7. Marshall Berman, *All That Is Solid Melts into Air: The Experience of Modernity* (New York: Simon & Schuster, 1982), calls this the "pastoral vision."

8. Examples are R. Hodge and D. Tripp, *Children and Television* (London: Polity Press, 1987); and D. Miller, "*The Young and the Restless* in Trinidad: A Case of the Local and the Global in Mass Consumption," in *Consuming Technologies: Media and Information in Domestic Spaces,* ed. Roger Silverstone and Eric Hirsch (London: Routledge, 1992), 163–182.

9. News characterization within the Pacific varied, but reports were more balanced in presenting matters in terms of Russian willingness for economic cooperation. See, for example, Griff Johnson, "Soviet Talks on Trade for Micronesian, Yes," *Pacific Islands Monthly,* July 1990; and Kai M. Schellhorn, "Politics in the South Pacific Region," *Contemporary Southeast Asia* 13:2 (September 1991): 188–199.

10. The U.S. Trust Territory of the Pacific Islands ended in 1986, although Palau continued to retain its status as a trust territory through 1994. In 1947 the United Nations authorized the U.S. trusteeship in the western Pacific of territory seized from Japan during World War II. Although there was an elected territorial congress, the governor was appointed. During the 1970s, districts that later became self-governing were formed. The areas are the Commonwealth of the Northern Marianas; the Federated States of Micronesia (Kosrae, Pohnpei, Chuuk, and Yap); the Republic of the Marshall Islands; and the Republic of Palau. With the exception of the Northern Marianas, all have a Compact of Free Association with the United States. Except for defense, they are fully self-governing.

11. For the Marshallese view of the *Times* "media editorializing," you would have to look elsewhere: Griff Johnson, "We're Not Anti-US, Says Marshalls," *Pacific Islands Monthly* (July 1997): 24–26. In contrast to the frivolous article by the *New*

York Times reporter, *PIM* dealt with more substantive issues of relations between the two sovereign nations.

12. Craig Skehan, "Land of Discontent," *Pacific Islands Monthly,* April 1993, 20–23. Out-of-region press continues to reinforce stereotypes of Fijians against Indians when the more interesting perspective is the internal shifts in chiefly power and influence.

13. Suzanna Layton, "Fuzzy-Wuzzy Devils: Mass Media and the Bougainville Crisis," *Contemporary Pacific,* 4:2 (Spring 1992), 299–323.

14. Makoto Katsumata, "Decolonization of New Caledonia and Independence," in *Prospects for Demilitarization and Autonomy in the South Pacific,* ed. Yukio Satow (Hiroshima: Institute for Peace Science, Hiroshima University, 1991).

15. Australia Department of Defense, *Australia's Defense Relations with the South Pacific,* Submission to the Joint Committee on Foreign Affairs and Defense Inquiry into Australia's Relations with the South Pacific, Hansard Report, vol. 5 (Canberra: Government Printing Office, 1987), 2ff.

16. Stephen Henningham, "Keeping the Tricolor Flying: The French Pacific into the 1990s," *Contemporary Pacific* 1:1–2 (Spring and Fall 1989): 97–132.

17. Herbert J. Gans, *Deciding What's News: A Study of CBS Evening News, NBC Nightly News, Newsweek, and Time* (New York: Viking, 1979).

18. Ibid., 36. See as well Philip Schlessinger, *Putting "Reality" Together* (London: Constable Press, 1978); and M. Rosenbaum, *Coups and Earthquakes: Reporting the World to America* (New York: Harper & Row, 1981).

19. Media specialists refer to this notion as "consonance." That is, news must partake of certain shared values, norms, and attitudes of the public to whom stories are directed.

20. In 1986 a twenty-six-hour state of emergency was declared when there was a brief disagreement between the French government and local traditional leaders concerning the expulsion of the second-ranking French official. Paramilitary police were sent from Noumea. Henningham, "Keeping the Tricolor Flying," 111. Wallis and Futuna briefly entered the news.

21. Masahiko Ebashi, *New Zealand Links with Asia,* Working Paper 92/3 (Wellington: New Zealand Institute of Economic Research, 1992), 4.

22. Ibid., 9. Professor Ebashi indicates that information on New Zealand in Japan is limited. "Since there is no Japanese correspondent resident in NZ, JETRO's *Daily Trade Bulletin,* which has a limited circulation among business people, is so far the only publication on NZ economy in Japan." Trade figures ibid., Table 1, p. 12.

23. The New Zealand–Japan Foundation established a media scholarship to enable New Zealand journalists to visit Japan for a two-week period each year to increase familiarity with Japan and the New Zealand–Japan relationship. Correspondence, Ian de Clive-Lowe, public affairs officer, New Zealand embassy, Tokyo, October 14, 1992.

24. Fifita Talagi, "Early European Contacts," in *Niue: A History of the Island,* ed. Terry Chapman et al. (Suva: Institute of Pacific Studies of the University of the Pacific and the Government of Niue, 1992); and S. Percy Smith, *Niue: The Island and Its People* (Suva: University of the South Pacific, 1983).

25. Radio Australia, "Pacific Service," September 22, 1992.

26. There are important exceptions to this generalization. Tonga and Samoa have full independence. Although both are poor, they have not suffered the large-scale immigration of such places as the Cook Islands, Niue, or Tokelau.

27. Asian Development Bank, *Annual Report* (Manila: Asian Development Bank, 1997).

28. This song was composed for the Hilo, Hawai'i, radio station KHBC, now KPUA, in 1936.

INDEX

About the Author

Robert Seward is professor in the Faculty of International Studies at Meiji Gakuin University in Yokohama and Tokyo. He has held positions at New York University, the University of Pennsylvania, and the University of New Mexico. He lives in Tokyo and New York.